Castro . . . and Cuba

"There was much on which we were to differ, but from the moment that he looked at us, his face unlined and young for his 47 years; from the moment that he shook our hands with his soft, almost gentle grip; from the moment that he first leaned forward to stress a point, his beard no more than six inches away, we knew that we were in for a fascinating interview and an exciting adventure. We were not let down."

ABOUT THE AUTHORS: FRANK MANKIEWICZ is the author of *U.S. v. Richard Nixon—The Final Crisis*. Former Peace Corps Director for all Latin American programs, he was also an intimate associate of the late Robert Kennedy. KIRBY JONES lived in Santa Domingo as a Peace Corps volunteer for two years and later traveled through fifteen Latin American countries for the Peace Corps. Both authors speak fluent Spanish. Their recent TV documentary on Cuba, from which this book grew, was awarded a Citation for Excellence by the Overseas Press Club.

Also by Frank Mankiewicz on the Ballantine Books list:

U.S. v. RICHARD M. NIXON: The Final Crisis

available at your local bookstore

WITH FIDEL:

A Portrait of Castro and Cuba

Frank Mankiewicz and
Kirby Jones

BALLANTINE BOOKS • NEW YORK

To my wife, Brandy, for making my life
Far more joyous than I ever imagined possible;
to my children, Eliza and Kirby;
and to the people of Barrio Simón Bolívar
in Santo Domingo, from whom
I received and learned so much

KJ

To Joshua, who cares a lot.

FM

Library of Congress Catalog Card Number: 74-33552

ISBN 0-345-24981-X-175

This edition published by arrangement with Playboy Press

Manufactured in the United States of America

First Ballantine Books Edition: March, 1976

Contents

135813

Acknowledgments

We are extremely grateful to many people who assisted in the preparation of this book. First, thanks are due to our partners, Ted Van Dyk and Bob Lifton, who, although unable to participate personally in the actual travel to Cuba, offered infinite patience, understanding, and support for the entire project.

This project could not have been undertaken without the help, assistance, and guidance of Saul Landau. Not only did he continually demonstrate his high proficiency as a film director and producer, but he also made the trip initially possbile.

To cameraman Richard Pearce, sound man Mark Berger, and unit manager Rebecca Switzer we offer our thanks for their companionship and the high quality of their technical contributions.

Marcy Wilkov deserves special thanks for enduring the writing and rewriting of the manuscript; for coping with our schedules; for her editing; and for undertaking and fulfilling several tasks at the same time—including taking care of the technical details associated with completing this book.

To Marylin Bitner for being cheerful and patient in helping to organize the manuscript and to Betty Plaseied for her transcribing and typing as we came down to the wire—thanks.

Several members of the United States Foreign Service helped to make our travels a lot easier: David Paton in Mexico City, Douglas Stevens in Nassau, and Lawrence Arthur in the Passport Office in Washington.

To Avelina Sabangan and Virginia Schofield we are indebted for their professional skill and patience in translating and transcribing the entire interview.

Few words can express our thanks and gratitude for

the many hospitalities and courtesies shown to us by our Cuban hosts. Under some of the most difficult and complicated planning circumstances, they never failed to try their best to make us feel welcome. To Teofilo Acosta, Alina Alayo, Daniel Rodriguez, and Nestor Garcia and their associates from the Cuban foreign ministry; to the officials from all parts of Cuba of ICAP (Cultural Institute of Friendship with People)—particularly Maria Elena Vallejera; to Andres, Barbero, Sergio, Ernesto, Ramon, Virgilio, and so many others—we are most indebted.

Some of the most pleasant times we had in Cuba were those we spent with the technicians of the Cuban Film Institute (ICAIC)—Raul Rodriguez, not only an excellent cameraman but one of the most knowledgeable people anywhere on movie trivia; Geronimo Labrada, sound man; Eloy Gutierrez, electrician; Guillermo Centeno and Adriano Moreno, production assistants. Their comradeship and willingness to be helpful in all ways are appreciated.

To the people of Playboy Press we are thankful for help and assistance in the preparation and editing of the manuscript: Ed Kuhn, Charles Whatley, and Morrie Goldfischer.

A special word for Bob Gutwillig of Playboy, who recognized at the beginning of our journey the value, meaning, and importance of an interview with Fidel Castro and who immediately demonstrated interest and encouragement while many others were tied up by their own and corporate policy.

We also want to acknowledge the contributions of CBS—especially Dan Rather, whose contribution in the second interview helped to complete the picture of Cuba and Castro.

Finally, no American politician was ever more generous with his time than Fidel Castro. We appreciate greatly the time he spent with us, giving us the opportunity better to know and understand Cuba and its revolution.

Washington, D.C.
February 1975

Introduction

This book is the result of three trips to Cuba in 1974 and 1975 by Frank Mankiewicz and Kirby Jones. The first trip lasted from June 29 to July 21, 1974; the second from September 28 to October 6, 1974; and the third from January 24 to February 4, 1975.

The main purpose of the trips was to conduct an in-depth interview with Cuban Prime Minister Fidel Castro for American television. Over the course of four days and nights from July 18 to July 21, we spent more than eleven hours in formal interview with Castro and another twelve hours in informal conversation and traveling with him by jeep throughout the Havana area. All conversations with Castro were conducted in Spanish. During the second trip, there were an additional two hours of filmed interview, and over six hours were spent meeting informally with Castro.

In addition to the interview and conversations with Castro, we spent twenty-four days traveling throughout Cuba. There were no restrictions of any kind placed on where we went, to whom we could talk, or what we could see. The Cubans provided buses, cars, drivers, and guides to help facilitate the program and to manage the scheduling. Often, we would change the day's itinerary and this would be done without protest or—as far as we could see—any advance preparation.

Portions of the interview in this book were included in a "CBS Reports" television special entitled "Castro, Cuba and the USA," which was aired on October 22, 1974; an excerpt was published in the January 1975 issue of *Oui* magazine and the foreign editions of *Playboy* magazine; and portions have been included in a television film entitled "Castro, Cuba 1974," which has been televised in several foreign countries and is distributed by Tricontinental Films, New York City.

Getting to Cuba

In early 1974, we formed a small company to produce exclusive television interviews with world leaders and personalities who hadn't appeared on U.S. television— or had not appeared for a long time. Fidel Castro was certainly one of them. We first contacted Saul Landau, a film maker and writer, who had been to Cuba many times and who we had heard had become a friend of Castro after producing a film, "Fidel," for educational television in 1968. We met with Saul, outlined our project, and asked him to produce and direct the film and the interview. Saul agreed to help.

We then wrote a long proposal to Castro describing our idea. We told him we felt that 1974 might be an appropriate time for the American people to hear not only what he had to say about international events, but also what was going on in Cuba today. We said we shared with many Americans a feeling that news about Castro and Cuba had been minimal and that what news appeared was based too often on ignorance and possibly even bias. We offered to conduct an interview in which the final product would be unaltered, so that Castro could be measured and judged by his own words.

After submitting this document, we received a request from Havana for additional information, chiefly about our own backgrounds, plus an expanded list of the possible areas to be covered in the interview. This second document was prepared and sent. By this time six weeks had passed.

About three weeks later, we were told that Castro had received literally dozens of requests from all three

U.S. television networks, several U.S. newspapers, and many foreign countries—all asking for an interview. Castro had rejected them all, but we were also told he had decided that if he were to accept any interview for U.S. consumption, it would be ours. The last word was that we could only wait and "that it might be two days, two weeks, two years, or never."

Much to our surprise, in the early part of May we received a message inviting us to come to Cuba at the end of June to do the interview.

The most convenient way to get to Cuba at that time was through Mexico City. (Now, a trip through Jamaica is cheaper and quicker.) We arranged for a crew, wrote the State Department for permission to travel to Cuba (it is almost always granted to journalists, and in this instance the State Department was quite helpful).

From Mexico City, Cuban Airlines flies a prop-jet Russian-built *Ilyushin 18* to Havana. The night we flew, the plane was jammed, mainly with an Argentine volleyball team, diplomatic couriers, and some returning Cuban film makers. The service on the plane was good. We were served a club sandwich; a choice of Cuban beer or pineapple juice; and deep, sweet Cuban coffee that shot through the body as though it had been injected directly into the veins. (On Cuban menus, coffee is listed under *Infusiones*—it is an accurate classification.) And, of course, we had our first Cuban cigars.

We landed at José Martí International Airport at 4:30 A.M., Havana time. Stepping out of the plane, we felt the hot muggy air of the Caribbean, and as we walked into the terminal, we came face to face with three wall-sized posters of Che Guevara. It was then that it really hit us where we were. For the only place one sees Che posters in the United States is likely to be on the dormitory walls of students who often pretend at their brand of relatively safe "revolution." But there in Havana it was no different from a foreigner's visiting the United States and seeing a picture of Abraham Lincoln or George Washington. In Cuba, Che Guevara is indeed a national hero, not a "camp" sign of protest.

2

We immediately encountered Cuban technology when we discovered that we had both forgotten our yellow International Health Certificates. Our first inclination was to try to bluff our way through. But we were quickly escorted into a small room at the back of the airport where we were met by a female Cuban medical technician who could not have been more than fifteen years old. It was our first exposure to the new Cuba, a Cuba run largely by people under thirty-five, building houses, teaching in schools, managing ports—and inoculating visitors.

Greeting us were the three people who were to be our companions for the next three and a half weeks. There was Daniel Rodriguez of the Cuban Foreign Ministry, thirty-three years old, married and the father of a small baby. He had rejected the life of his wealthy parents—the life of the *"burgesa,"* as he called it—and had completely committed himself to the revolution of Fidel Castro. Having seen so much of the U.S. protest of the sixties led by the sons and daughters of the rich, it was not hard for us to understand Daniel.

Alina Alayo, also thirty-three, is an official of the Ministry of Foreign Relations. Alina speaks almost perfect English and is, in fact, often used as one of Fidel's translators. She is a militant Marxist who understands Marxism-Leninism well, but whose ideology is tempered by a sense of humor. Alina was pregnant, her third pregnancy after two miscarriages. A strong advocate of women's rights, she told us she wanted a baby girl so she could "educate her child in the ways of men."

Maria Elena Vallejera, twenty-two, works with ICAP (Cultural Institute of Friendship with People)—sort of a national Welcome Wagon agency. A more bubbly, chubby, enthusiastic tour guide would be hard to find. Maria Elena has the voice of Tallulah Bankhead and the spirit of a college cheerleader.

After waiting for our thirty-five pieces of luggage and equipment to be processed, we finally boarded a Russian bus at 5:30 A.M. and headed for downtown Havana. As we left José Martí Airport, we saw the first

3

of hundreds of political signs—this one a picture of Ho Chi Minh calling for friendship with the North Vietnamese people.

At six o'clock on a Saturday morning, the Hotel Riviera seemed deserted except for a small night crew. Walking in, one thought of the Doral or the Americana hotels in Miami Beach. It was an appropriate comparison. The Hotel Riviera was built by Meyer Lansky and completed a few months before Fidel took power. Daniel proudly pointed to a closed door on the right. "The casino used to be in there in 1958, but Fidel closed them all."

Meeting Fidel

We first met Fidel Castro almost three weeks later. Although we had been expecting to begin the interview well before, we now waited patiently—and with little knowledge whether our filmed interview would last one hour or several—in front of the hotel.

As we stood at the curb, someone exclaimed, "Here comes Fidel." We looked left and there appeared, driving slowly up the half-circle driveway, one lonely jeep with a beared man in the front passenger seat.

The Cubans who were at the entrance just watched from a distance; some came out from inside, but there was no commotion. It was almost as if a taxi had delivered just another passenger.

Castro looked just the way he was supposed to look, but neater and more dapper. He wore the traditional olive-green fatigues, but they were well tailored and pressed and appeared to be made from an extremely lightweight material. His black boots were brilliantly shined and he wore a pistol belt—complete with pistol —around his middle. On each shoulder was the diamond of red and black with a white star in the middle signifying his military rank as *comandante* (major). His insignia was partially encircled by a gold braid, which meant *comandante en jefe* (commander-in-chief). There is only one of those.

There are some surprising things about Castro physically. He is taller than expected, and, for a forty-seven-year-old man who has been the leader of his country for fifteen years, he looks surprisingly youthful. At about six-foot-two and 190 pounds, he has the build of a cornerback, or maybe an Ivy League tackle. Considering the hours Castro keeps, his face is remarkably unlined, his eyes unpouched. The hairline is receding a trifle, and the beard is flecked with gray, but the midriff is flat, the eyes are clear, and he is remarkably unchanged from the young man whose last appearance in the United States was at the famous heads-of-state United Nations General Assembly in 1962.

Castro chatted briefly and then suggested that we all go for a drive. We were ushered into the backseat with Pepín Naranjo, Fidel's aide-de-camp and government minister without portfolio. Pepín has been a friend since Fidel's university days. Saul Landau climbed in front. Then Pepín noticed that there was not enough room for both Fidel and the driver. "I'll drive," Fidel said. He climbed behind the wheel and off we went.

The following entourage was a small Alfa Romeo sedan with one ministry official and one bodyguard. The jeep was Russian-made and equipped with a two-way radio placed between the front seats. On the floor was a box of six-inch cigars and a blue metal tin containing candy mints. Across the front dashboard, securely mounted, was a Russian-made AK-47 automatic rifle.

It is questionable whether Fidel Castro could pass a high-school drivers' education course. He has the habit —admirable under normal circumstances—of wanting to look a person in the eye when he is talking. But we were in the backseat.

There was no apparent itinerary. In spite of our wariness of his driving, Fidel stopped at red lights and obeyed traffic signs just as if we were out for a Sunday drive. People along the road waved and called out "Fidel, Fidel." Castro waved back most times. He was very busy talking and explaining everything.

As he drove he described the botanical gardens that were being developed outside Havana, pointed out a school, drove through Lenin Park and explained the facilities, and asked about our trip through Cuba. He seemed to know everything about everything we saw— and after subsequent trips with him we realized that he *did* know everything.

6

We stopped alongside a factory that was being built to produce radios, batteries, and minicalculators. He chatted a bit with the manager, asking him what the building was made of, about construction schedules, the number of workers to be employed, what the projected production schedule was, and if any problems existed. The manager replied that they were on schedule but would be able to move faster if they had more trucks. They talked as if they already knew each other, had talked before, and would again. We soon learned that this was the way most people talked to Fidel. They had seen him before, and they did expect to see him again. He was interested in everything about the factory, and it was something that he was not to forget. The manager knew that, too.

We soon arrived at Las Ruinas, a restaurant in Lenin Park which was built in and around the shell of an old hacienda. It was a fine building of whitewashed brick and stained glass, with plants growing in old stone pillars with holes drilled in them to permit watering pipes for the plants.

As we walked into the restaurant, Fidel stopped at a room in which several of the restaurant employees were seated in rows, as if in a class. "What are you doing?" he asked. "We are studying," they replied. He turned to us and explained, "Here in Cuba everyone attends some classes, everyone has the opportunity to learn."

Inside, the maître d' escorted us to a table as if we were ordinary customers. Daiquiris were served all around and for the next few hours Fidel quizzed us on Watergate and American politics with the same interest that he had demonstrated about the factory. This was July: John Ehrlichman had just gone to trial, the Supreme Court was considering the tape decision, and the Judiciary Committee was getting ready for public debate. "You Americans," Castro said after a while, "talk a lot about stability and the need to deal with stable governments. I think my government is the most stable in the western hemisphere." Then he paused and added with a slight smile, "Including, it would seem, your own."

He asked questions about the upcoming conspiracy trial, impeachment, who the Judiciary Committee members were and what they were like, what we thought Nixon's chances were of surviving. We answered all these questions with the easy wisdom that living in Washington seemed to require—wisdom built upon not much more than reading *The Washington Post* and being around some Democratic political campaigns. We never pretended to be experts, only observant amateurs. We told him we thought Richard Nixon was not going to survive and that indeed he might resign before the actual impeachment debate began in the House. "You might be right," Fidel commented, "but I think you overstate the case. In any event, Cuba must maintain a conservative policy and operate as if Richard Nixon is to complete his term."

After one and a half hours, he finally turned to the main purpose of our visit.

"What about this interview?" he asked. "A lot of the subjects that you want to discuss will require careful preparation and planning. I want it to be a good interview. Can we start on Saturday? That will give me a few days to prepare."

We gulped silently; we really did not particularly want to wait another three days. Landau finally asked whether we could begin that night and see how it went.

Fidel crinkled his forehead and finally said, "OK, why not? Where would you like to do it?"

"Anywhere convenient for you," we answered.

Fidel then turned to Pepín and suggested a room just outside his office in the Palacio de la Revolución.

"You people no doubt want to wash up and get everything ready, so why don't we begin around eleven tonight? Let's do the interview just as we have been talking here—informal, a conversation. Isn't that better than a formal question-and-answer session?

"One more thing," he added. "I'd like to invite you on an extended tour of some areas around Havana

8

before you leave. Would you like to take a jeep tour on Saturday?"

So it was decided we would spend three nights filming, and follow that with a day's informal tour. Things were looking up.

Comparing notes later, it seemed clear we had been with one of the most charming and entertaining men either of us had ever met. Whether one agrees with him or not, Castro is personally overpowering. U.S. political writers would call it a simple case of charisma, but it is more than that. Political leaders often can be and are charismatic in a public sense, but rather normal in more private moments. Such is not the case with Fidel Castro. He remains one of the few truly electric personalities in a world in which his peers seem dull and pedestrian.

Such personal feelings should not be confused with ideological or political agreement on our own part, for there was much on which we were to differ. But from the moment he looked you straight in the eye and spoke directly to every question, from the moment he first leaned eagerly forward to stress a point, his beard no more than six inches away, each of us knew we were in for a fascinating interview and an exciting experience. We were not let down.

The Interview

The crew—Saul Landau, Dick Pearce and Mark Berger—left the hotel early Wednesday evening to set up. We ate a leisurely dinner, showered, changed clothes, and waited to be picked up by Daniel and Alina at 9:00 P.M. We had dressed informally. Even a sit-down interview with Fidel Castro does not require a coat and tie in Cuba. At exactly 9:00 P.M., we piled into Daniel's Alfa Romeo and headed for the Palacio.

The Palacio is a well-cared-for structure with high ceilings, polished marble floors, and indoor plants. It was completed just before Castro took power, and had been destined to be the new headquarters for the national police. It now houses the highest government offices and the headquarters of the Cuban Communist Party.

Castro's study is a simple room with several couches, chairs, and potted plants spread throughout. Along one entire side is a bookcase filled with colorfully bound books in Spanish, a gift to him from the President of Mexico. Castro has no room for them in his office proper so he built a bookcase in this room for their display.

From this study, one door leads to the cabinet room, which contains a long chrome table for about forty people—complete, curiously enough, with simultaneous translation equipment—and another door leads to Fidel's office.

Inside the office, just to the left of the door, is a desk, uncluttered, but with several telephones. Behind the desk is a bookcase filled with the writings of Che, various books on Cuba, and a variety of highly technical works on agriculture, farming, and economics. At the far end is a small conference table for eight and on the right, a sofa, two large chairs, and a coffee table.

Three chairs were arranged in the center of the study for the interview: Cameras were placed, lights tested, all under the watchful eye of Fidel's staff. Everything we did was watched and checked out, not unlike the way in which the Secret Service watches over an interview with the President of the United States.

At exactly 10:45 P.M., Fidel walked in with Pepín. Gone was the pistol belt—and the pistol—around his middle, and his hair had been carefully combed. He greeted us warmly, surveyed the scene, and seemed to approve.

We sat down. Microphones were tested, and we began the first of what would be three nights of interview. The interview is included in other sections of this book. But a conversation with Fidel at close range should be described.

The interview was conducted totally in Spanish. No questions were submitted in advance, and Fidel answered everything put to him.

Castro speaks very softly. Contrary to the public image built up over the years in the United States, he converses in a relaxed, but serious, manner. He is the head of his country, and what he says is carefully thought out and logically presented. He knows what he is doing and saying all the time. He was completely aware of the camera, and demonstrated all the professionalism of a seasoned political candidate in the United States.

Our interview was really a conversation. Generally, Fidel sat easily in his chair, leaning back, legs crossed, and smoking on his ever-present small cigars. But when he wanted to place special emphasis on a remark, he would lean forward to within a few inches of his questioner, tap him on the knee, and look directly into his eyes. It bothered him when he was misunderstood. He did not at all demand agreement, but he would not

11

leave a point until he was satisfied that there was at least a basic understanding of what he was saying.

It was so easy to become engrossed in his style and logic that we often found ourselves starting from point A and within ten minutes agreeing with point B. Fidel is a former trial lawyer and he shows it. All his arguments follow a carefully structured presentation. By the time he has built his case, if you do not watch out, he has you convinced of things you do not believe.

(During our October visit, we were standing with Dan Rather of CBS, talking with Fidel. In the middle of a heated discussion between Rather and Fidel, Jones turned to Mankiewicz and whispered, "Frank, I'll bet within five minutes, Dan's head will begin nodding agreement."

Right on cue, as Fidel continued making his case, Dan's head began to move, and soon the words, "Yes, yes," were being uttered.)

Castro is not a passive talker. His whole body seems to become involved in what he says. His fingers stroke his beard, his arms and hands punctuate his points in a fluid manner. He often raises one finger against his face or in the air as he thinks and talks. Even as he sat quietly talking in his chair there was a magnetic energy and motion to him.

After ninety minutes we called a break. Immediately, frozen Daiquiris were brought in and served to everyone—guards, aides, and camera crew.

Fidel offered us all cigars from his leather carrying case. We emptied the case right away, whereupon from over Fidel's shoulder appeared the hand of an efficient aide who took the case and quickly returned it full. Fidel joked and tried to speak with the rest of our crew. He was interested in all of us and asked questions about our work and how we thought the interview was going.

As we sat down for the second session that first night, an aide interrupted with an urgent cable for Fidel. After reading quickly, he said, "Here, look at this. The Greeks have just overthrown the government of Cyprus." An update was handed to him.

"What do you think about this? It is a very serious situation now in Cyprus. . . . You know what I think," he said as he sat back in his chair, thoughtfully analyzing what he had just read. "I think that the action of the Greeks will result in an invasion by the Turks, the expulsion of the Greek troops from Cyprus, and will have serious repercussions in Athens—perhaps the end of the military junta."

After only a few minutes of reading and thinking about a situation many thousands of miles away, Fidel's apparent instinct about a distant crisis turned out to be right on the mark.

At about 3 in the morning, an aide signaled to Saul Landau that the time had come to stop.

"I don't think that we have nearly finished," commented Fidel. "Why don't we continue again tomorrow night and start a bit earlier—let's say about ten?"

Fidel offered us all a nightcap and, as we were about to leave, we presented him with a few gifts. We had heard that he liked mechanical objects and was fascinated with how things work, so we gave him one of the new Polaroid SX-70 cameras. He immediately wanted to try it out. We showed him quickly how it was supposed to work, but he was a bit impatient and it was not clear that he fully understood. He backed up, put it to his eyes, and clicked away. Out shot the picture, and everyone gathered around. The picture was miserably out of focus. Never one to be discouraged, he tried again. All of us assembled in a group, with Fidel Castro as the most unlikely photographer we had ever faced. Out came a second picture, somewhat out of focus but better than the first. He was like a small boy at Christmas, totally enthusiastic. After a third try and much laughter at what terrible subjects we were, he thanked us for the camera and left quickly by his office door.

To this day, we don't know if that camera ever produced a good picture.

Late Thursday, July 18, we picked up where we had left off. We had decided that the second night

13

would include all the tough questions—those things that bothered North Americans the most.

At 10:00 P.M. sharp, Fidel entered the room. He was never late at any of our agreed-upon hours. Indeed, promptness—a most un-Latin characteristic—seems a Cuban habit.

At the conclusion of the first interview segment, we asked him how he got his news about the United States and the world.

"I have a daily news digest," he answered. "Every morning at eight, there is a digest on my desk. Sometimes I don't get to read the entire thing until late at light when I do most of my reading, but if something important is happening, I will of course study the material."

"Might we see it?" we asked.

"Of course."

He motioned to an aide, who quickly brought in a one-and-a-half-inch-thick notebook containing cabled news stories from all over the world, all the news services from AP to Tass. Clearly indexed and summarized, it was broken down into various sections—Cuba, United States, Latin America, Europe, Third World. Each section was subindexed.

"Most of the time," Fidel explained, "I do not have the time to read the entire digest. But if an article seems particularly interesting or important, I do."

"When do you find time to do all this reading?" Mankiewicz asked.

"Mostly at night, usually after midnight. That's when I do most of my reading."

"Have you read any American books lately?"

"I've just finished *Jaws* and I liked it because of its splendid Marxist message."

We were surprised at this remark, as *Jaws* had seemed to us to be simply a first-rate adventure story. But Castro went on to discuss that part of the book where the local chief of police was urging the town officials to close their beaches while the great white shark, which had eaten a few bathers, was tracked

14

down. The officials refused, on the ground that the Fourth of July weekend was coming up and the bad publicity would ruin the season's business.

"Thus," Castro said, "the book makes the point that capitalism will risk even human life in order to keep the markets open." It was not a point made by many U.S. reviewers.

As we sat down after the break, Fidel again brought up the subject of Watergate.

"Yesterday, I mentioned that we in Cuba could not count on the impeachment of Nixon, but today something happened that seems very important. There was a Republican member of the Judiciary Committee who held what appears to me to be a significant press conference."

"Do you mean Congressman McClory?" we asked.

"Yes, exactly. He said today that he will vote for the impeachment of President Nixon. I think I now agree with you. For the first time I believe that Richard Nixon will not survive."

We ended at one in the morning, and Castro invited us to continue for a third session the following night. The final session, Friday night, was shorter than the previous two. At its conclusion, Fidel repeated his invitation to take us on a jeep tour the following day throughout the countryside surrounding Havana. Then, just as we were taking our leave, Fidel asked when we were planning to return to the United States. We said we would probably leave on Sunday, on the flight to Madrid.

"Do you *want* to go to Europe?" he asked.

"No, not at all," we answered, "but that is the only flight until next Wednesday."

"But, it seems a terrible inconvenience for you. Would you like to fly on my plane to Nassau instead? Would that be better?"

A four-hour flight to Washington via Nassau was infinitely preferable to a twenty-four-hour trip via Madrid. Fidel turned to Pepín and instructed him to call Foreign Minister Raul Roa and ask him to contact

15

the English ambassador for permission for the official plane to land in Nassau.

He then turned back to us, "Well, done. Until tomorrow, then." He departed quickly through his office door.

On the Road

Saturday, July 20, was one of those heavy tropical days, so hot and muggy that by 9:45 A.M. our eyeglasses steamed over upon leaving the air-conditioned comfort of the hotel.

Shortly after ten, three jeeps swung up to the Hotel Riviera, with Fidel in the front passenger seat of the first one. Fidel slid out to greet us, and the crew loaded their gear into the second jeep.

We had no idea where we were going until Pepín mentioned that we were off to visit Alamar, a large new housing development—actually a "new town" of some thirty thousand—outside of Havana. We had, in fact, visited Alamar before; it is a favorite showcase of the new Cuba.

Riding through Havana's streets in a Fidel Castro caravan did not really evoke the wild response that we had come to expect with some American leaders and politicians. Often we passed so rapidly that people alongside the road barely had a chance to grasp exactly who had driven by. But when we did stop for red lights or were forced to slow down, people waved at Fidel, called out his name, and smiled warmly.

At Alamar a crowd had assembled—but, as it turned out, not for us or for Castro. A delegation of South Vietnamese from the PRG (Provisional Revolutionary Government) on a state visit was due to arrive within a half hour.

The streets were filled with people waving PRG flags, and when they realized that our caravan included Fidel, they swarmed around him. Children brought him flowers and fathers hoisted the smaller ones onto

17

their shoulders for a better view. Fidel was gentle wtih the people as he shook hands, patted heads, and chatted informally. He asked the kids about the swimming pool, how often they swam, what hours it was open, and why there was no one swimming on such a hot day. The pool was due to open within the next few hours.

Disengaging himself from the crowd, Fidel walked with us toward a small ice cream stand. A woman— obviously a resident of Alamar he had met before— ran up and gave him a big *abrazo;* they warmly held hands for a minute. As they headed for the ice cream stand, Fidel's arm around the woman's shoulder, families began to appear on the balconies of their homes. There was no ecstatic shouting, but smiles were everywhere.

Fidel then suggested that we go visiting, and led us up the stairs of a five-story building. He knocked on the door of a third-floor apartment. The lady of the house opened the door and shouted, "Fidel, Fidel, come on in."

The apartment was like most in the Alamar complex—two bedrooms, living room, kitchen, bathroom, balcony, complete with electricity and running water. There were several chairs, a coffee table, a Russian television set, and a dining room table set for six.

Fidel's path was filled in by all of us, his aides, and an ever-increasing number of neighbors. Word had traveled quickly. Fidel took off his cap (but not his gun) and sat down. An old man in a straw hat squatted next to him, two small children sat down on the floor alongside, and the man and woman of the house seated themselves across from him.

"Quick," someone yelled, "get a fan; it's hot in here."

Immediately a light-blue table fan was placed on the small coffee table so that it blew in Fidel's direction.

"Does anyone have any rum?" asked Fidel.

A bottle and several shot glasses were brought in and we all toasted. And then Fidel and the family began chatting as if Uncle Harry had just blown in from Toledo after six years.

Apartment

CASTRO: How many people now live here?

#1: Seven hundred and seventy, with one hundred and seventy-five apartments completed.

C: How are you? How are you? Listen here, how many frozen custards are eaten daily?

#1: Three or four per person.

C: How many do you sell?

#1: Two hundred or so pesos worth.

C: You mean that you sell more than a thousand ice creams per day?

#1: Sure, a large amount.

C: Well, they're very good.

#1: We're located right next door to the dairy. The peasants like this housing complex. One hundred and seventy-five families have moved in already. We have a medical clinic, a pharmacy. . . .

C: And you're going to build a barbershop, a beauty parlor, and a movie house?

#1: But don't tell me that it's big, it's just right. It just grows and grows and grows.

C: You're soon going to start competing with Havana? Eh?

#1: No, Havana's bigger. Are you kidding?

C: How is the television reception here?

#1: Very good. They're trying a new antenna, *Comandante*.

C. You mean one central one?

#1: No, individual ones . . . one per each eight apartments for eight sets. In one building they're testing it.

C: Here's a toast to the success of your town, that it doesn't grow too large.

CRIES: No—here's to the change that's been made from before until now.

#1: And here's to the development of those countries that still haven't developed like we have—those still backward like we used to be.

C: He's in the political cadre here?

#2: Who couldn't be a political militant after undergoing the changes we've been through? Isn't that right, *Comandante?*

C: I think it is.

#3: Look, we've got more than a tableful of postcards. They say that all these big things we've done are making the Revolution.

C: From where did you receive those cards?

#2: From Mexico, from the Mayor of Morelia in Mexico, and all of the visitors that came here and then sent postcards about their impressions. We're going to answer them.

C: It's going to cost you a lot of money.

#1: Ah, no. The young French Communists who are in Jibacoa visited here three times. And now they have an impression of the community.

C: And who is going to fill these apartments?

#1: We are going to fill them up with peasants, but some are still on the ranch.

C: Grandmother, come here. I almost called you Grandpa.

#3: Go on, go on.

C: How big are the fields of the school?

#1: Imagine this, we have nine hectares of corn.

C: And what do you produce in all?

#1: Well, we had nine thousand last year, and this year thirty-six hundred and sixty-three worth, fifty thousand pesos.

C: And the vegetables that are consumed—tomatoes, peppers, onions—I'm not talking only about corn.

#4: We've loaded some trucks with our corn.

C: Have you sent it to other places?

#5: Yes, to the Mezorra Mental Hospital, to the workers' dining rooms.

C: Do you have all that you want here?

#1: Ah, yes. Plenty of corn given out every week.

C: Any complaints?

#1: No, things are going well with the Provincial Party people.

C: How many hectares do you have in the eastern part?

#1: Eighteen now. But we are going to develop more. A peasant lives on the land now, but he'll be moving to the apartments and we'll be able to work the land better.

C: How many students are there in the school?

#1: *Comandante,* do you want to eat a snack?

C: No, no, thank you. . . . What are those things?

#1: *Comandante,* they're sweet—corn with peanuts and eggs.

C: Yes, but I shouldn't eat many eggs.

#1: But it has only one egg, no more.

C: I like fried bananas better. . . . How many students are there again?

#2: We have one hundred and eighty-nine at this time who live in the community in this area, but this year we will have five hundred or a little more because of the peripheral residents. The preschool program will take kids from the outlying areas. This way these children also will have the opportunity to participate in the community.

C: And in the day-care center, how many children are there?

#1: One hundred and twenty.

C: How many women are working now?

#1: At this time one hundred and eleven women.

C: And what percent of the work force are women?

#1: We have more than eighty-five percent of the women working. Almost ninety percent. And we are building a new day-care center. It's very pretty in nice colors.

C: When will it be finished?

#1: In September it will open.

C: Very good. You really have everything here—day-care center, school, and now stores are being built.

#1: Yes, we have everything—and a medical clinic as well. We have a doctor four days here and one in Santo Cruz. He helps there, too.

C: And that doctor, how much do you pay for his services?

#1: We're going to pay him, *Comandante*. With our work, with milk. Ah, *Comandante,* don't talk to me like that. We'll pay for everything.

C: You're going to have to produce milk like crazy if you're going to pay for all that.

#1: Ah, *Comandante,* don't kid us like that. Nooooo.

C: One has to sell rum at very high prices to support the milk of all of you.

#1: No, it's not that way.

C: If you—your whole area—produces one half a million liters of milk, Havana'll be drinking a million. But we have a lot of dairy plants going. At least, you're not the only producers. Do you only have one child?

#2: Yes.

C: And you're not thinking of having more than one?

#2: That's right.

C: Good. If we keep producing kids the way we have been, they won't fit in this country.
(LOUD CRIES)

As we left the apartment we saw that a crowd had gathered from all over the huge housing complex. Alamar was being built to house over 125,000 people. It already contained 30,000, and it seemed as if most of them were in the street. We inched toward the jeeps. Fidel stopped to shake hands and to talk to as many as possible. But there were no requests for autographs and, unlike the case with popular American politicians, the people always seemed to leave a pocket of space around Fidel—not because of security guards, for there was only one directly with him. It was evident that he evoked a combination of feelings. Part of it was his own attitude of a visiting relative that allowed people

22

the informality and openness. But there was also demonstrated a feeling that people were in the presence of their liberator—the man who, they clearly felt, had led them from the miseries of the past into a new day. For that reason, they seemed to keep a step away as if afraid to puncture the bubble. Women would greet Fidel with a friendly touch or pat and then take a step back. The scene was warm and friendly, Fidel obviously was enjoying himself, and the Alamar residents were having the time of their life.

Fidel slowly climbed into the front seat of his jeep, the rest of us took our places, and off we went. As we drove down the road, a line of people thought we were the Vietnamese delegates. Amidst the Vietnamese flags, suddenly there were cries of "It's Fidel! It's Fidel!" Fidel acknowledged their greetings with a slight wave and joked, "They think we are the Vietnamese."

As with our car ride with Fidel the previous Wednesday, there did not seem to be any predetermined pattern or schedule to our journey. We just went where his whim took him. After a drive of about twenty minutes, we started to chug up a steep hill, on top of which was a beautiful modern house of wood and glass.

"Where are we going?" Jones asked Pepín.

"That is a government protocol house. It is where foreign dignitaries stay. The last visitor that was here was President Boumediene of Algeria."

As we stopped at the foot of some wide stone steps, Fidel turned to us and mentioned that he thought we "would like to see this new house we have built."

"But," he continued, "the Vietnamese delegation is expected here for lunch in a few minutes. I didn't know that, but maybe I can show it to you before they arrive. I certainly do not want to interrupt their schedule."

Fidel led us up the stairs and through a long corridor leading onto a veranda that overlooked a wide green valley. We passed the kitchen in which chefs were preparing a meal that, at least at a quick glance, included charcoal-broiled steaks. At the end of the corridor was a banquet table set for about thirty with stemware from eastern Europe, china and silver, and trays of different cheeses and fresh tropical fruits. Just as we walked out onto the terrace, cars appeared at the entrance and out stepped the Vietnamese delegation.

"Oh, oh," said Fidel, "now what are we going to do? I hope we haven't messed up their itinerary."

He immediately walked to the front door and greeted Madame Nguyen Thi Dinh, the deputy commander of the military forces of the PRG in South Vietnam. Accompanying her were two decorated soldiers from the PRG army. Both had been imprisoned from three to four years; both wore at least thirty medals of commendation; both were less than five feet tall; both were twenty years old and looked twelve; both were women. They were all escorted by Fidel's older brother, Ramon —as tall as Fidel, a bit thinner, his beard much grayer. "With his beard whiter than mine," says Fidel, "you can tell he is older." Ramon is director of one of four large animal husbandry programs.

Abrazos were given and received, and as Fidel and the guests came out onto the terrace, white-jacketed waiters passed trays of frozen Daiquiris, fresh fruit juices, and other cold drinks.

CASTRO: I came with a delegation of journalists and we were just passing by. How are you? Ah, here come the Daiquiris. Don't you drink?

MADAME DINH: A little bit.

C: Nor the others in your group? Well, a toast to the Vietnamese. We were at Alamar. We were there a little while before you.

D: How long have you been here?

C: Only five minutes. I'm with a delegation of journalists. They are North American, but good people.

D: Of the North Americans, there are many that are good.

C: I explained that in my interview—that there are many North Americans who fought against the war in Vietnam.

D: The bad ones are the rich ones and Nixon.

C: Where are the journalists? . . . Here they are. . . .

D: We hate Nixon, but have a great sympathy toward

24

the American people, and the American people have helped a lot to end the U.S. involvement in the war in Vietnam.

C: Look at all those medals on those two girls!

D: These two girls were in jail for several years and they do have a lot of medals. How long have the two of you been here in Cuba?

C: They have been here about twenty days. It's my fault they've been here so long—they've been waiting for me.

JONES: We're doing a television program for the United States. How long have you been in Cuba?

D: Three days.

C: We did not know that we were going to meet you and we just came from a place where there were a lot of people waiting for you. But I explained that the crowd was for you and not for me.

D: Have any of you ever visited South Vietnam?

MANKIEWICZ: Once in 1972 with Senator George McGovern—both Kirby and I were aides to him in his presidential campaign of 1972.

D: We wish you could come to the liberated parts of Vietnam to see the crimes committed by the Yankees.

J: We would like to go to Vietnam whenever it would be convenient for you.

M: When I was in South Vietnam, we were attacked in a church by people from Thieu's government, during a meeting with some anti-Thieu leaders.

D: The majority of the people in South Vietnam are against the current regime.

C: Look, Frank and Kirby, how many medals these two fighters have.

J: What are the medals for?

D: They wear these medals because for five years they fought bravely and helped to shoot down helicopters, planes, and to destroy tanks. One killed three soldiers before she was captured and spent two years in jail, but she maintained her spirits until she was freed.

25

C: Well, we should continue our trip. We have enjoyed our visit here, and the film they are making will be seen on American television by about ten to eleven million people.

D: When you return to the United States, please transmit our feeling of solidarity with all those Americans who have helped. Although the government of the United States continues to support the Thieu regime, we are sure we will be victorious over the Americans under Nixon's leadership.

C: Until later then.

(While walking out . . .)

D: It has been a surprise for us to see you today.

C: I had hoped to meet up with you, and we were lucky because those who were waiting to greet you at Alamar also greeted me. Have a good meal. Thank you all. I hope you will have a chance to rest. Are you returning to Havana now?

D: No, first we are going to the province of Oriente.

C: No chance for rest. It is very hot there—like in South Vietnam.

D: Yes, but we know the heat. Good-bye.

It was quickly back into the jeeps and on to the next stop, wherever that might be. Onto the highway, up more hills, and along some unpaved, dusty roads which led eventually to a rum factory in the final stages of completion—rows of warehouses holding thousands of kegs of aging rum. We entered the dark, hangarlike buildings where Fidel talked with the manager and the workers.

Rum Factory

WORKER: Fidel, Fidel, hello.

CASTRO: Good afternoon. How are you all? Do you have youth brigades working here?

W: Yes.

C: Are you accomplishing much here?

W: Yes.

C: Have they decided to build the building? All set with it?

W: Yes, already they have begun discussing it with Manolo.

C: It is coordinated. They are in agreement, right?

W: There is coordination between Levi and Raciel.

C: Prefabricated?

W: Yes.

C: For the people that are going to live here to work here? Are you going to produce liquors, too?

W: Yes.

C: And you haven't gotten that far yet?

W: That's going to be firmed up in August.

C: With the same capacity that we talked about, right?

W: Yes, with a hundred thousand tons, and it is possible that by next week the engineer will make the final analysis with Cointreau. They have many flavors—all kinds, including mandarin—and they're very tasty.

C: What I like about this is the smell. (laughter) One can almost get high on the smell, huh? I imagine that all of you who work here must always be a little tipsy. (laughter) And don't they ever give you a small bottle of *aguardiente?*

W: Sometimes.

C: But it makes much stronger Daiquiris, right? What a celebration the inauguration of this factory will be What an odor—so pleasant here. And how many workers are there in the microbrigade [special voluntary force]?

And this little girl—where is she from? Ah, you must be from right next to the house of your little friend, right? We're making here some propaganda about your rum.

W: That's very good . . . excellent.

C: It's for television.

W: Someone should have a bottle in their hand to show it off.

C: How much does this barrel weigh?

W: Fifty. It has a capacity of fifty kilos, one hundred and eighty liters, and weighs two hundred and fifty kilos.

C: You'll be the heavyweight lifting champ.

After we left the rum factory, back onto the main highway, Pepín mentioned that Fidel wanted to visit some vacationers on a beach. As we neared the coast, we drove along a road bordered by tall, skinny pine trees through which we could see the clear turquoise water of the Caribbean. We made several false stops as we looked for a place with lots of people. Finally, Fidel's jeep came to a halt and he led us through the shaded trees and back into the hot sun.

"What a beautiful place," he commented as the first bather cried out, "Fidel, Fidel. Look everyone, Fidel is here."

A rather portly woman was even more friendly, yelling, "Ah, Chico, how good to see you," as she engulfed Fidel in a warm, wet embrace.

The swimmers began to turn toward the shore to see what was happening. As each saw who was there, he or she swam in to join the crowd.

Fidel began to chat and joke with the people.

Beach

CASTRO: How nice, how nice it is here. Good day, good day.

CRIES: *Comandante*. Fidel! Fidel!

C: How are you? How are you? Aren't you going to swim in the sea?

#1: Yes, I already went.

C: Are you on vacation?

#2: Yes, we are the workers from nearby.

CRIES: Fidel! Fidel! Fidel!

C: Hello, hello, hello. I feel envious of all of you that have the chance to swim today. The water looks good today.

#3: Yes, yes, it is very nice.

C: How old is your child there?

#4: Five. His name is Ernesto, the same as Che.

C: More people come to the beach on Sunday, right?

#4: Yes.

C: And is the sea big enough for them all?

#4: Yes. (laughter)

C: How old are you?

#5: Twelve years old.

C: Which of you all swims the best?

#5: He does.

C: Your snow cone will melt. You better eat it. Eat it. (laughter) The water's very quiet now. Go in the water. It's no sin. You are not bored?

#6: No, no. We're so proud that you're here.

C: What grade are you in?

#7: Ninth.

C: That is a good grade. What do you want to study?

#7: Engineering.

C: And you?

#8: (a woman): Engineering also.

C: With so many engineers, we're going to have a problem. (laughter) Every once in a while, I stop by the engineering school. In what do you work?

#9: I work in an office.

C: Yes? Well, I just came to make a short visit with some journalists who are going to shoot some scenes of all of you. It's going to be on television.

CROWD: Yeah, yeah.

C: I just said that I can't go swimming here. (laughter) Are you a student?

#10: Yes.

C: What are you studying?

#10: Ballet.

C: Well, I'm going to leave so that you all can return to your swimming.

CRIES: No, no, no.

C: Until later, have a good time. Hearty appetite. Study hard all of you.

CROWD: See you—Fidel! Fidel!

As we left, Mankiewicz said to Fidel, "You know, you remind me of an American politician during a campaign, shaking hands with the voters at the beach"

"Yes," answered Fidel, "but American politicians only go to the beach on the eve of the election—never afterward.

"It's too hot and muggy today for the jeeps," continued Castro. "We really should be riding around in our cars. It's too bad they're not here."

A few miles from the beach, the jeeps came to a sudden halt. There—from nowhere—was a whole line of automobiles. Fidel motioned Landau and us into his car, and the rest of the crew got into Alfa Romeos.

"We're lucky," Fidel said. "This car is air-conditioned; it should be a lot more comfortable."

It may have been comfortable, but hardly cool. The car was a large black Russian limousine with tan leather seats. The AK-47 rifle was secured to the floor under Fidel's feet. The small box of cigars and the tin of mints had been transferred from the jeep. The windows were closed and we waited for the cool air. But it never arrived.

As Fidel described the scenery, the car got hotter and hotter. The air conditioning was noisy but broken, and on top of that we were all smoking cigars. The heat and stuffiness were unbearable, but hardly mentionable because Fidel had made such a point about the new air conditioning. Finally, Jones tentatively pressed a button to lower the rear window half an inch. Nobody noticed, and Fidel kept right on talking. What made it even worse, Fidel seemed to be the only one in the car who didn't perspire. Over the next few miles, that rear window got lower and lower with each "invisible" touch of Jones's finger. In the front seat, Saul had begun to do the same with his window. Fidel kept talking. Finally he said, "Why don't we open the windows a bit and let the fresh air come in?" All the windows immediately came down the rest of the way and Fidel never missed a beat.

"You know," he said, "it's close to four o'clock. If we went back to Havana now, all of you could take a

30

swim at the hotel and rest up for your trip home to-morrow. Or, if you wanted, we could perhaps have some lunch."

We really did not know what to say. Was the invitation real, or was Fidel only being polite? Did he want to go back? Who knew?"

"Well, either way is OK with us," Jones answered.

"I think there might be a new Arab restaurant around here somewhere, if you did want to eat something."

"If you'd like to eat," Jones replied, "it would be fine with us."

"Well, I'm not sure where the restaurant is; I've never been there. Are you sure you want to eat instead of a swim?"

"Sure, we are a bit hungry."

"Fine, then. Let's eat."

Fidel turned to the driver and told him exactly where to go and what turns to make. All along, it appeared, he had known where we were and how to get to this Arab restaurant out in the middle of nowhere.

The limousine, followed by the cars and jeeps, pulled up in front of the restaurant, and Fidel jumped out. At the top of a curved stone stairway two waiters were taking a break at the front door.

"Are there many people inside?" Fidel shouted.

One of the waiters answered casually that there were indeed a lot of people. Then he saw who was to be his guest and changed his answer.

"No," he said, "nobody's here."—A pause, then, "I mean, yes . . . or no," all with the implication that by the time Fidel climbed the stairs, he could have his choice. Both waiters ran back into the restaurant.

Fidel turned back to us. "Come on, let's go inside. Do you want to visit the kitchen?"

Did we have a choice?

He quickly led us into the small kitchen, filled with steaming pots and frying pans cooking on the stove. He met the chefs and began to remove the tops of the pots and look at the food.

31

"It all looks pretty good here. Do you have room for all of us?"

"Why, of course," answered the maître d', who had just joined us.

"Well, if you don't serve us, we'll lower your prices," he joked. With that, we were led to a large round center table. Fidel table-hopped, greeting all the patrons, and then joined us at our table.

The Arab meal was delicious—houmous, salad, shish kebab, 1971 (pre-coup) Chilean wines, dessert, and a large mild Cuban cigar.

But as good as the food was, it didn't compare with the conversation. We had just completed a fascinating day; the pressures of the formal interview were over; we all knew each other better and were more relaxed. As we finished our meal and lit up those long Cuban cigars, we launched into what was to become a three-hour discourse on revolution.

It began with a comment of Fidel's concerning the case of Lieutenant William Calley. "I just do not understand," he said, "why some men seem to like to kill just for the sake of killing. Why are men like that?"

Jones then asked Fidel about the system of justice during the revolutions. "Che wrote," Jones said, "that during a revolutionary war, traitors must be shot on the spot, without trial, to preserve the safety and integrity of the entire group. He called this the revolutionary system of justice. Did you face this situation in the Sierra Maestra?"

"Yes, we did. It was always a problem for us. Several times we found traitors or informers in our midst and they had to be executed. Some of those times, those fighters who were of the Calley kind were given those assignments. We never liked to do this, but it was forced upon us."

"Was the problem of traitors and informers a serious one?" followed Jones. "How did you know, for example, whether a new recruit was really on your side?"

"Well, it was a problem that we had to watch continually. I personally interviewed every person that came to the mountains to fight. I could tell after just a half hour's discussion whether that person was real or not. Not necessarily by asking him about his feelings and thoughts of the revolutionary struggle, but more by conversation about his background, his family, his past life. My intuition was very good and I just felt in the pit of my stomach whether a certain individual was on the level.

"I remember on various occasions the CIA tried to infiltrate our ranks with people who posed as journalists. And we always knew right away who they really were. You see, journalists are particular kinds of people. They always ask hundreds of different questions. They are very inquisitive. That is their job. A few of them did come to the Sierra Maestra. But a phony journalist—a CIA agent posing as a journalist— never asked questions the way an authentic reporter would. They couldn't play the role. A real journalist could be a CIA agent, but a CIA agent can never realistically appear to be a journalist."

"Was there ever a time during the early days after the *Granma* [1] landed that you thought you would not succeed?" Jones asked.

"No, never."

"Even after the Battle of Alegria del Pio?" [2]

"No, not even after that battle. You have to understand that we were right in what we were doing. Not only right in our cause, but correct in our overall method. Our basic tactic of beginning the revolutionary struggle in the mountains, at the time that we did, was correct. And we all knew that. Looking at events from a tactical point of view, we might have changed some things."

"Like what, for example?"

---

[1] *Granma* is the name of the boat in which Castro and his initial guerrilla force traveled to Cuba from Mexico in December 1956 to begin the Revolution.
[2] The first real battle of the revolution on December 5, 1956, in which a Batista surprise attack nearly decimated the embryonic guerrilla force.

33

"Well, I might not have chosen to attack El Uvero." [3]

"But wasn't that a great success?"

"Yes, we did win that battle. But in a revolutionary war, you must look at what you gained for what price. The winning of the battle for El Uvero cost us lives and equipment. You must always measure the possible loss against the possible gain. A rule of waging revolutionary warfare is to engage in only those battles in which there is the highest certainty that if you lose the battle the overall loss is minimal, but if the enemy loses the battle, their overall loss is great."

As Fidel talked on about the old days in the mountains, his mind began to wander, and a hazy look came over his face as he remembered what must be for him the most romantic days of his life and his struggle—"the good old days." He seemed to enjoy talking about the time in the Sierra Maestra. But it was time to leave. We never saw anyone pay the check; someone must have.

Back in the limousine, Jones continued to probe Fidel's memory and thoughts on revolution.

"You're very interested in this subject, aren't you?" Fidel asked Jones.

"Yes, I am. Ever since Santo Domingo in 1965."

"You were there during the Dominican Revolution, weren't you?"

"Yes, I was," confirmed Jones.

"Then let me tell you some things in more detail. You know there is a lot of strategy in waging a guerrilla war. For example, let me tell you about fighting in the mountains in difficult terrain against far better equipped forces than your own. There is a definite technique in attacking a column of approaching soldiers. You have to position your men well and know which part of the column to attack in what order. Almost the worst things that can happen to a band of

---

[3] The first major success of the guerrilla war, during which an army post had been defeated but at a cost of fifteen dead or wounded—or a little less than twenty percent of the entire guerrilla force at that time.

guerrilla fighters is to sustain a lot of wounded. That is really one of the greatest problems, because they have to be carried and cared for. It has a great effect on the mobility of the force and it is a serious factor."

By this time, Fidel's cigar was working overtime and he was oblivious to the passing scenery. His left hand was spread out to form an imaginary battlefield, and with the fingers of the right he began to diagram how to attack a column of enemy soldiers. It was a detailed lesson in guerrilla warfare, enthusiastically explained not by an army war college colonel reading from a textbook, but by one of the few men in the world who had successfully accomplished what he himself was describing.

The complicated explanation continued for the next half hour. Fidel then launched into an analysis of other revolutions—in Vietnam, China, Venezuela, Guatemala, and the Dominican Republic.

"Francisco Caamaño [leader of the 1965 Dominican Revolution]," he said, "was very much like Che. Both were valiant fighters, very courageous, with a lot of energy. Caamaño went back to the Dominican Republic because he believed in the people, he had confidence in the people.

"Some revolutionary fighters, though, let their enthusiasm for the cause overwhelm their tactical decision-making. A reckless fighter, even a brave and valiant one, can cause serious problems for the entire force.

"Let me give you an example. On several occasions when we would receive word that a column of Batista's troops was approaching, some of the guerrilla fighters would immediately propose an attack without really thinking about the possible outcome of that attack. That is what I was saying before about always judging the impact of any battle. There exist occasions when it may be wisest to let the column go through without attacking because the time, place, and tactical considerations are not the best. When everything is not just right, the possibilities for unforeseen events and for damage are greatly increased."

Back at the hotel, it was time to say good-bye; after all—although for nearly four days it had hardly seemed so—Fidel Castro did have other things to do than chat with a few Americans about guerrilla warfare and the state of the world.

A Brief Return

In late July, we returned to the United States, with more than seventy thousand feet of film taken in Cuba, including more than eleven hours of filmed interview with Castro. Since this represented the first serious interview with Castro to be made available to American television networks in many years—Landau's program had appeared on educational television in 1969 —we thought we had something in which the networks would be interested. We were in for a rude awakening.

For two "liberals," who had rather automatically defended American networks and their news policies over the years from attacks by the likes of Spiro Agnew, it was disquieting to discover that the networks did indeed have a news monopoly, one which they intended to preserve even at the cost of depriving the viewing public of a chance to see anything they themselves had not produced. The policy—adhered to at each of the three major networks—was simple: no news or public affairs program would be purchased or otherwise acquired from any "outside" producers.

In other words, if a news event occurred and a network cameraman and correspondent were not there to record and report it, it might as well not have happened. While this had very little to do with the claims of Agnew and others that there was a "pro-liberal" bias on the part of the network chiefs, it was nevertheless true that there *was* a bias, if only one which guaranteed that the way in which the networks chose to report the news would be the only way American audiences would ever see it.

In their defense, the networks say that because they are "responsible" for anything that goes out over the network as news, they must be able to control its con-

37

tent and method of production in order to be able to defend the product and their responsibility against the FCC, affiliated stations, and the public. But this is circular reasoning. The networks are "responsible" for the content of their news and public affairs programs because they choose to be. They are *held* responsible for content and production because they have *declared* themselves to be wholly responsible for content and production. Except for the five stations they each own, the networks are really responsible only to their stockholders. If they were to make some of their limited news and public affairs time available to outside producers, and state so on the air, there would be no problem of "responsibility."

But there is another problem that may be animating the networks in their restrictive news policy, and it seems a more likely cause. Each network maintains an elaborate worldwide news organization, and a top-heavy production and reporting staff in New York and in Washington. In addition, the amount of time available for the use of the product of this staff is sharply limited by network choice. One half hour of prime-time news per day and a few one-hour "public affairs" specials each month hardly constitutes full employment for the network news staffs. The result is that producers may produce only one program a year, and correspondents may go weeks without appearing on camera. If the networks used outside producers, it would increase underemployment and possible encourage the public's belief that "outsiders" are as capable, or even more capable, of presenting news and public affairs than the networks.

The president of NBC news, Richard Wald, had made his network's position rather clear before we left for Cuba in June: "If you come back with an interview with Khrushchev—now three years dead—we might want to look at forty-five seconds of it for the 'Nightly News.'" The president of ABC news, William Sheehan, said he didn't even want to look at the Castro film nor did he want to read a transcript of the interview.

That left CBS, where before our departure news vice-president William Leonard had indicated an interest in seeing the film and talking about a possible deal. Accordingly, we took the film and the transcript of the interview to CBS and began to talk to Leonard and to Gordon Manning, another news executive.

As it turned out, the day we went was the very day on which Nixon revealed the "smoking gun"—in the form of new and incriminating tapes—and it was clear that the President's resignation was imminent. Consequently, the meeting broke up and Manning headed for Washington. We did not resume our discussions with CBS until a week after Nixon's resignation, which turned out to be a very fortuitous circumstance.

Manning and Leonard suggested that in any event an additional interview with Castro would have to be held in order to bring the material up to date. After all, said the CBS executive, a network could not air, in October 1974, an interview in which Castro spoke of "the Nixon policy," or "the Nixon administration blockade," when the man had not been President for nearly three months. So we agreed to ask Castro if we could return for an updating interview as soon as possible.

But were it not for a CBS "personnel development," even the updated interview would not have made it. In the wake of Nixon's resignation, CBS News had pulled Dan Rather from his assignment as White House correspondent, under circumstances which gave rise to strong—and very believable—rumors in the industry and press that the action had been taken because of pressure on the network from affiliated local stations, angry at what they believed to be Rather's anti-Nixon role during the Watergate controversy.

Whatever the reason, Rather was gone from the White House, and CBS and Rather quickly joined in an announcement that he had been promoted. The proof of this, it was said, was a new "CBS Reports" program which Rather would anchor, becoming, as CBS put it, "the new Edward R. Murrow."

This turned out to be the key to the Castro interview, because CBS News president Richard Salant, citing the network policy against outside material, finally rejected the proposal of Manning and Leonard that CBS purchase our Castro interview, even with the updated portion. But when Mankiewicz, in the course of one last desperate phone call, raised the question of whether the network would be interested in the program "if a CBS correspondent went along for the update interview," the reaction was favorable and the deal was made. All that was needed was for Castro to approve Rather's accompanying Mankiewicz and Jones on the second interview, and CBS would then be able to "marry" our July interview with the Rather interview in October.

Although we had thought Castro might not approve the participation of an American network newsman, he agreed to Rather's participation, and we prepared to go back to Cuba at the end of September, bankruptcy at least temporarily averted.

All went well, except for one of those coincidences that come up now and then to thwart even the best and most carefully planned arrangements. Two days before Mankiewicz, Jones, Rather, Manning, and the crew from the earlier interview—Landau, Pearce, and Berger—were to leave for Mexico and Havana, it was announced that Senators Jacob Javits (Rep., N.Y.) and Claiborne Pell (Dem., R.I.), were to visit Havana on the same weekend. Their visit had been arranged, in principle, through the Senate Foreign Relations Committee some months before, but the senators had not been able to arrange their schedules until this time.

The visit of Pell and Javits would not necessarily complicate our interview, but the presence of American newsmen accompanying them certainly would. When we got to Mexico, the knowledge that twenty-three newsmen, including representatives of the other networks, were already in Havana made the CBS people nervous. Gordon Manning informed us just before our departure that CBS executives in New York had told him that our deal was off if Castro granted an interview of any substance to either of the other networks. We flew into Havana with some foreboding.

As it turned out, we need not have worried. Very few of the newsmen accompanying Pell and Javits knew anything about Cuba, and only a handful spoke any Spanish. Most of them had been recruited instantly from their newspapers and television stations when the Javits-Pell visit was announced.

For the most part, the newsmen acted in Cuba as though they were covering two American politicians in the United States, and this caused some friction with their Cuban hosts almost immediately. Not only did they complain a great deal about food, hotel accommodations, and the arrangements that had been made for their travels during the two days they were to stay, but at a session with Cuban Foreign Minister Raul Roa, one of them breached diplomatic courtesies and probably ended whatever opportunity any of the visiting newsmen may have had for an interview with Castro.

Javits and Pell were sitting with Roa, engaging in the small talk that usually accompanies such photo sessions. While Roa was in the midst of a polite answer to a polite question from one of the senators, Richard Valeriani of NBC news cut in with a shouted question: "Mr. Foreign Minister, what about relations with the United States?"

Roa turned slowly, as though something unpleasant had occurred—which, indeed, it had—and said that, while he was unfamiliar with the practice in the United States, journalists in Cuba waited until the foreign minister had finished his sentence before asking a question. With that, he, Javits, and Pell went into an adjoining office for their serious discussion.

There were fears on our part that Castro might still feel that it would be appropriate to hold a press conference with the visiting Americans, dashing the chances for ours. This fear was heightened on Sunday evening, when it was announced that Castro would meet with Javits and Pell for dinner in his office, and that there would be another cameras-only session in the outer office before dinner. One of the reporters told Mankiewicz there was a rumor in the American press corps that this would be the time and place where Castro would conduct the press conference. The photograph session was scheduled for eight-thirty in the evening.

At seven-fifteen, Jones came into Mankiewicz's hotel room, and a gloomy discussion followed of what might be salvageable if Castro were indeed to talk to the American press and television. Almost immediately there was a call from Daniel Rodriguez of the foreign ministry. Rodriguez asked Mankiewicz to stay in his room for another call "soon." Our thought was that Castro might summon us for a meeting before he met with the press, perhaps to discuss the ground rules for *our* forthcoming interview. Mankiewicz headed for the combination bath-dressing area—rooms at the Hotel Riviera are substantial—and said, "If we're going over to meet Fidel, I'd better shave." Clad only in a pair of shorts and a back brace he had been wearing for a few months, Mankiewicz was shaving when there was a knock on the door. Jones opened the door—and in came Fidel Castro! Mankiewicz stuck out his lathered face. Fidel smiled and said, "What's the matter, Frank, have you been having trouble with your back?"

"Uh—sort of—*Comandante*—" Mankiewicz stammered, and bolted back into the dressing room to remove the shaving soap and pull on pants and a shirt. When Mankiewicz emerged, Castro was telling Jones that "in an hour, I have to go meet with the two senators and also with the newsmen, but I wanted to say hello first to my friends."

The surprise visit lasted an hour and was most pleasant. Fidel asked us about Pell and Javits, but as we began a sort of standard American political briefing, Fidel interrupted and said, "You know, I think this is the first time I have ever been personally involved in a New York State election campaign." Mankiewicz and Jones looked at each other and realized that Castro hardly needed a political briefing. Javits at that time was in the final month of a reelection campaign against former Attorney General Ramsey Clark, and it was widely believed that Javits needed some shoring up of his liberal support, and that the visit to Cuba might be part of such an effort. In any event, Castro realized that whatever he did it would have some some impact on the election.

He then asked if we had any advice as to how he should deal with the American reporters. Mankiewicz, thinking about the possibility that the earlier interview might not get on the air if Castro were to have a full press conference, and not unmindful of the sure bankruptcy that would face our company if that were to happen, said to Fidel, "Well, if you have a press conference with them, we will be *ruined*." The Spanish word *arruinado* has a nice sound and is a strong word, and Mankiewicz thought it would be appropriate. He then added, "However, *Comandante,* you are not a shareholder in our company, and it might be in your interest and that of your country to talk the the reporters."

But Castro assured us that he had never had any intension of holding a full conference, and that this position had been reinforced when he had heard "that one of them was very rude to our foreign minister yesterday." He would merely permit photos, he said, of an informal chat he would have with Pell and Javits prior to their dinner. We felt more than somewhat relieved.

The rest of the hour was a conversation about the topics that would be discussed during the interview in which Rather was to take part. It was agreed that the interview would take place on Wednesday, October 2, and we indicated our desire that Castro discuss any changes he saw in U.S.–Cuban relations as a result of Ford's having assumed the presidency. We also said we would appreciate his response to the recent revelations that the United States had "exported revolution" to Chile, and that the CIA had cooperated in the overthrow of President Allende's administration there.

Castro agreed, and also offered to take all of us on another jeep tour on Wednesday. "I want to show you

43

our schools when the children are there," he said, and we readily agreed to the tour. Just as Castro was about to leave, he once again offered to fly us all back to Nassau in his airplane after the interview, and we eagerly agreed to that, too.

He then looked at his watch, rose from the chair, and said, "It's very late, I'll have to go or I'll keep the senators waiting. I'll pick you up on Wednesday." And with that, he was gone at a trot down the hall to where two of his bodyguards were waiting at the service elevator. After he was gone a few moments, Jones looked on the table and realized that Fidel had left his visored fatigue cap. His first thought was, "What a great souvenir"—his second, "I'd better try to catch him at the elevator and return it." He acted on the second impulse.

When Castro arrived to meet Pell and Javits, everything was arranged. The three of them were quietly talking while the photographers and cameramen began taking their pictures. Then, from the back of the room, a voice said, "Mr. Prime Minister, why won't you answer our questions?" Castro turned in the general direction of the questioner, and said—in Spanish, of course—"I would like to answer your questions, but I had a long interview in July with another group of journalists, and it is important that their interview be exclusive. If I answer your questions—they will be *ruined*." The word still sounded good.

"Is that other group the one involving Frank Mankiewicz and Kirby Jones?" asked another voice.

"Yes, that is the group," answered Castro.

"But that's unfair," called out David Binder of the *New York Times*. "*They* are amateurs," added Binder, "and *we* are professionals." Castro pulled on his cigar and replied thoughtfully, "Yes, I think you are right. They *are* amateurs—but they got the interview, didn't they?" At which, he turned and gallantly showed Senators Javits and Pell into his office and an aide closed the door. The danger passed.

The jeep tour on Wednesday was very successful. Castro was delighted to be able to show us schools in session this time, and we were able to visit a number of classrooms. At the interview itself, he seemed most anxious that we ask a question about Senators Pell and Javits as well as a question about political prisoners. When Rather finally asked about the prisoners, Castro seemed to welcome the question. He said that Senator Javits and Senator Pell had been concerned about the status of some Americans who were held prisoner in Cuba and, "as a courtesy" to the visiting senators, he said his government was considering the early release of some of them. It was thought at the time that this was Castro's way of smoothing over some bad feelings that had developed—the weekend of the Pell-Javits visit had also been one of the four weekends of the year when Castro delivers a major public address. This address was strongly anti-American in tone and devoted almost entirely to the U.S. intervention in Chile.[1]

As part of the conversation back in Mankiewicz's hotel room, Castro had been downright apologetic about attacking the U.S. virtually in front of the visiting senators.

"But what could I do?" he asked, rhetorically. "What would the people of Cuba have thought if, in my first public appearance since the revelations about the role played by the CIA in the overthrow and murder of Allende, I spoke entirely about other matters?" We got the distinct feeling that he wanted that thought conveyed to Javits and Pell, at least indirectly.

In any event, he had placed great emphasis upon the question about the prisoners, and the answer which forecast the release of some of them. He repeated the statement later, over a drink and some conversation after the interview, and even agreed to give CBS a beat on the opposition by notifying us the day before the announcement of the release.

He was as good as his word. Within a week word came that the government of Cuba would announce the release the next day, and four American prisoners were released on schedule.

---

[1] See Appendix 1 for complete speech.

The Interview

Author's Note:

The following interview is the result of almost thirteen hours of formal discussion with Fidel Castro. It is a combination of the interviews of July and October 1974. In the interest of clarity and continuity, these two sessions have been combined and integrated. No answer of Castro has been edited in any way that could change the meaning. Many of the sidelight conversations not pertaining to the formal question-and-answer sessions are contained in the preceding chapters.

Fidel

Q. You visited the United Nations in New York to attend the heads-of-states session in 1961. Have you wondered where they are now, after thirteen years? Everything has truly changed.

A. That is true, the panorama has certainly changed.

Q. I am thinking of Macmillan, Kennedy, Khrushchev. . . .

A. I think there was also Sukarno.

Q. And De Gaulle?

A. De Gaulle. Yes, things have changed, for one reason or another. Some have died, others were assassinated, like Kennedy.

Q. You are almost the dean.

A. Some heads of state have been in power thirty years—more than thirty years. I don't consider myself the dean. In a way I still consider myself a pioneer.

Q. How old were you in 1961?

A. In 1961 I was thirty-four years old. Time passes; a few years have gone by.

Q. Does the state pay you a salary, do you receive a check every month or every week?

A. Of course I do. We don't have many expenses. It is the same salary former ministers used to receive, divided by half. Of course, all taxes, social security, and Party dues are deducted. You don't have to pay personal taxes, but of course our salaries are not very high.

Q. What is the highest salary that a Cuban can earn?

A. A minister earns around seven hundred pesos.

Q. Seven hundred pesos monthly?

A. Monthly.

Q. How much does an engineer or an architect earn, for example?

A. It depends. You could be talking about a doctor with a specialty. I don't recall exactly, but I believe a specialized practitioner will earn between four hundred and five hundred pesos.

Q. What about a cane-cutter?

A. Depends on how much work he does. Some cane-cutters will earn two hundred, up to three hundred pesos, depending on how much they cut. . . .

Q. Is there a great gap between the lowest salary and the highest?

A. There are no large salary differences, and in general the salaries for the factory managers and the unit chiefs are not that high. We have tried to keep the differences small, and some of these salaries, such as university professors, are high because they date far back.

Q. High?

A. Yes, like the doctors, based on their specialty and their studies. They start working with a certain salary, and as they study and specialize their salaries are increased. Since we are always attempting to encourage betterment and further studying, each

47

higher classification means a higher salary. In some cases, salaries are related to productivity, amount produced, but the professional classification is also paid for.

Q. Do you do a lot of reading?

A. All that I can.

Q. What type of books do you like to read?

A. Political literature and Party literature as well as economic and historical, for which, regrettably, I don't have all the time I wish I did. Sometimes I read classical novels also. . . .

Q. Which authors?

A. I will say practically all the classical authors. Actually a great number of works. Economic topics, about energy, monetary crises, and development in general. A lot of books are published now and we always have more than we can keep up with. The President of Mexico and a Mexican publishing house gave us a complete library recently, and I wish I had sufficient time to read all the very interesting books that comprise that collection. Of the American authors, Hemingway is one of my favorite writers. He was very close to us.

Q. Did you know him personally?

A. Yes, I met him after the triumph of the Revolution, when we were handing out the Hemingway Awards for a fishing competition. But I knew his works from before the Revolution. For example, I read *For Whom the Bell Tolls* when I was a student. It dealt with a guerrilla group and I found it very interesting, because Hemingway wrote about the rear guard fighting against a conventional army. I can tell you that of the works that helped me develop tactics for fighting against Batista's army, this novel by Hemingway was one of them.

There were other very important works in which we learned about the War for Independence, especially the history of Máximo Gómez. One of the topics that I have always liked was Cuba's history during that period—the writings of the men who were making history then. I have read practically everything written by the men who participated in the struggle for independence, Máximo Gómez, Antonio Maceo, and other patriots.

From all that, there was one unresolved issue—how a revolution can be carried out against a modern army. There were modern writers who even during the Paris Commune had concluded that it was impossible to fight a modern army. Someone said, I believe it was Mussolini, that the revolution had to be carried out with or without the army, but never against it. They were struggling with the difficulties of carrying on a revolution against a modern army, and we found ourselves in the same situation here in Cuba—fighting against a relatively modern army which had absolute control of the arms. The methods other men used to solve this problem helped us considerably to develop an intuition of how to do it. These elements were in the book by Hemingway, *For Whom the Bell Tolls*.

Q. Interesting. Did he know you felt this way?

A. He never said so. He traveled a lot and lived only a few years after the Revolution. He had his home near Havana, and today we have turned it into the Hemingway Museum. And let me tell you this, he is one of the world's most admired writers. He is greatly admired in the Soviet Union and in the socialist countries. Many people who come here as members of delegations, sailors, visitors—the first thing they want to do is visit Hemingway's house. It is incredible how widespread his popularity is. Everything in his house remains intact—his rooms, his library, the table where he used to stand and write for hours every morning. He wrote standing up, and everything is perfectly well preserved there.

Q. Are there some manuscripts there?

A. I don't know if there are any manuscripts there, but I do know that there are a lot of personal belongings of his.

Q. If you could spend a night talking with three historical figures, alive or dead, who would they be?

A. Do you include everyone in history?

Q. Yes.

A. Well, I will begin wtih the Cubans I admire the most. In the first place, José Martí, an extraordinary genius. As a warrior, Maceo, Máximo Gómez, Agramonte. Other historical figures that I admire very much are, of course, Lenin, Marx, Engels, and if you ask me for an American that I deeply admire, I would say Lincoln. I believe he was one of the most moving characters in history—especially how he worked in the fields and cut down trees; how he was so poor and lived under such difficult conditions; how he had to go through so many hardships in order to learn to read and write, to study; how he picked up the banner of justice during his time and so bravely and wisely struggled against all these difficulties; how he became the President of the United States; how he had to carry on a war, when he so loved peace.

It must have been a real struggle for such a peaceful man to find himself involved in a civil war. And then for his life to have ended so dramatically, so unfairly. All these elements make Lincoln's life one of the most moving biographies in history. There is no doubt about that, especially considering the cause that he espoused.

I also admire, of course, the great men who fought for the independence of Latin America—Bolívar, San Martín, Sucre, Juárez, and Tupac Amaru, the Peruvian who was one of the heroes of the struggle for independence. These are the men I admire the most.

When I was a boy I read a lot of history books and stories of warriors, as most boys do. I also read a great deal about Napoleon, Alexander the Great, Hannibal, etc.

Q. Who were your boyhood heroes? Soldiers?

A. Soldiers, yes, but this was typical of most boys, not of me alone. When we started to study history—Alexander the Great, Caesar, and Hannibal . . . well . . . boys always felt a great deal of admira-

50

tion for these heroes of antiquity, not because I aspired to become a warrior or had the warrior's spirit.

As I grew, I developed a deep admiration for the men in our history, because our country has a beautiful history. It was the last colony to gain its independence from Spain—it fought Spain for thirty years. We can call Cuba the Vietnam of the nineteenth century because we barely had a population of one million and we had to fight nearly three hundred thousand Spanish soldiers. This gives an idea of the magnitude of our fight without logistics, without a supply of arms, without help of any class. Extraordinary pages of heroism were written. Ours is a beautiful history. I understand that of all the countries of this continent, Cuba had to launch the most difficult and hardest fight for its independence. The wars of independence in Latin America started at the beginning of the nineteenth century when Spain was occupied by Napoleon, and the Latin American independence movement was widespread throughout the hemisphere at the time when Spain was very weak. It, too, was an heroic struggle; but the Latin American countries did not have to fight with the enormous disadvantages Cuba had to face. That is why I call it the nineteenth-century Vietnam.

Q. One question people always ask in the United States is why you always dress in guerrilla garb.

A. It is a habit. I feel more comfortable because I got used to it, and it seems more practical for me to dress this way. It is cheap clothing and very practical. Kirby was asking me why I was wearing this jacket and I told him to protect myself from the heat. (laughter)

Q. Do you intend to write your memoirs someday?

A. Actually, I believe I should. Not out of personal vanity, but rather out of a sense of obligation toward future generations, to let them know how things actually happened. When someone else writes their version of certain historical events,

51

they don't seem to adjust too closely to the truth. I agree with Martí that all the glories of the world could be written on a grain of corn.

We have documents, which I have saved since the old days for when I have the opportunity, the time. (laughter) Life teaches us that as time goes by we have less and less time, because we have more work. Work is more complicated, more rigorous, but some of us should find time to write.

Q. If you had one word of advice for revolutionaries, what would that be.

A. No, no one (laughter) will pay much attention to my words of advice, because no revolutionary listens to advice. I don't wish to pass off as an adviser of revolutionaries. I tell you the truth, we are satisfied with the way things have gone in Cuba. We are pleased, we believe we are accomplishing something, that we are achieving something long-lasting, the best that we can. I believe that some lessons can be derived from the Cuban experience, but it has also been a learning process. What we were supposed to do was never written anywhere. We had to learn as we went along, and we gained experience.

Q. And you continue to learn. . . .

A. Of course, we continue to learn. . . .

Cuba

Q. Fifteen years have elapsed since the Revolution. Would you summarize for us what you think are major achievements of the Cuban revolution? Its failures as well as its strong points? But first, the achievements . . .

A. We have had major successes in some areas. To understand this it is necesary to imagine Cuba as it was before the Revolution. We had, for example, close to six hundred thousand unemployed men out of a population close to six million, a little over six million. We had a thirty percent illiteracy rate, more than a million illiterates. We lacked sufficient schools; more than fifty percent of the children did not attend school. We had a very bad public health situation, a high infant mortality rate, other very serious problems, such as prostitution—close to one hundred thousand women lived off prostitution. We had gambling, and beggars on the streets.

In today's Cuba you do not find any of these problems. Unemployment among the male population has disappeared. And close to half a million women have joined the work force in addition to those women who were already employed. Prostitution, gambling, begging were eradicated. Illiteracy was overcome. Today we are the country with the lowest illiteracy rate in Latin America.

Q. What about infant mortality?

A. Infant mortality was reduced to 27.4 for each one thousand live births this past year—27.4.

Q. How does this compare to the rest of Latin America?

A. It is the lowest in Latin America. There are countries such as Brazil which have one hundred and forty. That is, one hundred and forty children out of each thousand born per year die during their first year of life. We now have close to one hundred percent of the children attending school. Not a single child in the country is denied the opportunity to go to school. And the quality of education has improved considerably.

Q. And public health?

A. At this time hospital facilities are available to all corners of the island, and many diseases have been eradicated.

Q. How many hospitals?

A. I can't quote you an exact figure, but we used to have very few public hospitals. Before the Revolution there were private hospitals and clinics supported by membership. To give you an idea of the average life span of the Cuban, it was approximately fifty-four years when the Revolution triumphed. We presently have an average of close to seventy.

Q. That is sixteen years' difference. . . .

A. Almost sixteen years gained in fifteen years. Of course, it would be pretty difficult to improve that average much more, because we now would start in a much better situation. We can say that in the fields of education and health, we are the most advanced country in Latin America.

We have also encouraged sports in Cuba. Professional sports disappeared, and Cuba now has a very favorable reputation in international sports events. In many major sports it rivals the United States. That is one of our major goals. Our great goal is to surpass the North American athletes. It is not easy, but we are trying.

We can also say the following—our people have a greater political conscience, a sense of dignity. For example, before the Revolution in Cuba we had racial discrimination; it was quite strong. Women also were discriminated against. We have overcome these problems. Cubans live in equality, in true equality. Another area which has seen considerable improvement is that of social security. In the fifties, very few workers could retire with the benefits of social security or a retirement plan. Today, every worker is covered by workmen's compensation for accidents, has guaranteed retirement and pension in his old age, and is insured against accidents. In other words, we have very advanced legislation.

We cannot overlook having withstood these past fifteen years—the enmity, the hostility of a country as powerful as the United States. Let us say that the mere fact of having been able to carry out the Revolution and to consolidate it is also a major achievement of these past years. Today the Revolution is a political reality, and the continuation of the revolutionary process is totally guaranteed. The Cuban government is probably the stablest of governments in Latin America. We have achieved a very high political stability and have set the basis for working in future years.

Q. What would you say about the spirit in Cuba? How would you compare the spirit of the country in 1958 and today?

A. The difference of spirit? Well, in 1958 we were struggling for the triumph of the Revolution. In those days it was the enthusiasm of the people. Today it is a conscious enthusiasm resulting precisely from experience, victories, and political consciousness gained over the years. You can sense this spirit on the streets, everywhere. We can say that today the large majority of the population actively participates in the Revolution. Almost eighty percent of the women belong to the Federation of Women; nearly eighty percent of all Cubans are members of the Committees for the Defense of the Revolution; and all the agricultural and other workers are organized. The students and even the children are organized. They have a place and they work together and are very optimistic about the future. We could call today's Cuba an optimistic Cuba.

I don't mean to imply that we have no difficulties. I don't suggest that our road is an easy one. But what I can say is that we have a very optimistic people, confident that it will overcome difficulties and the country will forge ahead. I can assure you of this, but anyone visiting the country can also capture this feeling.

Q. Well, after the Revolution triumphed, would you have changed or reversed any of the political decisions made during the sixties?

A. I believe that, in general terms, the events developed in an inevitable way. We, of course, did not have the experience we have today. It was not possible. In the handling of political, economic, or diplomatic affairs, we had no experience. And the United States had no experience in handling such revolutionary situations as that presented by Cuba.

It was the Foster Dulles era. It was also the era

55

of Nixon in the vice-presidency, of Eisenhower as President. All that led to a very hostile attitude toward us from the very beginning. I do not believe, therefore, the manner in which our relations with the United States developed was avoidable. And looking at it from the other side, if you analyze the revolutionary position, we were hypersensitive to any show of enmity, hostility.

Events, therefore, followed an inevitable course. We had to fulfill our revolutionary program. We could not fail to do this. It was a firm decision.

We had to start and pass the agrarian reform immediately, but at a time when no one could speak of agrarian reform in this hemisphere. After the Cuban revolution, yes, some North American politicians started talking about the need for agrarian reform in Latin America, but at that time the term agrarian reform was forbidden. The reality was that a major part of Cuba's land belonged to American companies, and what really started the conflict between Cuba and the United States was the Agrarian Reform Law.

Q. How?

A. Because it affected the interests of large American companies—owners of land in Cuba.

Q. Sugar producers?

A. Sugar producers mostly, because, for example, some American companies had as many as two hundred thousand hectares. Today, it is considered an average agrarian reform, in which the maximum ownership of land is limited to fifty hectares, sixty hectares. When we passed our Agrarian Reform Law it was not a very radical law, because we allowed up to four hundred hectares, and exceptions up to thirteen hundred hectares. But, of course, our law clashed strongly with the interests of some of the American companies which owned the best and greatest portion of the land we had. Of course, when people in the United States speak of agrarian reform in other countries of Latin America, the U.S. investments in those countries may not be mainly on land, but rather in other industries and mines.

Q. Can you tell me what percentage of the land belonged to Americans—to large landholders, to the North Americans?

A. To the Americans, I would say about forty percent of the best land. And in total, seventy percent of the land was in the hands of the large landholders, and thirty percent in the hands of small farmers—either tenant or squatter farmers. Even the land in the hands of small farmers, however, was not their property, but they had to pay with rent or produce or they were judged to be on the land illegally.

When the Revolution triumphed, one of the major steps was to limit the size of farms. This had already been provided for in our constitution as well as in almost all of Latin America's constitutions. The other major step was to give title to small farmers for the land they occupied. We gave them title. That is what the agrarian reform consisted of mainly, but that caused the conflicts. But we had to carry out the agrarian reform; it was inevitable.

Q. Speaking the Revolution, what was life like? For those of us who have never participated in a revolution, it is difficult to imagine what life is like for a band of revolutionaries, a band of seven men fighting on mountains for twenty-five months, without beds, without showers. . . .

A. Well, the group of seven men soon grew. We had our first succesful battle on January 17, 1957, when no one believed we were still alive. It was our first successful military operation, and we carried it out with eighteen men. As a matter of fact, we adapted to that way of life. We identified so completely and so well with the natural surroundings of the mountains that we felt we were in our natural habitat. Now when I go by those mountains, or if I fly over them and remember those days, I think we identified with the forest as much as the wild animals that live there.

We were constantly on the move. We always slept in the forest. At first, we slept on the ground. We had nothing with which to cover ourselves. Later on, we had hammocks. And nylon, we had not yet come to the energy crisis. (laughter) And it seems that polyvinyl was abundant. We used plastic covers to protect ourselves from the rain.

Later we organized kitchen duty by teams. Each team would carry the cooking equipment and the food uphill. In the beginning, we had to stop at houses to eat, but later on we freed ourselves from this. And, of course, there was another factor—we did not know the region well. We had practically no political connections in that region. We were the ones who established the relations with the population, studying the terrain as we fought. Besides the difficulties, Batista was carrying on a fierce repressive campaign, and there were many houses burnt and many peasants murdered. We dealt with the peasants in quite a different manner from the Batista soldiers, so that we slowly gained the support of the rural population, until that support became absolute. Later on, our soldiers came from that rural population as well as from the workers of the large sugar and rice plantations near the Sierra. From them our army was strengthened during the beginning.

Q. Did you base your actions, your military campaign, on the writings of anyone in particular?

A. No, not really.

Q. Were there any writings at that time?

A. There were some writings, but we did not have access to them. And then later on we did receive some writings and classic works on guerrilla warfare. But in the end, we had already faced the problems and found their solutions. As the fighting progressed, we developed our own tactics; we learned the art of fighting the enemy. In the beginning we really did not know, but we acquired experience. This is very important: we did not arrive there with the specific purpose of creating a center of disturbance, but rather with the very clear idea that we could win by forming a new army, and we did form a new army. We were certain that we would not receive aid from anyone, that we would have to take the weapons from the enemy, and that we would have to solve our problems from our own resources. There were different criteria—there were those who thought that the formation of a guerrilla front would create a national disturbance throughout the island and that in the end the problem could be solved by a military coup d'etat. But we saw clearly the danger, and we always fought the idea of a coup. Yes, we were aware of the need for support from the people, not only of the rural population in the Sierra Maestra, but also of the workers and the students, of the entire population. That is, we had to rely on the masses. We assumed we represented the true cause of the people and that we would obtain the backing of the people.

The alleged theorists on whom we were basing our struggle were correct. We did gain the support of the people, and that support played a major role, because in the end our army consisted of three thousand men against Batista's army which comprised seventy thousand men. But our three thousand men had experience and a lot of initiative. We had managed to form a small army which divided the island in two, so that in Oriente Province we had seventeen thousand of Batista's soldiers surrounded. That was when Batista's government finally collapsed. We had already defeated Batista's operations army, and the rest of his army was an occupation force in the cities where they had to watch everything. In the end, a coup was attempted which, according to the documents now available, was with the participation of the American embassy.

Q. How?

A. It seems that the American government realized that Batista was in a total crisis, and that a change was necessary. Batista asked the U.S. to let him

59

wait until the twenty-fourth of February because he had organized some fraudulent elections and they had elected a new president who was supposed to take over in February, and Batista asked the American government to let him stay until February twenty-fourth. But during the last three months of 1958 our forces started a strong drive, which provoked a crisis during the month of December. There was, therefore, no time for political maneuverings and no time to wait until February. But then at the last minute, in order to prevent the triumph of the Revolution, there was an attempted coup d'etat in Havana. When we received the news of the coup, we mobilized all our forces, and seventy-two hours later we had defeated the entire army.

We were then under new conditions: the old army was gone and the people had the weapons. Without that very important factor the Revolution would have been impossible, because at that time the strength of the Revolution was underestimated. No one—including Batista and the American government—believed that our strength could develop to the point that we could defeat the army. They thought they had time, but they did not. In our favor was the fact that we had the offensive, and this was constant. That is why the war lasted twenty-five months. There was no time for political maneuverings or for saving the old army.

Without these conditions being present, of course, the Revolution would never have been consolidated and it would have taken the same route as in Guatemala or what has happened in other countries.

Q. Or what happened in the Dominican Republic?

A. The Dominican Republic was another matter. American intervention decided the Dominican revolution by preventing the triumph of the popular will. As far as I know, the United States has yet to be condemned for intervening in the Dominican Republic.

Q. If you, hypothetically, had to face again the conditions of making a revolution in the fifties—able to foresee the results—would you make any changes in your decisions? How would you go about it?

A. There is no doubt that we would have followed the same route. We would have made the same decisions. Of course, we were less experienced in every sense. We had no military experience, but I believe we made the right decisions.

Q. The basic decisions?

A. Yes, and that we followed the correct route adjusted to Cuban reality. I am convinced we had no alternative. Perhaps if we had to go through that experience again, with the same hypothesis, during those years, we would have succeeded more rapidly.

Q. How?

A. Well, now that would be a matter of philosophizing a little over our experiences. If we speak, for example, about the armed struggle. We started at the Moncada barracks,[1] continued with the landing of the *Granma,* and went on with the guerrilla struggle in the Sierra Maestra. A shorter route would have been to start in the Sierra Maestra. Because when we tried to take over the Moncada, we attacked two barracks with a little over one hundred sixty men. I believe today that we had a good plan basically, that the attack was well organized, and that it was possible to take over the barracks. But we were unable to overtake the barracks. In an operation of this nature there are always the imponderables, the unexpected which can arise. Later, when we planned the struggle in the Sierra Maestra, we calculated that we would need three hundred armed men with automatic weapons, and in reality we were able to start with eighty-two men without automatic weapons. I think we had one automatic weapon. After the first few difficult days, when we

---

[1] The Moncada barracks was the second largest army barracks in Cuba. Located in the city of Santiago, it has now been converted into a school.

suffered great setbacks, only a few of us remained. We were forced to start fighting again in the Sierra Maestra with only seven men. If we had studied the region, if we had had with us the men we had in the attack on Moncada and the *Granma* landing, if we had taken them with us to the Sierra Maestra, we would have had a much firmer beginning in the military field. We would have started the struggle with a good supply of weapons, we would have had the arms for an entire regiment, the population of Santiago de Cuba. We would not have had to attack the Moncada or land in the *Granma*. We would have spared ourselves the long road. Therefore, if we had to relive those days and that situation with today's experience, we would have started fighting directly in the Sierra Maestra.

Q. Would it have been shorter?

A. Yes, it would have been shorter. But let me add that when we landed we did so on very difficult terrain. Had we landed on some other places, we would have kept the eighty-two men we had initially, and the fighting would not have lasted twenty-five months. It would have lasted fourteen, fifteen, sixteen months. I am not including the learning period, because it was experience that could only be obtained on the march and in the struggle.

Q. We have noticed since our arrival that while there are some similarities in Communism Cuba style with those other Communist societies, there are more things here that strike us as unique. There's a different feel to Cuba and to the Communist government here as opposed to other socialist countries. Could you define for us, in your judgment, what the difference is between Communism Cuban style and anywhere else?

A. We all start out with the same principles, the same basic ideas. They are the ideas of Marx, Engels, Lenin. Now then, each country has to apply these ideas to its own concrete conditions. What we have done is to interpret these ideas and to apply them

62

to the concrete conditions of Cuba. Undoubtedly, each country has different traditions, different idiosyncrasies, different customs, and I think that all these factors influence the form and manner in which a given idea or doctrine is applied. I would say that in reality, we have much in common—the concept of society, the concept of the state, the concept of history, the concept of economics, the organization, the planning of the economy, all these things we have in common, and also the role of the Party has similar criteria.

The origin of our revolution is different: the revolution takes on different forms in each country. It is the first revolution to take place in a Latin American country. Maybe the differences you observe relate to the character of our people, to the idiosyncrasy of our people, to the customs of our people. But the differences that may appear to you are not ones of principle but rather of one's own style, if one may call them so.

This educational program, for example, has been developed entirely on the basis of Cuba's needs, of Cuba's aspirations. And it is a very, very uniquely Cuban program. It is not a program that is similar to that of other countries.

Q. More Cuban than socialist?

A. I can tell you it is as much socialist as it is Cuban. This program is an adaptation of socialist and Martí's ideas to the concrete conditions of our country. For example, we have large mass organizations. The Committees for the Defense of the Revolution [CDR] do not exist in other socialist countries. In this manner, we not only have a party, but we also have very powerful mass organizations that embrace all the people. This has contributed to creating greater unity and greater strength of the masses. That is to say, these are peculiarities of our own, but based on the same socialist principles; even though the Cuban is very cheerful, smiling, and very enthusiastic, this has nothing to do with doctrine. It has to do with the character of the people, with the idiosyncrasies of the people. All we have done, really, has been to apply the revolutionary ideas to the conditions of our country. We did not seek to invent anything new.

Q. I suppose that what you are saying is that in a certain form, the socialist government of Cuba involves itself in the ordinary life of the Cuban in a more or less easygoing way—a less demanding way than other Communist governments, right?

A. I don't know, maybe it is the outward appearances.

Q. What about the areas of music, art, and movies?

A. We had some difficulties with that, but actually very little. You must also take into account that in the future I believe we will have to pay more attention to all these aspects. Actually, during all those years the Revolution was fighting to survive, we brought education, a higher political level, and a great culture, to the people. Maybe these could consititute future problems, but they are not current problems. It is true that we are, of course, trying to maintain, trying to enable the individual to feel the greatest freedom possible. We are opposed to the interference into the personal life of people, even though the Revolution assigns many tasks to everyone and gives a lot of work to all. Students have a lot of work, but they work in production, they study, participate in cultural, artistic, and sports activities; in brief, they have not a minute free during the day. Women do a great deal of work as workers, as members of the Federation of Women or trade unions, as housewives, and as members of the CDRs. If they are also active members of the party, they have a lot of activities. I hear that people are complaining, for example, that the teachers have a lot of work—in the schools, the programs, and the teachers' union; that the women also have many meetings. So I must say, in truth, that everyone here has many social obligations and many political obligations.

But this is also bringing about the feeling of being a part, being a participant. No one feels alienated from the process or feels indifferent to the state. Everyone here identifies with the revolutionary state. Today, each Cuban citizen can say as Louis XIV said, *"L'État—c'est moi"* [I am the State]. And this identification between the citizen and the power is decisive, for without it the Revolution could not have maintained itself.

It would be a great lie to assume that the Revolution is maintained by force; the Revolution has to develop strength to defend itself against the external enemy, but our internal revolution defends itself with the masses. In Cuba, there has never been a state of siege. Cuba has never had searches, and you will not see any inspections on any of the highways. Cuba never had a state of emergency, Cuba never had to take a soldier out into the street —never. There has never been a conflict between the government and the workers, between the government and the students, between the government and the peasants, between the government and the masses. Never. Never has a soldier been used against the people. In more than fifteen years of Revolution, there has never been a conflict between the government and the people. Why? Because the people, the masses defend it. It is their government. And this is a very solid thing. It gives great strength. We have achieved a great union of all the people, and had we not been able to achieve this unity and this support of the people, we would not have been able to resist the hostility of the United States. How many governments did the United States destroy! How many governments did it overthrow! In how many countries did it intervene during the past seventy years! And we have successfully confronted the opposition of the United States. It was the first time in the history of this hemisphere that a government was really able to resist the hostility of the United States government.

Decision Making

Q. Many Americans see Cuba not as a government, with a council of ministers, nor as a proletarian dictatorship, but as a government of Fidel Castro. What is your role in the government?

A. That is a much-used cliché to refer to the Cuban government. Sometimes I read references to 'Castro's government,' but there is nothing further from the truth. This is not a personal government. Not a single decision is made unilaterally, but rather, collectively, according to Party lines, involving the heads of the Party, the political leaders of the Party. All fundamental decisions are discussed there, the basic political decisions.

Q. But you are the head of the state and the commander-in-chief?

A. That is one thing.

Q. Which is first?

A. Head of state.

Q. Head of state?

A. Sometimes, of course, President Dorticos represents the country, and sometimes I represent it. Sometimes I go, somethimes he goes. Depending on the decision reached by the central government.

Q. But you are the head of state and of the Communist Party?

A. Yes, first secretary of the Party.

Q. In India, in the fifties, it was said that Nehru was like a banyan tree, under the shade of which nothing grew. Do you see a similarity in today's Cuba?

A. Well, we have just the opposite here, and my major activities have to do with the functioning of the Party in my capacity as first secretary of the Party. But I can say that there is great decentralization of responsibilities and functions within the government and that each one of the ministers has certain authority and acts with ample freedom within the areas that correspond to them. We have to attend to the political matters, to administrative matters, and to economic matters. This is precisely because the economy is in the hands of the state—this is a socialist economy. These matters are not managed by particular individuals, and this requires a great deal of effort on the part of the men who work in the central government. If they, therefore, do not limit themselves to certain fundamental matters, they could not do a good job, not even a bad job. I can assure you that I participate minimally, and even that minimum sometimes seems to me to be excessive. The day is only twenty-four hours long, time is short, and we have too much to do. I don't think you can apply your quote to the Cuban government, because many trees have grown—not under my shade, but under the shade of the Revolution. Many leaders, many cadres have developed.

Q. For example, what?

A. Suffice it to cite the army—our army has nearly twenty thousand officers trained under the Revolution in a country that had no army, that is, where the old army was totally replaced and dismissed. Numerous organizational leaders, administrative cadres, labor leaders, and political leaders have emerged under the shade of the Revolution.

Don't forget that all those who had administrative training in Cuba left the island. They went to the United States, and Cuba had to train its new cadres. We have withstood all the tests and continued forward. This has been possible because a new generation, a larger number of men have been trained. Under the shade of the Revolution many minds have flourished and new personalities have emerged. This would not have been possible were the Revolution controlled by individuals. I believe history is always impartial, and when the history of these revolutionary years is written, it will be clear that this was not a government of one person. I am really opposed to that. I don't believe in that.

67

I don't believe any man has all the qualifications and all the talents. We believe in collective capabilities, collective merit, and collective intelligence. The total sum of these minds will produce better results than the minds of a few individuals.

Q. If this is so, then how did people think that Cuba is a one-man government?

A. We are not the ones who seek all the glories, because it is the American press which, when speaking of Cuba, refers to Castro! As if Castro could do everything. What happens is that people seek symbols in men and to attribute to these men the efforts which other men did. At least, when we receive some honor or recognition, we think it is an honor and a recognition of the efforts of millions of people. One man or a few are too insignificant to perform the miracle of the Revolution; it is the people who performed the miracle. There is no doubt about that. It would be very sad if the Revolution depended solely on one man, and I would be the first one to be saddened because one always wants one's efforts to have some continuity.

Q. Then the problem of succession is a matter of—

A. It is an institutional matter, problem, concern. . . .

Q. —Of the Party? What is the form of succession within the Party?

A. Undoubtedly, within the revolutionary process, some men gain more prestige, and these men with greater authority are most likely to be selected. This is not a matter of my designating a successor. It is the Party that decides who occupies which position; and besides, we have no successors, because it is the collective which leads. If a member is missing, the collective continues to exist. Someone takes his place. The Congress elects its central committee and the central committee elects its political bureau, and it assigns the different positions to each one. We are not dealing with an absolute monarchy where the absence of one man is serious. It does not really matter who is the first secretary among several secretaries, a member of the political

68

bureau among several members, a member of the Central Committee among several members, and it brings us peace of mind to know that any impartial, objective observer of the Cuban situation would conclude that the survival of the Cuban revolution would not depend or be influenced by the death of one or two men. This is crucial.

Q. Doesn't anyone worry about this problem?

A. It is a problem that concerns the Party and the Party leadership. But as revolutionaries it gives us a great feeling of satisfaction to know that the revolutionary process is assured. This government belongs to no one in particular.

What many times happens in Latin America will not take place here. Often, when a man disappears from the scene, the system also perishes. What we claim with great satisfaction is that any one of us could die and it would not change things within the revolutionary process. I sleep well because I know that beyond us the Revolution continues and that the work of the Revolution is not in the hands of individuals but of the community. We say it with the phrase: "Men die—the Party lives on."

Q. How many members does the Political Bureau have?

A. Eight members, and it is mostly made up of all the ones who participated in the revolutionary struggle. Some go back to the era of the Moncada attack, such as my brother Raul, Ramiro Valdez, and Juan Almeida. We were together in the Moncada, in the jails, and later fought together in the Sierra Maestra, four of us. Others, such as Armando Hart, joined us after Moncada, but before the Sierra Maestra; Guillermo García, the first young rural peasant who joined us, and Sergio del Valle, who participated in the fighting in the Sierra Maestra and fought with Che, too. There is President Dorticos, who fought with us in the underground. So that the eight members of the Bureau, the Political Bureau, have this background. We get together regularly and discuss all the important

69

issues. Issues of lesser importance are decided by each one in his own area.

Q. What is the next level?

A. We have another unit within the Party, and that is the secretariat of the Party, which deals with certain types of problems. The more important ones are handled by the Political Bureau, and the major decisions are taken by the leaders of the Party. But from the point of view of the state, the laws, the agreements, these are decided by the executive committee of the Council of Ministers and by the Council of Ministers. The highest decision-making body is within the Party and is made up of this group who study the issues and make decisions collectively. We have no type of personal government and we are very pleased with this, because we believe that eight men think better than one, and that a single man, no matter how experienced he may be, is likely to make mistakes often.

Q. Was this system developed recently?

A. Even when we organized the Twenty-sixth of July Movement we set up a small group to head the movement, even before the Moncada assault—and although I had an important role within the organization, the planning and the preparations for the Moncada assault, we had a small group which discussed the issues jointly. Later we had another phase—after the attack on Moncada—which was called the Movement of the Twenty-sixth of July. This movement had national leadership which was overseas and organized the landing. During the fighting in the Sierra Maestra it functioned just like any military organization.

Q. And after you came to power?

A. After the triumph of the Revolution, we had various political organizations, although our movement certainly had the support of the majority of the people. We tried to unite all the revolutionary forces, and when this was accomplished, we had collective leadership, and all the problems were discussed jointly. This type of political leadership for running affairs of state will become more and more ingrained, and I don't believe the style or the concept can be changed.

Q. Have you ever suggested some measure that has not been adopted?

A. It can happen, it can happen. This is possible. I can have a particular opinion on a subject, and others differ and may be right. Many times, of course, we come to an agreement. Often it is the others who take the initiative, as I am not the only one who can take the initiative on any particular issue . . . everyone is involved in decision making.

Q. What role will these assemblies and councils which were elected in Matanzas play?

A. It is a pilot project insofar as some ideas that we plan to implement in the future. We want to test them in actual practice so that at a specific time we can carry them to a large plan, the national level.

It is related to the process of decentralization of public administration. The idea is that each locality manage its own services, its own production centers, and everything related to that locality.

Q. This pilot program in the Matanzas province. How did that election go, and will there be other elections now, soon?

A. Actually, the elections went perfectly well. The neighbors could nominate anyone, and there was one candidate to elect from among seven or nine. Then he had to obtain a majority plus one. When no one got a majority plus one, then runoff elections had to be held all over again the following Sunday. There was heavy popular participation in the nominating assemblies, and in the elections. Approximately ninety-five percent voted on the first round and nearly ninety-four percent during the second round.

We intend to analyze all the results and to apply these same principles nationally. In a year, more or less, we shall be able to collect the results of this

71

experience, and then at the end of 1975 we will hold the first Congress of the Party. The Party Congress will decide whether in 1976 it is possible to apply this procedure to the entire country.

Q. Is voting mandatory?

A. No, voting is not compulsory. No one is fined for not voting, because we believe each citizen is entitled to the right to vote, and it is his prerogative to exercise this right or not. We had a very high participation. Never in Cuba's history has there been such a high participation in an election. Before the revolution it usually was around seventy to seventy-five percent of the population, including when the dead cast their votes, because in Cuba the dead sometimes voted.

Q. And in some American cities, too . . .

A. Also?

Q. Sometimes.

A. And here we had ninety-five percent of the electorate participating on the first round, and ninety-four percent voting during the second.

Q. Why so high?

A. The revolutionary masses welcomed this initiative with great enthusiasm. Besides, it was organized by them, and they participated in the entire process. They understood how important it was to establish these organisms of popular power which will manage the communities' activities. All the mass organizations participated, the workers, the women, the defense committees, the rural organizations, the student organizations. The students elected members of the student groups. The military also voted and elected representatives from their groups. The results were very interesting. We were testing this mechanism because we had no electoral mechanisms and it was necessary that we create them, using the identity cards of each citizen, and everything went smoothly.

Q. What powers do the elected representatives now hold as the "Popular Power" in Matanzas?

A. They absolutely administer everything that has to

do with the province, with the region, and with the municipality. The public health program and the public health institutions of the province, for example, are all administered by them.

Q. Under the administration of the "Popular Power"?

A. Yes, of the "Popular Power." The educational program and all the educational institutions—including the type of schools we have visited—they have them under their administration.

Q. How about the appointments of teachers?

A. Yes, they appoint the teachers, too. And the doctors.

Q. According to certain standards, right?

A. Yes, of course. They must follow the same educational program, the same public health program, but they are responsible for all these programs. The taxis, the buses, the trucks for local transport, they administer them all. All the network of sports facilities and sports programs, all the restaurants, and recreation centers, the chains of movie theaters, and the cultural programs are administered by them. But, they do not administer, for example, the large basic industries such as the national railroads, or the sugar mills, which are run by the national exports industries.

Q. Construction?

A. No. They are in charge of part of the construction, not of the large-scale construction work that is done by the central government, but everything regarding maintenance and the construction of many facilities for local services are their responsibility.

Q. But you spoke of national elections—in 1976, did you say?

A. Yes.

Q. Yes. Now, these elections would be for what kind of office? Could you give us an example of the kind of office that would be open to the election?

A. Well, to organize the entire state. The municipal, regional, provincial, and national "Popular Power." As a result of this process, we will have a National Assembly which will have the power to pass laws

73

and which will have the authority to govern the state. From this National Assembly will come forth the Council of Ministers, the Executive Power. It will be the supreme body of the national "Popular Power."

We already have a Commission studying the constitution. It will be analyzed on the occasion of the Party Congress, and afterwards it will possibly be submitted to a national referendum for debate by all the people. In this manner, during the next two years we shall be taking a large step forward towards the institutionalization of the country. That is to say, the revolutionary government will cease to be a provisional revolutionary government.

For many years the Revolution had to fight for survival; the Revolution has succeeded in surviving. And now, it marches on at a marvelous pace and we can fulfill these tasks of giving the Cuban state a definitive form.

Q. The province is the largest unit?

A. No, after that comes the nation. The base for the organization of the state is municipality, region, province, and national state.

The municipality will, for example, have control of the administration of the schools, of the municipal hospitals, of the commerce or trade, transportation, and services. There will be municipalities in the country where the central state will not have anything to do with administration. Of course, if there is a sugar mill within the municipality, then that sugar mill will be administered or managed by a national organization. That will be where an industry operates or produces for the entire country, for export It will remain under the management of the central state.

The region will manage the regional enterprises, the hospitals, the industries that service several municipalities. Of course, the bakeries, the pastry shops, the stores, the recreational centers, the sports centers, all those will be managed at their corresponding level. The region will administer every-

74

thing that has to do with the region, and the province will manage everything that has to do with the province. For example, provincial transportation.

Q. What will this new stage of administration mean to the existing structure?

A. The local managers or administrators still exist and they have a series of obligations, but not as wide-ranging as they will have now. The schools were centrally administered. That is, the ministry of education administered the schools throughout the island. A school could need repairs or more teachers, but they were centrally managed.

Q. Who selects teachers?

A. Traditionally, that has been the responsibility of the ministry of education. Now, the teachers and the schools for teachers will be within the provinces, and the teachers will be selected by the corresponding administrators. There will, however, be uniform central guidelines. Guidelines are not decentralized; it is administration that is decentralized. It does not mean that directors of schools, or that a certain municipality, can change the educational programs or establish criteria which differ from that of the rest of the country. But the schools will be managed and run by the communities. If a school has a problem of maintenance, personnel, or whatever, the community will deal directly with this.

To be practical, there are national organisms which will remain with no provincial representation. The ministry of education will be a central ministry without provincial delegates. And so will the public health ministry. Of course, they will have relationships or ties with the responsible public health officers in the province, so that there will be certain participation on the part of the ministry in naming or appointing the party responsible for public health in the province, and, in the same manner, the province officials will relate to the regional officials and the regional officials to the municipal officials, but each one will have its own autonomous functions. The central organisms will establish the guidelines and develop plans for services, supplies, for all that is necessary. They will have to work jointly in this planning process, but the state will be decentralized. In the case of transportation, for example, the ministry of transportation will remain in control of railways, the interstate transports, and those transport bases in the provinces which are connected to the railways. All other transportation will be in the hands of the communities. The city of Matanzas, for example, will manage the taxis and its own urban transportation. Of course, electric plants, sugar mills, and the mining industry will remain in the hands of the central government.

We see this as a large school of government, because everyone will have to participate in the organization, direction, and control of all these activities. There will be a provincial assembly and the people will not only elect or appoint the executives for the province but will be responsible for a large number of activities. Of course, it won't be that difficult because, for example, the ministry of education personnel, the offices, the warehouses, the transports, will all be turned over to the provinces for them to do the administering at the provincial level and so on.

Communist Party

Q. After the elections for the "Popular Power" in municipalities, provinces, and the nation, what will be the role of the Party?

A. The Party will give the direction to the state and to the whole society. It will hold the supreme political command. The Party's role will be included in the constitutional precepts of the country: because the Party will play a political role, a role of uniting the people, of educating the people, of guiding the people, and the guiding of the state.

Q. But not the administration?

A. It has no administrative functions. In the municipality, the municipal Popular Power will administer all that is related to the municipality; the regional Popular Power, all that is related to the region; the provincial, all that is related to the province; and the national Popular Power, all that will remain in the hands of the nation.

The administrative functions belong to the state. The Party is in charge of the highest political guidance of the society, of the mass organizations, and of the state.

Q. Who is in the Communist Party?

A. The Party, which is at the revolutionary vanguard, is made up of exemplary members, the most revolutionary . . . elected by the masses, because to be a member of the Party you have to be nominated at your place of employment.

Q. And this structure will disappear one day—Marx has written there will be no state, no structure?

A. You are presenting a problem that not even the theorists have solved yet. It is possible that, at a given time, all the societies will form part of the Party, that there will be total identification among the societies and the Party. This is a stage at the vanguard, however, a revolutionary vanguard; but you are presenting a theoretical problem which has not yet been resolved.

Q. This disappearance of the state gives us a bit of trouble. . . .

A. (laughter) Well, look, the state has historically had the purpose of maintaining a given social system. The Athenian state—the famous Athenian democracy—with which they tried to fool us during the first years of school. What was this Athenian democracy? It was an enslaving society, and just a few had the right to gather in the public plazas to talk, to argue everything. The large majority was made up of slaves, people deprived of all rights, and the minority ruled. It was a patriarchal society, a society of proprietors, an enslaving society.

In Rome they had a similar situation. There was the famous Roman senate, and yet Rome had its nobility, and its commoners, and its slaves, and a republic with all the trimmings. The goal of that state was to maintain the privileges of the ruling classes. This no one will deny.

We had the era of feudalism. After the feudalist era, we had the feudal kings. They wanted to maintain a system of privileges of the landed gentry, the aristocracy. That society was replaced by another. It was the capitalist society, which maintains the capitalist society by force. For example, the United States. It doesn't only wish to see capitalism in the United States, but throughout the world—in Cuba, in Latin America, in Africa, Asia, Europe, everywhere . . . because then why else does the United States spend eighty billion dollars per annum on the armed forces? Why do they spend thirty billion on foreign military aid? What role does this huge army and those powerful armed forces play if not to maintain capitalism outside the boundaries of the United States? Of course, within the United States there has been no need for the use of force because it is maintained through its laws, judges, tribunals, Congress, the Senate, its police force, the FBI, the CIA, and that huge mechanism, the entire defense apparatus. Force then is used to maintain and preserve the interests of the capitalist system.

We utilize force to maintain the collective ownership of the means of production. We do not deny this, and our laws, our institutions, our policy, and our state institutions all have the goal of creating a new society—not perpetuating a society of patriarchs, of slave owners, of feudal lords, or large monopolies, nor large owners. Our goal is to establish the society of the workers. Our society today is not maintained by force. If it had been imposed by force on the people, the Revolution would have been overthrown. The United States intervention would not have been necessary to overthrow the Revolution, because our people are armed, the soldiers are our workers. Our organizations include everyone, the workers, the women, the agricultural workers, the students, the large majority of the population. So that internally, our State is supported by the general consensus.

We also have the strength to defend ourselves. The job of the army is the defense from foreign attack; it is not to defend the Revolution, because the Revolution needs no army. In the fifteen years that the Revolution has been in power we have never had a stage of siege. You see in Chile where they have just had a coup d'etat, they have been under a state of siege for months—people have to go to bed at ten o'clock at night. We have never enforced this here, because the people defend the Revolution, as workers, as soldiers, as agricultural workers. We have armed forces to defend us from foreign attack. Actually, against the United States, because if we did not have the United States as close as we do, we would not need an armed forces to protect us.

That is what I mean, that historically, each type of government has sought its historical role. This state does not believe in supporting the division of classes, but in the disappearance of class distinctions. . . . The state has been maintained as a tool for the domination of one class, so that when there are no exploiting classes nor exploited classes, the state as a coercive force will have no *raison d'être*. Do you understand?

Q. Yes, but if all the means of production are owned by the state, how can the state disappear?

A. They belong to the people, to all the people. In this case the state represents the producer. In a school there is need for . . .

Q. There is need for administrators?

A. Professors and teachers and administrators, but it is not a weapon to maintain the system. I say that

79

the classist societies were maintained by force and that the state was the instrument of the ruling classes, of the patriarchs in Rome, of the feudal lords in Europe, of the absolute monarchies in history, and of the capitalist classes in the era of capitalism. Then the first state, the first society without classes, will be the socialist society, the communist society in which there is no need for a coercive instrument to protect the interests of one class, because there are no classes. So that this coercive role of the state disappears.

Q. But if there is no state, who will decide what the priorities are?

A. There has to be an administrative body, because undoubtedly the economy, in our opinion, belongs to the people. A factory, a hospital, a hotel, belongs to the people. The means of production belong to everyone. If you give it to a group of workers, then you form a group of owners. This does not fit within our concept, that everything belongs to everyone. The people need an administrative tool. Well, it needs administrative mechanisms to manage the collective property. That is, I don't believe we can do without the mechanisms that a society needs to manage its economy.

Q. But the administration, isn't that a state? Mustn't it be coercive?

A. No. It is no longer an instrument of oppression. The concept changes completely. I must add that this topic has not been fully developed. This idea of Marx, Engels, and Lenin must be developed.

It is assumed that a community of men no longer has classes, has no need to defend the interests of one class to the detriment of other classes. It is no longer an instrument of power over society. Political parties have historically represented the interests of various classes, and the workers of this country have their own party, but the landowners have none and the owners of large industries have none and they can have none.

Q. Why?

A. They cannot have them. We do not allow it and we consider our state a coercive one until we complete this phase of transition from capitalism to communism.

Q. And afterwards?

A. There will be no exploiting classes, there will be no opposing interests within the society. There will be no need for a state with coercive powers.

Individual Freedom

Q. Another immediate thought regarding Cuba is the whole area of personal liberty or freedom—i.e., speech, press, etc. What does "personal fredom" mean to you?

A. I don't think that we could summarize it here in just a few words. I could ask you, "What does individual freedom mean to an American?" I could ask you what individual freedom means to a man who is discriminated against in the United States? For a Chicano, a Puerto Rican, to what is individual freedom reduced then? Freedom to vote, say, every four years for the two candidates chosen by the two major parties. The freedom to write. You write. I don't deny that there are groups of people in the United States who write freely, but in the end freedom of expression is that of the owners of the major newspapers who delineate the policies of the newspapers. In general, really I am not going to deny that there exists in the United States a fairly free press.

Q. There are many owners with many points of view.

A. But I don't see the freedom that the humble man of the United States has to change the system. I can give you the example of the McCarthy era in the United States when you had the liberty to think freely, in accordance with certain political criteria, but if you had different political opinions, you could be fired from your job or the newspaper. Everything, everyone was persecuted.

In summary, I believe there are two different conceptions of freedom. You believe that freedom can exist within a class system, and we believe in a system where everyone is equal, where there are no superpowers because there is no pyramid, no millionaires, no multimillionaires, where some don't even have a job. I wonder if you can compare the freedom of the millionaire with that of the beggar or of the unemployed. However, you believe this is freedom. We believe that is all false, and we believe that without equality there is no freedom because you do have to speak about the freedom of the beggar, the prostitute, the exploited, the discriminated, the illiterate. Freedom to write and speak for a man who cannot write, who cannot read? . . . Freedom for an illiterate who does not have any opinion or who cannot even differentiate between good and evil? We believe man can be free only if he is equal.

Q. Is there freedom to be a millionaire here in Cuba?

A. I believe that is a negative sort of freedom, the freedom to be an exploiter.

Q. Some value it highly.

A. I believe the freedom to be a millionaire is very bad because one has to take into consideration that in the United States many are millionaires because they inherited their money from their grandfather, their greatgrandfather. They did nothing but are millionaires by inheritance. We do not agree with that sort of freedom. It is the freedom to pile up money and exploit others. This is why it is so difficult to answer your question, because we take off from two different points of view and we don't believe freedom can exist in a society with exploited and exploiters.

Q. If a group such as ours, for example, went to the United States and interviewed an American President, would you allow it on Cuban television?

A. Cubans? They would probably not be granted the interview. (laughter)

Q. But supposing a president gave the interview and he was critical of Cuba, would you show this interview?

A. Yes, we would.

Q. The interview?

A. I am going to answer you. Personally, I would not object, and I don't think anyone else would object even if he were critical of us. Truly. We are not afraid of that. (laughter) So that I, at least, would be in favor of showing it.

Now, you ask me, do we bring attacks from our enemies here and publicize them? No, we don't do that. In all honesty, I tell you, it is not our custom. We do not use our means of expression for that. I am not going to lie to you.

Q. Could an opposition group publish a newspaper in Cuba?

A. No. We believe in a concept that the newspapers belong to the workers. There is a socialist system here which operates coercively in the name of the majorities, and within our concepts we do not allow the existence of a press that is against the revolutionary class or that publishes anything against the Revolution. I do not ask that you think like we do, but we have nothing to hide nor are we going to deny our beliefs. We have a theoretical concept of the Revolution which is a dictatorship of the exploited against the exploiters.

Q. Who is the exploiter and who is the worker?

A. The exploiters were the owners of the means of production who enriched themselves with the work of the exploited social classes. We consider the exploited those who used to live with a salary and work to enrich others. We believe the Revolution changed the structure of the society, and we consider this a dictatorial process. We take off from the historical concept that the controlling classes maintain their system by force, and that the exploited classes must, during a period of transition,

83

maintain their system by force and thereby deprive the enemy classes of their rights in general.

Q. And is Cuba at that stage now?

A. Well, we cannot say that we have totally passed this stage already, but I can say that we have made great advances. We are now in the process of institutionalizing the Cuban state through the elective process, and we are doing this in the province of Matanzas. But I want to say to you with total frankness that in general terms we don't understand the concept of liberty in the same way as you and, as a matter of fact, the opportunities to carry out opposition against the Revolution are minimal. They do not exist legally. I tell you this in all sincerity how it is.

Q. They exist illegally?

A. Well, illegally, very few. In the beginning there was a lot of opposition, in this period of transition. Because there were a lot of counterrevolutionary activities. They are minimal now. But I was giving you the example of how, as the class differences disappeared, a true equality among all the citizens became a reality—all these citizens have equal rights, and I was giving you the example of the elections in Matanzas. It is not easy to understand these things. You are used to different systems, different methods, which are totally different from ours.

Q. Can there be opposition?

A. Opposition within the context of classes as you know it does not exist. But yes, opposition exists. One carries it out within the Party, within the organizations, the factories—as the nationally organized Party which represents one class. It has to be within the Party because the essence of the Party is precisely its democratic spirit, the election of its leaders, its direction, the right to criticize and the duty to carry on self-criticism. What matters is that the democratic mechanisms function within the revolutionary institutions. This is what is important and essential. This is what we have fought for and to what we aspire. Our popular organizations are also organized in this manner, but we believe in the principle of central democracy. What does this mean? That while the right to have an opinion and to disagree exists, when the majority reaches a particular decision, the minority must accept the decision of the majority. There exists the right to disagree. . . .

Q. Without talking?

A. Without talking any more, that is correct. They argued and argued within the municipal assembly, provincial, or Party leadership. One side, everyone, gave their views and their opinions, and the majority decided. It is the duty of the minority to follow the decisions of the majority.

This is a very broad subject. I could be talking about it all night long. It is one of the most difficult points to understand, because our outline is different from yours. I respect the right of others to think that it is not the best way. That is how the Cuban people think, and Americans may think differently.

Q. And if there is a small group that wishes to speak out? How do they do it?

A. And who does that little group represent?

Q. A group consisted of three, four, ten, twelve men. *One.* Is it a risk?

A. No, it is not a risk. Where are they going to speak out? They may speak all they wish to. They do so already. No one forbids that. Everyone talks; in reality, that is a Cuban custom.

Q. But for the opposition to meet, to form opposition groups. . . .

A. No.

Q. To publish their own manifestos?

A. No. In reality, no. It isn't a risk, per se. It is a matter of principle. If those elements are going to weaken and split up the people, then we believe that the unity of the people is more important than that activity, and besides, who are they going to represent? Are they going to represent the workers?

Or are they going to represent the enemies of the workers? We, for example, do not agree that they should organize like that. A newspaper to defend the point of view of the United States like *El Mercurio* in Chile—we do not accept it, simply do not accept it.

We have other more important things with which to concern ourselves. Especially at this stage we are in. The only really important enemy we have had has been the North American imperialism, a powerful enemy who would have liked to have opposition parties here against the Revolution—newspapers, radio stations speaking out against the Revolution—to use them against the Revolution. Look at the Chilean example. Allende respected all these rights. The opposition press conspired. There were newspapers clamoring for a coup d'etat every day, and they finally gave a coup. Everyone had the right to conspire and the results were that they overthrew the Allende government and set up a fascist regime.

Q. Is that why there is no similar opposition allowed in Cuba—is it too risky for you?

A. We do not run that risk because our Revolution is incomparably stronger than the Chilean revolution. In the beginning we could have, but to a much lesser degree than Chile. The difference between Cuba and Chile is that we had a people's army. But Chile had an army which supported the interests of the oligarchy, the landed gentry, and the wealthy, and they overthrew Allende.

There is a principle we believe in, and that is that we do not allow the activities of the enemies of the Revolution. I say it with all sincerity; you ask me and I tell you there are no risks involved and that there is no need to take the chance. This is our concept. This is how we believe we should run the Revolution. We do not aspire to convincing the Americans of all this. I am only trying to explain how we think and how we see things.

Q. Well, in the United States, for example, there are

various points of view, there are newspapers who speak out against the government.

A. There are millions of opinions and there is the right to say the greatest lies that anyone may wish to say (laughter), and many times this right is misused.

Q. Yes, but there are newspapers, powerful ones. They don't call for a coup d'etat, but they vigorously oppose the President and call for his impeachment.

A. There is no need for a coup in order to defend capitalism. But if someday there should be the need for a coup to protect the capitalist interest, there will be a coup. There is no doubt about it. Besides, what would the Pentagon wish for a coup? It has all the funds it wishes, all the weapons, all the privileges. What does it want a coup for? It is hypothetical.

Even in Europe, no one knows what would happen if Socialists and Communists united and won the elections in Italy. What I say is that what happened in Chile is not going to repeat itself exactly.

Does the military/industrial complex exist or not? They are are a reality, and they are superpowerful. They have enormous influence in the United States. The capitalist system does not run any dangers in the United States. There is no powerful Socialist party. The Republican is not a Socialist party; the Democrat is not a Socialist party; the Communist Party is relatively small. I don't know how the Pentagon would react if there were a powerful Communist party competing in the elections. If success came I don't know what the reaction would be. I am not saying that what occurred in Chile will occur. There are doubts as to what will happen if French Socialists and Communists were to unite and win over the majority, as to whether the military establishment would allow that. And I ask myself if a majority party in the United States attempted to set up a socialist system, if the military would allow it, if the financial oligarchy would allow it. You have never gone through that experience.

Q. Several months ago, the new Chilean government challenged you to release what they say are political prisoners in this country, pointing out that they had released some political prisoners in their own country. Are you willing to meet that challenge?

A. No, we do not intend to enter into any kind of arrangement, of discussions, to traffic with the Chilean fascist junta, because the fascist Chilean junta is a despotic government, an illegal government, an unpopular government, which destroyed the constitution, liquidated the *Unidad Popular* government, incarcerated thousands of people without any reason whatsoever—and all this simply because they supported Allende, because they were revolutionaries. What, then, does the fascist junta want? That we recognize the right of some fascist clique to make a coup d'etat and to kidnap the revolutionaries, so as to later demand the release of the CIA agents and the counterrevolutionary agents in exchange for the release of the imprisoned revolutionaries? If they believe it would be just that these men be free, let them release them. This is a moral qustion and if they don't believe that it would be just, then let them keep them in prisons.

But according to their statement, it seems that they think that the fascist regime is not facing any risk, that the fascist regime can release them. Then why don't they release them? We have counterrevolutionaries in prison; we don't think that they should be free. We don't consider it just to give them freedom. And, therefore, we cannot release them. If we would consider it just that we should release them, we would release them without demanding any conditions.

At present in Cuba for example, there remain in jail about twenty percent of the counterrevolutionary prisoners that we had in the first years of the Revolution. We released eighty percent, we did not put any condition on anyone to release them.

We believed that they could be released; there is a part that we believe should not be released as yet. It is a moral question, an issue of justice, not a question of negotiation. I believe that this attitude of the Chilean government is simply a demagogic attitude. Without any hesitation we absolutely say NO; and besides, the Cuban revolutionaries themselves agree with us that this blackmail of the fascist junta in Chile should not be accepted. This is our position.

Q. Senators Pell and Javits, by chance, were here in Cuba on the twenty-eighth of September, the day of the meeting at which you spoke in your speech about Chile, and they were interested in U.S. political prisoners.

A. Unfortunately, and much to our regret, their visit coincided with the date of that speech. We highly appreciated the visit of Senators Javits and Pell to Cuba. They were received in our country with great hospitality, they talked with all the people they wanted to talk with. They amply expressed their points of view and we presented our points of view. I must say that Senator Javits is a very eloquent man, a very intelligent man, and a man with strong convictions, no doubt. Senator Pell is a very civilized man. The situation of Javits was undoubtedly different from that of Pell, because Javits was facing an election campaign and the trip to Cuba meant a risk election-wise. Actually, I am of the opinion that it was a courageous attitude on his part. He took a step such as the visit to Cuba which could have led to discussions, contradictions, and polemics in his election campaigns. But actually, we have a good evaluation of this visit. We are satisfied with the visit and we believe that the visit of these senators to Cuba has been positive.

They did show interest in some North Americans who are imprisoned in Cuba. We analyzed what we could do in consideration of this interest that they showed for the North American prisoners. We will set free some North American prisoners in a few days, not all, but some will be released, and the senators were interested in this.[1] This could, of course, be considered as a gesture on our part toward the senators and also toward public opinion in the United States.

Q. When many Americans think of Cuba, one thing that comes to mind is the 1959 executions. Why did this occur?

A. The executions? During the war we had discussions and we agreed that excesses were to be avoided, such as men being dragged through the streets and lynched. We always told the Cuban people during the war, when daily assassinations were being committed, that there would be justice when the Revolution triumphed, and that no one should take justice into his own hands. Revolutionary laws against torturers and criminals were passed.

During the Batista dictatorship, many crimes were committed, and our people suffered all sorts of tortures, killing of students, women raped, tortured, crimes of all sorts, and they had to be punished. So that according to the strict spirit of the law, when the Revolution triumphed, all those who had killed and tortured were arrested, tried, and executed.

Of course, I can't understand some people who lived the experience of the Second World War when with no prior laws the Nuremburg trials were conducted and the war criminals were arrested, tried, and executed. So that I don't understand why it should be expected that a people should undergo the horrors of a tyranny, the crimes that a tyranny commits, and not apply justice to those criminals.

One can argue about the penalties imposed. As you know, there is a great debate going on in the United States about the death penalty. But a lot of people have been executed in the United States. I can assure you that no one in the United States has

---

[1] This answer was part of the October 2, 1974, interview. True to his word, Castro released four U.S. prisoners a week later.

been sent to the electric chair for crimes comparable to those committed by the men we sentenced to death. I can assure you of this, because these men committed dozens of crimes in cold blood. And I ask, what is a country to do with these murderers? Forgive them? Should they be tried or not, should they be punished or not?

Anyway, I can tell you that there is one thing worse. You welcomed many of these criminals to the United States. Some of Batista's worst criminals fled to the United States and live there calmly, with impunity, and sometimes they also violate North American laws and no one has bothered them. In any case, between the extreme of punishing these criminals and protecting them, between the extreme of punishing or pardoning the crime and helping these criminals, I think that what the United States did—the government of the United States—was much worse, because it protected, sheltered, and helped these criminals. We arrested them, sentenced them, and punished them. And more than that, our position is unchangeable in that regard. We understand what we did because we needed a punishment model.

Today, everyone is horrified at the crimes and tortures that are committed in Chile. Everyone is horrified at the crimes and tortures that are committed in Brazil. So I ask myself, what are we going to do with the criminals? And with the torturers? Do you have to protect them? Do you have to shelter them? How does humanity gain most? By letting torture and crime go unpunished or by setting an example of punishment for these torturers and criminals? That is the question that one has to ask.

The attitude or philosophical position that one might have about the punishment that is applied, or about whether one should or should not apply capital punishment, is a different question. It is open for debate. But there can be no debate to the fact that the criminals must be punished. This was the type of punishment that the laws in Cuba provided for those crimes. The victims' families demanded it and the public unanimously asked for it because our people were tired of seeing so many crimes go unpunished.

We hope that history will never again repeat itself, that our country will never again know torturers, assassins, murderers. But for the first time they were punished in Cuba. This is the truth.

Q. Was it also the last time?

A. I am sure this was the last time that something like this will take place in Cuba and that we will never return to the injustices of the past.

The Workers

Q. What are the differences between the two economic systems, socialism and capitalism, as far as productivity of the workers and working conditions?

A. Well, the first thing we must mention is that under the capitalist system work discipline is very strict. Man has to work under competitive conditions. First, he is competing against the unemployed. The capitalist system requires a certain level of unemployment, an available work force which can take the place of the absent workers in the event of lack of discipline in work. But conditions are not identical in every country, because in some countries protective legislation and better working conditions exist. When unemployment disappears, for example the worker no longer has to compete with someone who is ready to move into his job. Under capitalism, the worker depends mainly on his wages for the support of him, his family, his children's education, their health. Under socialism, the problem of education for the children, for example, is no longer dependent upon his income. Health and education do not depend on his income, because the state gives free education and medical assistance. Social security is much greater and the family is protected against accidents while working. So that under capitalism the worker depends much more on his salary. If he fails to pay his rent, for example, he is evicted from his housing.

Under capitalism, discipline is maintained through a man's needs, and under socialism discipline is basically dependent upon a man's conscience.

Well, let's look at a specific situation, a specific case, such as that of the workers of the copper mines in Chile. Under the Allende government they had greater freedom . . . they had more guarantees at work. In other words, they could organize strikes. They were not dismissed from their jobs, there were no longer ten unemployed for each working man. The fascist regime has imposed very hard conditions—the prohibition of strikes, bloody repression as a response to workers' protests, and dismissal without any sort of consideration of mine workers.

This explains the reason for higher productivity under the fascist military junta than under the Allende government. Conditions are much harder and the worker who does not produce at a maximum is fired, the worker who does not accept a job or assignment is fired, the worker who dares protest is fired, and the worker who organizes a strike is shot, so that the fascist junta can brag about its higher production at the mines than that achieved by the *Unidad Popular* government because the workers received other treatment, other rights, and Allende was respected. It is obvious that the Chilean working class was still evolving. It had just left capitalism, and it was, of course, gaining a higher conscience as a result of being educated under new working conditions. This is why we have established in Cuba a combination of work and study.

Q. Can a Cuban worker change jobs?
A. Yes, he can change jobs. There are required steps. He requests a transfer at the factory, and there is a waiting period.

Q. Can he also move from one city to another?

A. Of course.

Q. Then how is it determined that so many workers will be in this factory or in a crop or in various sectors?

A. In general, you know that—

Q. Is planning difficult?

A. We have a labor shortage, more acute in some regions than in others; for example, in Havana, which developed faster than the rest of the island. Now our development projects tend to involve construction of plants in Oriente, or the interior of the island. We tend to decentralize industry, because in the past industry was concentrated around the capital. That is why in Havana we don't build industries except those that we have no other choice but to build here.

We had to set up in the western region, for example, a cement factory near the raw materials; a pasteurizer for milk distribution to the capital. Industries are only built near the capital if they produce for it or get their raw materials from that area. The Oriente has the highest rate of population growth—almost four percent per annum, which is much higher than the western region. We, therefore, have a greater labor force in the eastern region, and this is the reason for seventy-six to eighty percent of our development efforts being concentrated in Oriente.

Also, every year a certain number of young people are added to the labor force, and we keep these statistics. Of course, some of the young people remain students, and we cannot expect them to work until they finish their studies; others join the armed forces. We have to estimate the young people who reach working age, and then they are offered the alternatives of working in a cement factory or a textile factory, of the various types of jobs available in those industries. Sometimes the factories begin recruiting ahead of time. For example, construction workers are needed for certain

94

types of jobs for which it is difficult to find workers. Electrical installations, these are always more difficult. We carry on campaigns among the youth. We utilize the incentive system when there are difficulties to take the working force out to a certain area. We also use political means to develop the young people's conscience about the importance of work and ask them to do these jobs. Then the working force that each year reaches the working age is distributed through these means.

One of the problems we have is labor shortage, and this is aggravated by the fact that since the educational system has improved considerably, a lot of young people decide to continue studying, so that the available work force is reduced.

Q. In almost every country one of the demographic problems is that of rural migration to the cities.

A. Yes.

Q. Do you have that problem in Cuba?

A. Relatively little. Since people can find work in any of the provinces, in any city in the interior, we do not have this type of migration to the capital, and the capital even has a lower rate of population growth than the rest of the island. The Oriente has an average growth rate of approximately two percent. It isn't very high, because some other countries, such as Mexico, for example, grow at the rate of four percent. Mexico adds approximately two million to its population every year, and we grow at the rate of approximately two hundred thousand per year. At the beginning of the Revolution our birth rate went up, and it has been going down ever since, so that it is now at a rate of approximately two percent. We have not carried out a birth control campaign because we have had no need for it, and we expect that with economic and educational development, a spontaneous reduction of the population will be reached.

We have had no unemployment problems and we anticipate none. On the contrary, we believe it is a basic duty of the state to find employment for its population.

It may be that in the future we will have to develop jobs for women. There are three times as many women working now in Cuba, but actually the difficulties women face, insofar as work is concerned, are related to their families. In other words, day-care centers for the children are needed so that the mothers can go to work. We are building these centers and expanding that program, and we expect to expand it much more in the future. We have been developing a program for school lunches for elementary school children whose mothers work, and for those under six, the day-care centers, but we don't have enough of the latter. Women are a major labor reserve. That is to say, we could incorporate many more women to the working force if we had enough institutions to take care of their children.

Q. Do you have jobs for them?

A. Yes, in general, especially in the western region. They work in textile industries, clothing factories, stores, public offices, in administration, in schools, in the day-care centers, in the hospitals. Education has approximately 230,000 workers, approximately sixty percent are women. In public health, there are about 140,000 workers, and more than sixty percent are women. Our female population consists of about twenty-four percent of the work force. They, therefore, are a reserve if we can create centers to look after their children. Up to this point, we have not had the problem of not enough work, rather not enough workers.

Q. What do you do if you need workers in a province and not in the other?

A. Well, we generally try to set up industries where the workers are located. Sometimes we set up an industry in an underpopulated area, and we have greater difficulties meeting our labor needs, but we recruit workers through the youth and labor organizations. We are introducing economic incentives with the purpose of solving these problems because some jobs are harder than others and we want better to distribute them fairly. One always has to resort to economic stimulus to solve this type of problem—they are not easy.

Q. Does the Cuban worker have the right to go on strike?

A. I have yet to hear a worker say he wants to strike against the Revolution. We see a strike as a struggle between the worker and the industrialist.

Q. Well, let's say, a worker or workers from a particular factory due to working conditions want to express grievances—don't they strike?

A. No, there has never been a strike. Here in Cuba, no policeman or soldier has ever intervened against the workers. Never. If the workers identify with the revolutionary cause, it is because the Revolution is theirs, and if they identify with the economy it is because they know that the production is for them. They do not think of harming production or stopping production. It is not that they are forbidden, it is that they do not conceive of this.

Q. And are the workers now organized in any way?

A. They have unions and the unions are in charge of watching over the interests of the workers and seeing that labor laws are complied with.

Strikes take place where there is injustice, exploitation, but here any injustice or mistake can be corrected. We have workers' tribunals, a labor legislature. These labor or workers' tribunals are formed from the workers, and the workers are the judges of any conflict, injustice, act of aggression, or violation of labor laws or workers' rights.

Q. And how do these tribunals work?

A. It is very simple. There is the labor legislature, and any fault expressed by a worker, if not decided by the manager, is brought up before the workers' tribunal. If it is considered that the worker has not fulfilled his duty, or if the administration has committed an unjust act, the worker appears before the tribunal. The tribunal decides. If the decision is against him, the worker can appeal to a higher workers' court.

Q. Who makes up the tribunals?

A. They are elected from among the workers. Once elected they receive special training for their work as labor judges. Labor justice is in the hands of the workers and of the judges elected by the workers. Injustice against a worker, a conflict within a factory, or a worker being fired is very unlikely.

Q. Is there a tribunal within each factory?

A. There is practically one per factory.

Q. What size?

A. It is very difficult or unlikely for a conflict to arise that will not be correctible there. And what could that be—what is it that we do not give the workers? We don't give them what we don't have or what we cannot give them, and the workers know this. We never take any steps without prior discussion with the workers.

Right now the economic plan for 1975 is being discussed at the work centers. The five-year plan for 1976 through 1980 will be discussed at the factories so that the workers become concerned about the production goals, plans, and production commitments. That is their life, because they feel fully integrated into the system. They are the system. The large majority of those who run the factories were former workers. We don't have to forbid strikes, because no one thinks about striking, it seems an absurdity to him.

Q. Who selects the administrators for the factories?

A. It is the responsibility of the corresponding organization. Of course, they have to meet certain requirements, training. . . .

Q. The worker or the organization?

A. It is the responsibility, of course, of the worker . . .

Q. Can a worker rise to form part of the management of a factory?

A. Of course he can. When all the managers left, then, those that emerged were former workers in the factories. We have production assemblies where all the production plans and goals are discussed with the workers, and the workers bring up any problem—any managerial deficiency—within the factory.

They are alert to any problem of this type, but the factory manager is not elected. He is appointed by the organization under which the particular industry may fall.

The Family Code [1]

Q. Well, could we talk about the proposed family code?

A. The family code is being discussed at the present time with the people. It is pretty advanced; let's say, very advanced. It establishes complete equality among men and women. We had an old civil code dating back to the time of the Spaniards, and this new civil code of the Revolution is being submitted to criticism by all the people—by the workers in the factories, the peasants, the students, and the neighborhoods. Once the neighborhoods have gone over it and gathered general opinions and made known their findings, if there are modifications or variations which are backed by the majority of the people, then they go into effect before they become law.

It is really a very advanced code which puts women on the same plane with men, and I understand Cuban women are very satisfied with the draft code and are defending it.

Q. But who is responsible for having written it?

A. A committee of lawyers. They drafted the project in accordance with Party lines, no, Party policy. Then it is discussed by everyone. All important laws are subjected to public discussion. Those that have a great impact on the population—we always discuss them first with the people.

Q. What form does this discussion take?

[1] See Appendix 2.

A. It is planned, over a period of time, through the various organizations. Information on the proposed law is disseminated, and the organization sets up assembly meetings to discuss the law. Later, we hold conferences, and make television appearances so that everyone will be aware of it. You can go and visit any Cuban home, anywhere in Cuba today, and they will talk to you about the family code, and they will give you their opinion on the points they like and the more polemic ones.

Minutes are kept of all the assembly meetings to gather all the various opinions.

Generally, after discussions, the law comes out pretty polished. When there is a major issue, the people as a whole bring it up. Their opinions are listened to and incorporated prior to being approved by the Council of Ministers. The National Assembly has been organized as the popular national center of power for the future. It will be there that laws will be approved, because it will be given the authority within the Council of Ministers. When that transition period is over, it will be the National Parliament which will approve the laws. But even with a National Parliament, laws will be discussed with the people. I think it is a very important, a very useful mechanism which we have set up, very progressive, and we intend to continue to abide by this principle of discussing important laws with the people.

Q. Why is a new family code necessary?

A. Because there has been discrimination against women. A woman works in a factory, and when she returns home she has to cook, clean, wash, do everything, attend to her children. She does all the work and we believe a man also should know how to do this type of work and help his mate in the home. If we do not start by teaching young men how to clean their rooms, to do the dishes, everything, it is conceivable that a young man will refuse to do these things. I think teaching a young man these chores should be an integral part of his education. At work it is the same thing. You learn to work. You try to choose whatever job you like best, it could be trimming trees, planting, any such type of activity. You are actually asking me something we have not had to face. We have met no resistance from the young people, because they are brought up with this sense of duty to work and to work with his hands. He is aware of the fact that it is a social obligation to work.

Q. Is there overall agreement with this family code?

A. Some do not agree with this, because there remains a certain discrimination against women. It is still very real, and the Revolution is fighting it. Although we are winning ground, it undoubtedly will be a long struggle. This discrimination against women is manifested in many different ways. Even within the Party, where we have only thirteen percent women.

Q. Thirteen percent?

A. Yes, and only five percent of the leadership consists of women, even though the women contribute a great deal to the Revolution and have sacrificed a great deal. They often have higher revolutionary qualifications than the men do—a sense of responsibility, of discipline.

You find some organizations, such as education and public health, where sixty percent of the workers are women and yet they hold a lower percentage of the administrative positions, much less than the percentage that make up the mass of workers. Labor organizations, however, have a fairly proportionate percentage of women participating: twenty-four percent of the labor force is made up of women, and approximately twenty-four percent of the cadres are made up of women. Although now, in the popular elections held in Matanzas, I believe the percentage of women elected was only five percent, more or less.

Q. Yes, we noted that.

A. So that, undoubtedly, it went down.

Q. Why was that?

101

A. Because women are still discriminated against. They are not elected. It is a struggle which both men and women have to deal with. If women are half the population and half the voters but only five percent women were elected, there is an indication that even the women share the same discriminatory mentality of the men. So that it is a women's struggle. It is not only necessary to change women's mentality of the men. So that it is a women's is a struggle the Party must carry on and it is doing just that. I believe this will be one of the major topics at the next Congress of the Federation of Cuban Women. These problems will affect us strongly, and will have to be faced by the Congress of the Party.

Q. Within the Political Bureau, are there any women?

A. No, it is true, we don't have a woman member. It is a major problem and we are aware of its existence. . . . The Women's Federation is a strong organization with grass-roots support, and it functions very well. One of its major tasks is to bring up this problem at its Congress. It was organized regionally and then the percentage of women working was relatively low—twenty-four percent.

Q. A committee within the Political Bureau?

A. It is more or less one within the Political Bureau. The problem is that when election time comes, they cannot be elected merely because they are women but must have some experience. We cannot fall into demagoguery over the issue.

Q. What about quotas?

A. If we establish quotas, then we cannot keep in mind the experience requirement. We have to wait for the women themselves to develop into cadres.

Q. Are we also talking about a Latin American phenomenon, *machismo*?

A. It is certain that Cuba participates in this phenomenon in a similar way as other Latin American countries. But such activities as the efforts of the Party, the family code, the meetings of women's organizations, the struggle women carry on—all of these factors will help eradicate this type of mentality. We must point out, however, that Cuban women enjoy a special position now. Before they were an adornment, a pleasure object, an instrument for exploitation. As I mentioned before, prostitution was wide-spread. Women were not protected at all. They worked mostly as domestics, in the bars, the brothels, and had limited access to the universities. You visit a university today and you will find a high percentage of women there.

Q. And what are the provisions of the family code that arouse the most discussion?

A. Women are awarded certain rights, involving divorce and their children, for example. The man's obligations are established in connection with housework, too. This is one of the points brought up most often, because it is a fact that men should share in housework, and many men don't like this because they can't see themselves washing dishes, cleaning a house, cooking. So that the end result is that women work more than the men do. This is one of the major issues. Of course, a man has obligations to support his children in case of divorce, but a woman's obligation toward a man is similar. Under the old laws, the woman was seen as dependent on the man. The laws never accepted the situation where a man could be dependent on the woman. Instances may occur where the man needs the woman's help. These issues are also a matter of equality. But one point men don't often bring up is the obligation on their part to do housework. All the laws on this subject attempt to protect women and affirm their equality.

Q. Are there any women's organizations?

A. Yes, of course.

Q. But not of men . . .

A. No, because men perhaps did not need to organize to protect their rights as men per se. They are in control.

The Military

Q. Does Cuba spend a lot of money on their military?

A. The United States has forced us to spend large sums of money on weapons for the defense of our country. There is no doubt about that. We have a modern army, well disciplined, with thousands of cadres. We have defense mechanisms but they have cost us much, and we have invested considerable energies, too.

We are not like the United States, which spends so much on arms and thus contributes to inflation. The military budget of the United States is the same as it was during the Second World War. However, there is no world war. The resources we spend on defense are a drain on our economy and our development, but we do it because of the aggression of the United States. We aspire to peace.

Q. What percentage of its budget does Cuba spend on armaments, on the armed forces?

A. Our budget comprises the entire economy, but at one time we were spending close to five hundred million dollars on defense. Today we are better organized, better equipped, and we spend less than four hundred million dollars, and we spend two and a one-half times that on education and public health. We are actually spending close to one billion on public health and education. This includes current expenses as well as investments. As you can see, I am not keeping secrets.

Education

Q. There seems to be a lot of emphasis placed on the value of work—does everyone contribute? What about students?

A. All our new schools, the ones we are building, all the polytechnical institutes, are built next to factories. The student works four hours and studies four hours. All our high schools are being built in the countryside—near citrus plantations, vegetable farms, tobacco plantations.

Each high school student works fifteen hours a week and studies the rest of the time; he participates in cultural activities, sports, and study activities. The most interesting aspect of this experience is that already more than a hundred and fifty thousand students are participating, and the academic results are far superior than those under the old system. The student utilizes his time much better.

Q. Why?

A. Because undoubtedly one of the basic drawbacks of the traditional system, wherein the student just goes to school in the morning and returns in the afternoon, is that psychological factors lead to his exhaustion. He tires of excessive intellectual work during the day. He becomes bored with just one type of effort, intellectual work. When he is also engaged in physical labor, he begins to develop a social conscience of the importance of work. He benefits from the education of work. Otherwise, he gets used to being given everything good, clothing, shoes, without having to produce anything himself. I believe the old system is deforming.

We are applying the system of work and study and obtaining excellent results. For example, last year ninety-five percent of the high-school classes in the fields passed their final exams. Historically, it has been seventy percent in the cities. Results have been indeed impressive. We are applying this system at the universities, and, when we can, in elementary schools. There are, for example, vegetable gardens in many schools. We are developing them in the elementary schools where the children of fourth, fifth, and sixth grades work for one or two hours in productive activities. We are expanding this program because of the academic results we are obtaining and because we believe it innovates the academic system.

Q. How did this system get started?

A. We take off from the principle that our country is poor. To be able to offer greater universal education and give every child and young person an opportunity to obtain an elementary and high-school education, work has to be generalized, because our societies are too poor to be able to generalize education.

In the second place, if the young people do nothing but study, there exists the risk of having a society of intellectuals only—of men removed from the social duty that is work. For us, a part of education is teaching the young person to do productive work with his hands. And we are very optimistic from the results of this concept of education. By 1980 we expect to have at least one million students involved in this work/study program.

Q. What happens if a student does not like doing agricultural work or anything else and he is in high school in the countryside and has to work in agriculture?

A. In general, we do not have those problems. Because the young person, for example, chooses to go to these schools. On the contrary, we receive a great number of applications for scholarships to these schools, which are very well equipped. These schools are in great demand among our youth and are very prestigious. In reality, we never have had these problems.

The services at the schools are provided by the students, and I think that part of a young person's education is learning to fix his bed, to clean his room, to serve his own food, to wash dishes. As I just mentioned, one of the problems in our society is that, for example, housework is still considered exclusively a woman's job. This program falls entirely within socialist concepts. That is to say, education for all the people.

Q. But could this educational system exist in a non-socialist country?

A. It is not easy, it is not easy. In those schools that you saw, for example, students are working on agricultural projects which belong to all the people. If you were to compel the students of a school to work for private ownership, the students would not agree. . . .

Q. Nor would the unions . . .

A. Nobody would agree. In a system of private ownership, this educational program could not be applied.

Both Marx and Martí insisted on the idea of combining study with work, and we have developed this idea further and are universalizing this principle, applying it in a general manner, with fabulous results—academically, educationally, as well as the training of the man. I am certain that this system which we are putting into practice in Cuba will greatly increase our prestige. There is great interest, growing interest in the educational system of Cuba.

Tourism

Q. We saw and visited several construction sites of new hotels. Can we discuss the plans you have for national tourism?

A. We are developing plans. We have been developing internal tourism for the workers and their families. Of course, our present facilities are inadequate. Even by limiting stays to about a week at the beaches, etc., the hotels are insufficient. We are now building hotels—around nine or ten microbrigades are building hotels—at natural sites, beaches, the Escambray mountains, the Salto de la Hanabanilla. Also, since we are building new schools, we are vacating old structures. In Topes de Collante in the Escambray mountains, for example, what had previously been a hospital was turned into a teachers' college. But since we already have several teachers' colleges in Santa Clara province, five to six thousand people can vacation and stay in Topes de Collante.

Q. Are all these for adults—what about children?

A. We are also organizing vacation camps for pioneers. In Tarara, which used to be a resort town—later a teachers' college (we now have other teachers' colleges in Havana), we are developing a vacation spot for the pioneers which will have a ten- to twelve-thousand-children weekly capacity throughout the summer. Nearly eighty thousand children from Havana can go there during the summer and stay for a couple of weeks, and during the school year we will have approximately five thousand each fifteen days—a whole school or various schools. There is a sports field, the sea, etc. We estimate that each year about a hundred and fifty thousand children can utilize the facilities.

We will also have the "Palace for Pioneers" in Lenin Park which is now being designed and will start next year. You saw such a camp in Camaguey which has a two thousand seven hundred capacity. It is in Santa Lucia Beach, which is a very good beach. Good sand and tranquil waters, because it has a breaker close by and doesn't allow strong waves to reach shore. Camps such as those will be built also in Santa Clara, Oriente, Matanzas. The one in Matanzas will be built in Varadero Beach, and the one in Pinar del Rio will be built near the San Diego River.

We are paying a great deal of attention to vacations for children. We also intend to use the high-school facilities in the countryside, because they have good sports facilities for the children of working mothers. During the school year the children of working mothers are either boarders or semi-boarders, but in the summertime they are home and the parents' vacations do not always coincide with that of their children.

For the first time, we are beginning to build hotels. Then, in 1976, we will organize ten more hotel-building microbrigades. We will have nearly twenty microbrigades building hotels. We may expand this in 1978. These are more or less our plans for internal tourism, but they may be available for foreign tourism. We are already receiving tourists from Canada and Europe, and some from Latin America.

Q. But foreign tourism isn't yet sizable, is it?

A. No, it does not amount to much. What happens is that Cubans don't go to the beaches during the winter months—December, January, February—because we consider it too cold. When Europeans come in winter they marvel at our beaches. We have to teach children here that they can swim in winter water perfectly well. The facilities that we are creating for internal tourism, therefore, are underutilized during the winter months which is when the northern countries' tourists take their vacations. We are thinking of the possibility that these tourists could use these facilities which are of the highest quality—although we have not yet decided about foreign tourism on a large scale. Someday we will have to reach a decision. Opinions are divided, because some people remember the old days when the tourists who came were looking for gambling, prostitution; and these memories are not very favorable. Cuba's tourism in the past was tied up with gangsterism, because some well-known mafia figures from the United States operated here in Havana.

Q. When?

A. During the Batista years, to be precise.

Q. During the 1950s?

A. Yes, from 1950 on there was a proliferation of casinos, drugs, etc., and the image was not very favorable. The Canadian and European tourists that come now leave a very favorable impression. It is

109

another type of tourism. If we make a decision about massive tourism it would be for economic reasons, but there is resistance among the people.

Q. I know of no other Latin American country with national tourism. Our large hotel is full of couples, honeymooners, and workers. Everyone can use the facilities now at reasonable prices.

A. In comparison to prices elsewhere, they are cheap here, and the demand is much greater than the supply. So that whatever recreation centers and hotels we build will always be occupied. We have emphasized the construction of schools and hospitals, but we want to encourage, stimulate, internal tourism.

And it is possible that these facilities may be used by foreign tourists. But we don't anticipate having to make a decision in less than three or four years.

Q. If relations are resumed and the blockade lifted, do you think about tourism from the United States?

A. If that occurs, this will be a possibility and we will have to reach a decision. The only massive tourism we can anticipate is from the United States, and we will have to face a serious problem—(laughter) —how we will handle that type of problem, because two different mentalities are involved, customs are different. Two different cultures will be facing each other.

The United States and Cuba

Q. How can ties between Cuba and the United States be established?

A. Ah, which ties can be established? First of all, we are neighbors. Independently of our will, our geographical location and that of the United States makes us neighbors. We cannot move, nor can the United States. This is speaking realistically, that someday some sort of ties will be established between the United States and Cuba. It is dictated by geography, history, and the very interests of Cuba and the United States. Of course, we think of the future of Latin America, and we believe that the Latin American countries should unite, and we believe that in a not-so-distant future, Cuba will form part of that integrated community of Latin American nations. That someday we will have not only economic, but also political unity. And, as I said earlier, I don't believe there is any future for a small, isolated country in this hemisphere. But even under those conditions, there will have to be relations between the United States and that community of nations. And Cuba, either as a single separate state or as part of that community, is a neighbor, one of the closest neighbors of the United States, and logically, sooner or later, economic and political relations will have to develop between Cuba and the United States.

We, of course, will not plead with the United States to renew relations, economic relations; nor are we going to plead to reestablish political relations. I see this as an inevitable historical necessity, when circumstances change, when passions die down, and when men can think more calmly and coldly, so that someday they will take place, and those ties will develop.

They will be very different ties from those that previously existed between Cuba and the United States. First of all, they will have to be ties with a truly free country, which ours regrettably was not.

Q. How do you mean?

A. Even though Cuba fought very valiantly for its independence for over thirty years during the nineteenth century, in the end the United States intervened. That intervention meant the occupation of Puerto Rico and the Philippines, the intervention

111

in and the establishment of large economic interests from the United States in Cuba; a growing political dependency; the Guantanamo base was established—a piece of our territory was occupied; the Platt Amendment was passed, which gave the United States the right to intervene in Cuba. This the United States knows and historians know— many have written about it. No country fights for decades for its independence to have a Platt Amendment imposed upon them. Besides, for a long time, many American Presidents considered the occupation and absorption of Cuba as their destiny. And that danger existed until the end of the nineteenth century. During our War of Independence, the purchase of Cuba from the Spaniards was discussed more than once; to buy her for a certain price and thus solve the problem as had been done with Florida and Louisiana. That was an old expansionist strategy of the United States. And I would say that what saved Cuba from annexation to the United States was the patriotic fervor of our people, the fact that they fought for so long for their independence, and had a national conscience. Then things changed. The intervention took place, the Platt Amendment was imposed, and the right to intervene legally to maintain order, and all those excuses. There was a real political domination and economic domination of the United States over Cuba.

But this situation will not return. When there are men in the United States who understand this reality, our relations should be based on absolute mutual respect and equality. We are patient, and we will know how to wait. We are in no hurry. We are also very realistic and we will therefore wait for the right historical conditions for the establishment of these relations.

But also from a realistic point of view we believe that those ties will develop. They could be economic ties, people-to-people relations, cultural exchange, technical exchange: but from the politi-

112

cal standpoint it will be an exchange between two different cultures. It will be the culture of a free-enterprise, capitalist society and that of a socialist country.

I do not know when the United States will change its present system of free enterprise for a different social system, for a socialist system, but I am certain that it will be decades, many decades. But someday the economic and social system will change—I am sure. Someday the social systems of Cuba and the United States will meet, when the United States changes its social system. The capitalist social system will not be eternal.

Q. How will relations develop between the United States and Cuba?

A. The course of relations? Look, I think that any step taken must first be taken by the United States. Because the major, fundamental problem is the economic blockade. It was a decision taken by the United States, which it has maintained, for the purpose of preventing the economic development in Cuba and of choking the Revolution. To tell you the truth, it has been a hard struggle, the fight against the blockade, but we have survived. The Revolution was not asphyxiated, the country is developing at a satisfactory rate, and we believe that nothing can prevent our country from maintaining this level of development in future years.

So that now we are used to the situation and all our plans have taken the economic blockade into account, but in our opinion it is up to the United States to put an end to the blockade.

We took an important step when we signed the hijacking agreement. We have no major airlines, and the hijackings were affecting, hurting, the United States and not us. The determining factor that led us to sign the agreement was really a concern for international public opinion—for the people of the United States. It was done in a favorable spirit in an attempt to help solve a serious problem which could result in many catastrophies and the

113

tragic loss of lives. This was the basic reason, not a special desire to make a gesture towards the government of the United States.

We took this constructive step in order to find a common solution with the government of the United States. We now wait for the United States to take the next step. That next step would have to be putting an end to the blockade. This is a *sine qua non* condition, because the blockade, in our judgment, was an unjust act, which lacks logic and morale. It maintains a hostile cold war policy toward us, and the United States is involved in a demeaning fight with us, of course. It is more and more criticized throughout the world. The Latin American nations remove themselves more and more from this policy, and I don't think that these trends of reestablishment of economic and political relations between Latin American countries and Cuba can be stopped. It is a powerful movement. Therefore, the United States's policy toward Cuba is discredited, morally weak in every sense.

Q. What does the blockade mean? What effect has the blockade had on Cuba's everyday life?

A. The blockade affects us in many ways, and I can explain some of them to you in a practical sense. First of all, the transports—there is a blacklist for carriers. And Cuba has to export all its products by sea and import all the products it consumes by sea. It has to charter ships, and the fact that any ship traveling to Cuba is put on the American blacklist makes things quite difficult for us and the price of sea transportation is very high for Cuba. It is one of the difficulties.

Many of the world's industries produce goods with North American technology and have direct or working relations with North American patents. We do not. Whenever we try to purchase a certain type of equipment, we face the problem that we have no business relations with North American industries and we don't have their equipment. The United States has always hampered our development efforts because they have exerted pressure on other countries to prevent them from trading with us. Also, the United States makes it very difficult for us to have access to loans.

Q. What about international organizations?

A. We cannot rely on any organization because they are always dominated by the United States. There is also a technological problem. That is, we are deprived of access to the technological achievements realized by the United States.

And finally, from the commercial standpoint, there are problems in obtaining certain supplies. The United States is the source of some products, some agricultural techniques, some raw materials, and some products which we cannot obtain. All our purchases that we need have to take a long voyage to reach Cuba. Therefore, we cannot deny that the economic blockade is a very heavy drain on our country, but it has not prevented the consolidation of the Revolution, nor the development of our country, because our development will continue. But it does constitute an economic drain. The importance of the blockade for us cannot be underestimated, and they, of course, know it. They know well the figures and they know that the United States creates many difficulties for the Cuban economic development. The United States not only refuses to trade with us, but it takes punitive measures against the ships that come to Cuba, against the countries that trade with Cuba. Now, here you have a recent example: Bangladesh. A small country with fifty million inhabitants that has suffered a great natural catastrophe, enormous floodings, which is in need of food. Then the United States, in order to grant Bangladesh certain shipments of foodstuffs—I believe, one hundred thousand tons of wheat and some other foodstuffs —it set a condition to Bangladesh that it break its commercial relations with Cuba. In reality, actually, it is a great shame that in order to be able to extend a certain assistance to a country very much

115

in need of it, you impose on it a harsh condition, a humiliating condition. I don't know what Bangladesh is going to do, but, of course, if Bangladesh stops trade with us because of a situation of *force majeure,* because they are in a situation of hunger and because they are going to receive food from the United States, we cannot criticize Bangladesh, because we understand its special situation. But isn't this really a shame, isn't it conceited, isn't it ridiculous that the United States, in order to ship a bit of food to a country which has faced a very great natural catastrophe, forbids it to trade with Cuba, because it is selling Cuba some jute bags, and henceforth Bangladesh won't be able to sell jute bags to Cuba? It is because of this that we are establishing the condition that there cannot be, that there cannot be an equality of circumstances for negotiations, so long as one of the parties maintains a coercive measure against us. And we have posed as an indispensable condition that the blockade must cease.

Q. Could you tell us some of the specific results of the blockade during 1959, 1960?

A. It was very serious, because all of Cuba's industries were American-made. Our transportation means came from the United States, and all of a sudden we found ourselves unable to buy spare parts for vehicles or for industries.

There are many countries which at first did not dare trade with us for fear of the American prohibitions. Slowly, trade developed, and it is much greater now. We trade with almost all the Western capitalist countries. Our trade with Europe has increased considerably, and our trade with Japan as well, and we are receiving better terms. Our means of transportation have slowly been replaced. Our industrial equipment has slowly been replaced. That is why in the beginning, the blockade hurt us much more than today.

The United States has always exerted pressure on other countries to prevent the establishment of trade. The financial resources of the United States have also exerted pressure to prevent the obtaining of financial resources on the part of Cuba. The blockade has also forced us to develop a policy of austerity, to be more careful with our resources; we had to try harder. But it has also had a positive effect, because we had to force ourselves in the midst of all these difficulties. We wonder what would be the conditions in other countries with a similar blockade as that imposed upon Cuba by the United States, by the most powerful country, financially, economically, technologically.

One should ask therefore, not how much Cuba has developed, but under what conditions Cuba has developed during these past years. Of course, Soviet aid has been very valuable to us. That has been a determining factor in our fight against the blockade. For example, with the energy crisis, which has presented such a problem for other countries. We did not suffer an energy crisis. We continued to receive, as in the past fifteen years, all our energy sources from the Soviet Union, in spite of the blockade. We have received food items, the wheat we consume, fertilizers, considerable transportation equipment, agricultural and industrial equipment, and a lot of basic materials. Our electric plants have been installed basically with Soviet equipment, and we produce more electricity now than before the Revolution. Our workshops are equipped with Soviet tools. It has been not only our effort, but the fact that we have the support of international solidarity. While from the United States we received only aggression, from them we received aid. We have received ample proof of their friendship and solidarity. And I must mention this in all fairness and sincerity. Although I think we will profit from the lifting of the blockade, so will the United States.

Q. How is it in President Ford's interest to change relations with Cuba and lift this blockade?

A. Look, first of all, I believe that those who can

117

actually make a better evaluation are in the United States, right? But I believe that in the first place, to abandon the policy pursued against Cuba is to abandon a policy that today cannot be morally or politically defended, that is devoid of ethics, and that has no justification of any kind. At a moment of international detente, of disappearance of the cold war, what sense does it make to maintain a micro—cold war with Cuba? It really is ridiculous. I believe that, first of all, the United States would benefit morally and would gain politically.

In the second place, take relations with Latin America. There is in Latin America a growing feeling of rapprochement and of solidarity with Cuba. As long as the United States maintains a policy of hostility towards Cuba, its relations with Latin America will become more difficult. I have no doubt about it.

There is another element. Cuba will not be the only revolutionary country in Latin America because the history of the United States is not going to repeat itself in Latin America. Latin America is not going to find a solution to its problems along the roads of capitalism. We have talked of the important changes that are taking place in Peru, in Panama, in other countries—and these are the realities that no one can prevent from occurring, the United States cannot prevent them. The United States has to learn to develop relations with revolutionary countries in this hemisphere, and I believe that the form in which the relations of the United Stated and Cuba will develop will serve as example; the solutions found with Cuba will be solutions similar to the ones the United States will have to find with other countries in this hemisphere. The United States must learn to deal with the community of Latin American countries on terms of equality. And it must develop amicable political and economic relations with this community.

The United States has to learn to live in peace

Havana skyline.

Cubans and tourists enjoying swimming pool at Hotel Riviera, Havana.

Dining Room of Gran Hotel in Camagüey.

Renovation-construction site in Old Havana.

Fidel Castro, in Russian Jeep, arriving at Hotel Riviera to
meet authors. At left, film producer Saul Landau.

Street scene in Ciego de Avila.

Piece of U.S. equipment, captured at Bay of Pigs, on display at Museum of the Revolution, Havana.

Soviet freighters in Havana harbor.

Carnival float, July 26, 1974.

Rural street scene in Oriente province.

Rural housing in Sierra Maestre.

Small market-town street in Las Villas province.

Child with carnival-season toy, Havana.

José Martí housing complex outside Santiago.

Micro-brigade construction crew outside Havana.

New apartment houses near Havana.

New housing construction in Santiago.

Woman cooking in kitchen of Alamar apartment.

Students outside work-study school.

Mural in psychiatric hospital.

Ward in psychiatric hospital.

Mental patients exercise on Olympic-sized track at hospital.

Salvador Allende school at Alamar housing project.

Sugar cutters cleaning cane.

Left to right. Castro, Madame Dinh, behind her Ramon
Castro, an interpreter, Kirby Jones, Frank Mankiewicz.

Fidel Castro greeting students.

Primary-school students.

"The Power of the People; that is power."

Train unloading at sugar plant.

Young campers during two-week vacation at Santa Lucia Pioneers camp.

Guide Anna Serrano stands outside Moncada barracks.

New hotel-construction for domestic
tourism near Camagüey.

Kirby Jones and Frank Mankiewicz (r) interviewing
Fidel Castro.

Fidel speaking on July 26, 1974, the 21st anniversary of Cuban revolution in Matanzas province.

with the rest of the world, because peace interests all of us. The United States has to become interested in peaceful relations with Latin America, with the socialist camp, with Africa, with Asia, with the whole world. Because war and conflicts have not produced any benefits for the United States. That is to say that all this policy of repression of change, all this policy of the international policeman, have not only cost the United States hundreds of billions of dollars, but many other countries as well. The cold war, the arms race, inflation, poverty in the world, and many other problems are all the result, in part, of this policy which the United States pursued in earlier years. It is impossible that the North American politicians do not think rationally that these errors of the past must be overcome and that the United States and all the other peoples have to learn to live in peace. Because there is no alternative to peace in today's world, and I believe that the manner in which the problems with a country such as Cuba are approached will indicate the extent to which the United States is really adapting itself to today's world. The United States must be capable of developing friendly relations even though they may have different social regimes, even though it may have a different political ideology. The United States will have to face the fact that in the future Cuba will not be the only revolutionary country in this hemisphere.

Q. Not the only country?

A. It will not be the only socialist country in the hemisphere.

Q. In this hemisphere?

A. Yes, because I am convinced that in one way or another, the people of this hemisphere are headed toward socialist systems of production. Be they the same as Cuba's, be they different, more or less radical. So that in the future, the United States will have to deal with one, two, ten socialist countries in this hemisphere, and maybe even with a union

119

of these peoples. Relations with Cuba will be more or less the beginning of a form of relations with revolutionary countries. The U.S. cannot continue with other countries the policy it applies to Cuba.

It was, for instance, an error to keep the Soviet Union isolated during such a long time. Commercial trade relations could well have been developed. It was a mistake to keep China isolated for such a long time. Extensive economic relations could have been developed with these countries, which need equipment, which need technology, and which in turn had products of interest to the United States. And so, the policy towards Cuba is an absurd policy.

There could be other benefits, of an economic nature, even of a material nature—which I have left for last. The United States might be interested in some of Cuba's products and some of the raw materials Cuba is producing. Historically, the United States was a buyer of our products. We were their principal source of sugar. We do not aspire, of course, to return to being their principal source of sugar supply, because we have also developed commercial relations with other countries and we sell sugar to those countries. Our tobacco enjoyed great acceptance in the United States.

Q. We like Cuban cigars.

A. Tobacco was in high demand. They tried to produce the same tobacco in Central America, Santo Domingo, and they were unsuccessful. They took the seeds from Cuba, but failed. Probably due to the climate. The quality of the tobacco is dependent upon the climate, and we remember that even Kennedy would ask his friends to bring him Cuban cigars because he was fond of them. He was an *aficionado* of Cuban cigars. We also exported seafood, lobsters, shrimp, which are in high demand in the United States. We also produce some raw materials which are very important for industry. For example, we have large nickel deposits and we export it. Today, the United States follows our

120

nickel all over the world to stop its commercial use, when in reality nickel is one of the raw materials that it needs for its industries.

But we are also a potential market. We buy in Japan, in Europe, and in many parts of the world. We buy construction equipment, for example, transportation equipment, raw materials, foodstuffs, from countries that are much further away than the United States. So that there is an economic advantage for commercial dealings between the two countries. It would be based mostly on economic exchange, the relations between the two countries. I think we would both have to live within international norms of mutual respect.

I am not going to say that the United States is going to get rich trading with Cuba; materially, the United States can well disregard trade with Cuba, just as Cuba can also disregard trade with the United States; but this is not reasonable. I believe that it would bring about advantages of a material nature. Now, the most important advantages are of a moral nature and of a political nature, because if you are doing something wrong, something unjust, and you rectify it, you gain from this. And all that policy has no moral justification at all at this moment. Besides, sooner or later, it will have to do it.

The important thing that I want to point out is that we are not impatient; time is in our favor. The Revolution is more secure today than ever. The people are more united than ever. And so, we can wait all the time that may be necessary until the United States makes the corrective change, because we have nothing to rectify. What would we have to rectify? All we have done is to defend ourselves, we did not seek to change American society. Nor to impose on the United States an economic and political system, a social system. We have sought to change Cuban society and to establish an economic and political system in Cuba, not in the United States. So, we do not have to change anything, it is our right. Now, the United States does not have

121

any right to impose upon Cuba an economic, social, or political system, and it has no right to interfere in the politics of Cuba. It is the United States that must rectify its policies. We are not the ones to carry on a blockade, nor are we the ones who impose conditions; this is reality. But we can wait.

Q. What will happen after the blockade is lifted?

A. Once the blockade stops, then we can start discussing all the other problems as may be desired. There is the 'Guantanamo base—it is one of the problems to be discussed.

Q. Guantanamo?

A. There are two types of problems. Guantanamo is a piece of the national territory of Cuba. It is occupied by the United States, but we do not pose as condition that they must—that in order to start discussions, they must withdraw from Guantanamo; rather we have posed a single condition, which is that the economic blockade be stopped. I can imagine that they have things to claim from us. We have things to claim from them. But in essence, we have not taken any measures against the United States. They, the United States, have taken them against Cuba. We do not have a piece of territory in the United States. We have no base in Florida, or in Washington, or in New England, or in California, or anywhere. They have a base here.

Q. What are the other problems?

A. The United States has to account the amount their interests were affected by the nationalization laws of Cuba, and we have to account the amount of economic damage done to Cuba by the economic blockade. This is without counting the Bay of Pigs, without counting the counterrevolutionary gangs the CIA organized in Cuba which cost us hundreds of millions of pesos, without counting the expenses the United States has forced us to spend on defense, without counting the sabotage. There have been almost fifteen years of hostilities against our country, which have affected us economically. All these questions we can discuss . . . but I believe that also we are interested not only in the problems of Cuba, we are also a Latin American country, and we are also interested in what is the political attitude of the United States toward Latin America. Because while the United States takes for itself the right to intervene in any country of Latin America, I do not see any form in which the relations between Cuba and the United States can improve, because we are not going to neutralize ourselves, we are not going to remain silent. We are not going to cross our arms, because we regard ourselves as part of Latin America, economically and politically. We are interested in the attitude of the United States toward Latin America and nothing would please us more than to know that the United States is going to follow with regard to Latin America a policy of respect and a policy of nonintervention.

Q. Some North Americans say that the United States should not renew relations with Cuba until Cuba stops "exporting revolution," as they charge you are doing.

A. That is inaccurate. I can assure you that Cuba is above all an exporter of sugar. (laughter) It is an absurd assumption, that revolutions can be exported, because they either spring from the people of the nation or else no one can carry them out for them. I don't quite know what is meant by exportation of revolution. That we sympathize with revolutionaries. Yes, we do. That we have aided revolutionaries as much as we have been able to do so, yes, this is true. That the influence of the Cuban revolution can be felt in the revolution of another country. Yes. But that cannot be labeled exportation of revolution. It is an impossible task, to export revolution.

Q. For example, in my country, when we refer to exportation of revolution, we refer to Che Guevara in Bolivia.

A. Right. And what type of exportation of revolution was involved there?

123

Q. A Cuban, a revolutionary leader . . .

A. Right, Che Guevara. He was born in Argentina and fought in the Cuban revolution. It can then be said that Argentina exported revolution to Cuba, and there is nothing further from the truth. A revolutionary with a Latin Americanist spirit fought with us and was willing to die for the Cuban revolution—and he was determined, even while we were still in Mexico, that once he had fulfilled his obligations insofar as the Cuban revolution was concerned, he would fight in Latin America. This was an old dream of his, and he always used to say to us that after he had fulfilled his obligations toward the Cuban revolution, we would allow him to continue his revolutionary struggle. And he followed his ideal. We are not going to say we did not share his beliefs. We did, but the decision to continue with the revolutionary struggle was entirely his. He wanted some of the Cubans who had fought with him in the Sierra to accompany him, and they did. They were Cubans and they were revolutionaries and they agreed to go with him, and we had no objections.

Q. What support do you give to other revolutionaries?

A. Well, for us to support revolutionaries it is essential that they be fighting. When they do fight, we help them.

Q. How

A. Morally and materially, because we had no commitments of any sort that we had to abide by, because if they wanted to export counterrevolution, if they wanted to crush the Cuban revolution, if all the Latin American governments with the exception of Mexico yielded to the orders from the United States and joined the economic blockade and the efforts to destroy the Cuban revolution, we were not going to remain with our hands tied, tied to an international norm. We, therefore, felt that we had the right to help fighting revolutionaries who were trying to carry out a revolution in their countries, because we had no ties with those coun-

124

tries which were trying to crush the Cuban revolution through the blockade. What cannot be said is that Cuba violated its normal relations with any country. That is, if a nation abides by the norms in their relations with us, we reciprocate. Those countries that do not interfere in our internal matters have our highest respect with regard to their internal affairs. But those that violate the international rules in their relationships with us, who attack us, who interfere in our internal affairs, those do not have our respect. I believe we are very explicit with regard to this policy.

Q. Some liberals in the United States will say that we are the exporters of revolution—Chile, for instance.

A. Against Chile it was counterrevolution, it was the export of fascism.

We cannot have any illusions from the point of view that our relations would improve while the relations of the United States with Latin America worsen, because we are a Latin American people and we are not going to hold to a selfish position, because we will be in solidarity with the other Latin American countries. When the blockade of Cuba was actually implemented and when they cut off our sugar quota, the United States distributed the quota among many Latin American governments, a certain form of bribery to many governments, handing over to them the sugar quota of Cuba. I understand this to be an act of betrayal of another Latin American country by these governments, but we are not disposed to act in this manner—we are not willing to turn traitors to the interests of our Latin American peoples.

Q. But do you think that without betraying the positions of the Latin American countries the relations with the United States could improve?

A. I believe that if the relations of the United States with the rest of Latin America are bad, then we cannot improve the relations between Cuba and the United States.

Q. You speak of the intervention in Chile, then, from

the Latin American point of view, not from that of your country, but overall. . . .

A. No doubt, in this position, I reflected a Latin American sentiment, not only a Cuban sentiment. And we have no fear of voicing criticism, because the improvement of the relations with the United States, the possibility that the relations between Cuba and the United States would improve, cannot be advanced on the basis that Cuba renounce its principles, that Cuba renounce its honesty, and that Cuba abandon its solidarity with the rest of the Latin American peoples. If we are going to obtain an improvement in the relations with the United States at the cost of betraying our principles, then we could not have any improvement in the relations with the United States.

Q. You have read what President Ford said about Cuba at his first press conference, saying that our blockade policy is actually the policy of the OAS. If they don't want it, then we shall follow them.

A. The first statement Ford made ratified to a certain extent the prior policy in which he said that there was no change and there would not be any unless there were changes in the attitude of Cuba. Later, referring to the OAS, he said that in this matter he would follow the measures taken by the OAS. Of course, within the Latin American countries, there is at present a very strong movement against the isolation of Cuba which, in my judgment, is irrepressible and cannot be contained. If the United States attempts to check this movement, it would expose itself to a defeat, because either it would find itself in the minority among the countries making up this organization, or even if it were to maintain a minority sufficiently large to prevent the lifting of the isolation and of the blockade of Cuba and it were to succeed in this, many more countries would move to establish relations with Cuba, in spite of the OAS.

The winds of history are blowing in our favor, and therefore I believe that if, in fact, the United

States follows this feeling of the majority of Latin America, it would be acting in an intelligent manner. If it does the contrary, it would be acting in a manner that is greatly mistaken. Of course, up until now, the OAS has always done what the United States says, and it would really be interesting to see if, for the first time, the United States would do what the Organization of American States says.

Q. Under what conditions would you meet with the President of the United States?

A. Two people are not going to sit down to talk with a knife at one's throat, and to talk with the blockade still being imposed is precisely that. If the blockade is ended, then we will sit down to talk, and we would then do so with whomever represents the government of the United States. We could then have an open agenda to discuss the issues that interest the United States, but the requirement for all this is the lifting of the blockade.

Q. Have you ever met President Ford?

A. No. Not that I recall. I did not have an opportunity, because when I was in the United States many years ago in 1959, I did not meet with members of Congress.

Q. Have you read anything about him?

A. Not much, only what has been published in the papers.

Q. What is your impression of President Ford, so far as you can determine, what he is like, and what he is doing?

A. My personal opinion?

Q. Yes.

A. It seems to me that during the first days he acted with great caution, with much discretion. It seems to me that he found almost unanimous support in the United States. However, as you know, some things have happened. I have read a good deal of criticism because of the pardon of Nixon. I also think that this posed a moral problem, because it is difficult to understand that Nixon be pardoned and all the rest of the people be left to be punished. This does not seem to be very just. This is, of course, a matter of the internal policy of the United States and I imagine there must have been certain reasons for taking this decision.

From our point of view of foreign policy, there are two statements that concern us. One was his justifying statement on the intervention of the CIA in Chile. And the other was his speeches in the United Nations and in Detroit on the energy issue, in which he used what seems to us very strong, pressuring language, and in a certain form threatening, to the oil-producing countries. This reflected a certain political style, from positions of strength. These two international events are, to the Cubans, to the Latin Americans, to the countries of the Third World, something that worries us. Of course, on the other hand, he has made other statements, favoring the continuation of the policy of international detente, which we regard as positive pronouncements. Still, it is much too early to be able to make an evaluation of what will be Ford's path in the presidency of the United States, but up until now we have observed some positive deeds and others which, from our point of view, are negative.

Q. I know that it's early, but have you seen any indication that President Ford might be the kind of President with the courage to change his mind and question his own policies?

A. He is not involved with the Cuban counterrevolutionary elements. Nixon was personally very much involved with them. And we have seen in Ford a man who is above this, these relations of friendship.

We think that the policy of a large and powerful nation such as the United States cannot be determined by reason of personal bonds with certain people.

From the Cuban point of view, we see Ford with a certain hope in the sense that he may, after all, adopt a different policy towards Cuba, and at least

128

he does not have the personal involvement that Nixon had in this regard. This is a positive point that can be pointed out from the Cuban angle. That is all I can say in fairness, but I have no elements to form an opinion.

Q. Have you ever met Rockefeller before?

A. No.

Q. No?

A. No. Rockefeller is known, because a lot has been written about him.

Q. And he has written a lot, and has talked a lot with—

A. He has some relations with the Latin Americans, but with us Cubans I think he has had no relations.

Q. Under what conditions would you consider meeting with Secretary of State Henry Kissinger?

A. Well, if Kissinger wishes to come to Cuba as an individual, as a tourist, like all of you come, we would not object. In general, we think highly of his capabilities. He is an intelligent and realistic man, and truly able—so that we are favorably disposed toward him. The day that he comes to speak for the government of the United States, he would be speaking as its representative, but our condition would be that the blockade be lifted, and then we could discuss as equals. Otherwise, it would be like saying, "We have you blockaded, but let's sit down and discuss our differences."

Q. Do you see any problem with the fact that Kissinger was also President Nixon's foreign policy adviser?

A. It seems to us that there was not always total agreement between the policy of Kissinger and the policy of Nixon. You see, I do not believe that Kissinger has a personal position that is hostile toward Cuba, while Nixon undoubtedly had a personally hostile position toward Cuba. Besides, Kissinger has shown himself to be a realistic politician who undoubtedly has fought for international detente. And I must say that the positive facts that Nixon has shown in international policies are to a large extent also to be attributed to Kissinger.

Q. What about Dr. Kissinger's involvement in the CIA activities in Chile?

A. Well, according to the North American press, he was the head of the Committee of Forty, and according to this information, he has a responsibility for this CIA participation in Chile. The fact is, of course, that this is a blow to his prestige. It is a blow, because international public opinion certainly always regarded Kissinger as a man of peace, and this episode in Chile is considered as an act in contradiction with the opinion held of him internationally. But it could also have happened that his enemies, that is, the enemies of international detente, might try to exploit, might try to take advantage of this episode to weaken Kissinger's position and to combat Kissinger's policy. In spite of all of it being very lamentable that he might have had any part in the events in Chile, I believe that he is no doubt the most realistic politician, and one who has made the greatest effort to find a solution to the cold war problems in recent years in the United States.

Q. Do I understand, then, that despite the revelations about Dr. Kissinger's role about what happened in Chile, that you still consider him a man to respect?

A. I am not going to say, of course, that because of that, the image that I and many others had of him, has not been hurt. I will tell you very frankly, for me this was disappointing. Objectively and independent of these unfortunate events, I continue to have a positive evaluation of his international role.

One cannot deny the role he has played in international politics because of a single factor, because of a single event. I believe sincerely that in United States politics, Kissinger is a fighter for detente and for the improvement of international relations. Maybe there are within the government of the United States tendencies favorable to cold war and favorable to international tensions; it is because of that that I consider—I tell you in all honesty—that the role of Kissinger was in general a positive role, and that it will continue to be a positive role in international politics.

Q. If you did sit down to discuss with Kissinger, what would you say to him?

A. (Laughter) I have not thought about it. We have not thought of it as an immediate possibility. We know he has been successful in diplomatic negotiations and we have spoken to people who have relations with him and who esteem·him and consider him a highly intelligent and capable man. He enjoys high international prestige.

Q. Also in Cuba?

A. In Cuba he is considered a very capable man for his activities in international diplomacy.

Q. Our secretary of state believes in a policy of linkages—

A. What?

Q. Linkages . . . that one policy links up with another. In your point of view, is there merit in viewing foreign policy under this light?

A. I really do not quite understand the meaning of the theory. Perhaps if you were to explain it better. . . .

Q. When he speaks, for example, of Vietnam, he speaks of Vietnam tying in with the Soviet Union, China, Thailand, Cambodia. Foreign relations are not isolated, but each country and each problem is a link with another.

A. Well, then, I understand you in that sense. I believe problems are interconnected, and that there was a great linkage among problems. There is no doubt that the problems of Vietnam concern the Soviet Union very much, as they do China. This is to say that the act of aggression against Vietnam was a typical example of aggression against a socialist country, and it was seen badly, annoyingly, by all the socialist countries, and we did, too. In that sense, as you explain that problems are interconnected, there is no doubt that it is so. I don't un-

131

derstand in what sense Kissinger meant it, though. Is this the same theory as Metternich's?

Q. Well, they are related, no?

A. Then it is obvious that we must study Kissinger's theory in order to be able to criticize it.

Q. But if we are speaking of linkages. . . .

A. Lenin said, for example, that the Czarist empire was the weakest link in the capitalist world, and that therefore the revolution could be started. Cuba did not seem to be the weakest link the United States had in Latin America.

Q. Which link is?

A. The weakest link? It is the link where the chain breaks. On the contrary, however, Cuba seemed to be one of the strongest links.

Q. If Cuba maintains its socialist path, how can Cuba take advantage of an end to the blockade and a renewal of relations with the United States?

A. The socialist path is not in question.

Q. Without compromise? How can the peoples from such different cultures learn to come together in a new way?

A. Of course, we are speaking of two different political cultures—one with a socialist mentality and the other with a capitalist one. It is a fact, and we have to remember that it is precisely the material base, the bases for production, which determines habits. For example, I imagine it would puzzle an American to see how a socialist restaurant, a socialist hotel, factory, store, functions. Americans are used to seeing the proprietor of the restaurant running it, although we should not forget that in the United States there are also private organizations which resemble socialist organizations very much. For example, restaurant chains. The restaurants, the stores, are run by administrators who work for these large companies that own the chains. That is why in general the Marxist theorists, and even Lenin, said that capitalism, when highly developed, created organizations similar to those of a socialist state. But one has to realize that other forms of administration still function because, next to the large enterprise, there is the small company, where everything is run by the owner, so that in a capitalist system, a more individualistic attitude is developed. In general, man depends on himself and on himself alone. He does not really rely on others; he expects little from others. Under socialism, a spirit of solidarity results and people work with a feeling of community, and we can see it in the way our people's mentality has changed over the years. Our people now have a socialist conscience, a very high sense of solidarity. In the United States, individualism has been emphasized from the very beginning and it is the type of society that developed. Culturally, we may have similar traits, others that are very different. I am referring to political terms.

Q. How will these two mentalities relate to each other in closer contact?

A. It will be a problem. We will have to analyze the implications this will have for us, as the Americans will have to consider the effects it will have on them.

I give you the example of Teofilo Stevenson, who is the Olympic boxing champion. He was offered a million dollars and he refused it, and in general we have many athletes who have been invited to join the professional ranks with excellent remuneration but they turn these offers down easily. Why? Because their mentality does not have room for professionalism or earning large sums of money. They have other moral values which prevail, and as a result it is natural for them to turn down a million dollars. I would imagine it would be much more difficult for an American athlete to turn down a million dollars. This is why I believe there are two different ways of thinking and they will come into contact in case we had a massive exchange in the future—traveling between the two countries. But we have to think of the future and be prepared. I prefer the people to be prepared for all contacts rather than an isolated, as-cetic people with no contact.

Q. And how can they be prepared? What will you do?

A. I think through education based on socialist think-ing. This is a way to prepare man not to see work as a burden or as a punishment, but as a natural, logical activity to which he becomes accustomed at a very early age. I believe a deep sense of convic-tion based on socialist values is developed through this type of educational system.

Q. Have you developed such an effective new educa-tional system in fifteen years?

A. I think so. If we believe we represent a just society, a superior society with higher spiritual values, which we consider higher than those of the capitalist so-ciety, there is no reason for us to fear contact with a capitalist society. The new generations must be educated in that spirit. When I speak of education, I do not speak of indoctrination, because I don't believe ideas can be imposed. One can develop ideas, one can give people access to them, and if these ideas are superior, they will prevail.

Q. Are there many in Cuba now who are undergoing this educational preparation?

A. By 1980 we will have a million youths integrated into the work/study programs. When the Revolu-tion triumphed in 1959, we had seventy thousand. Besides, we now have more and more professors with more experience, and they are very young. By 1980 the average age of high-school professors will be twenty-four years. So you can see what it will be like when we have professors with ten, fifteen, twenty years experience. I think we will then have a very well-educated generation, polit-ically as well. Cultural activities are encouraged in every aspect. I think we are prepared to face the future, a future not made easy by being neigh-bors of the United States.

Q. Is there not a danger that because of this educa-tional process, all Americans will be seen as enemies of Cuba?

134

A. I think our people can distinguish, discern the issues clearly and they are not confused as to who is guilty of certain wrongs. In our political relations we do not blame the people of the United States, but rather the system, the capitalist system, the imperialist system. But we can say with great satisfaction that our people do not hate the people of the United States. Because we have had many friends among the Americans. Young brigades have come here year after year to help us with the crops. Our people have not been left with the memory of Bay of Pigs alone, of the infiltrated spies, the blockade, the sabotage. We also have fresh memories of Americans citizens who have opposed all this, who have approached us and made a great impression on us. This is a point which we always want to make clear—that we do not confuse the people with the system, and we do not blame the people for the system.

Q. What do you mean by the system, because the people are part of the system?

A. Well, the people are part of the system and they are the victims of the system. Was not Cuba a country that lived under the capitalist system? Didn't we live under colonialism? Are we to blame the people for the colonial system or the capitalist system?

Q. Don't you think people, though, may be the creators of their system?

A. I do not believe in the maxim that each country has the government it deserves. Because why should we blame the Dominican Republic when it tried to liberate itself with the American troops there? We cannot say that the Dominicans do not deserve a more advanced, socialist system than the one they now have. Are we going to blame the colonized for the colonization system? And are we to blame people who live under a certain social system for the existence of a social system with such historical background? Capitalism in the United States goes back two hundred years, and it flourished there

135

due to the geographical and natural conditions. The North American was brought up under this system. They have lived well, materially. The Americans never knew the famines of Europe nor the devastation of war. The Soviet poeple know what it is like to be invaded by Nazi troops, the destruction of its cities. They lost twenty million lives in the Soviet Union. The European countries know war. American soldiers have participated in wars, but not on American soil.

Q. What, then, does determine the system?

A. Historical, geographical conditions determine a social regime or system. One cannot blame the people. Besides, there are millions of people in America who have known discrimination—manual workers, intellectuals, scientific workers, artists, students, blacks, Puerto Ricans, Chicanos. We do not confuse the American people with the large monopolies, trusts, or with the financiers who dominate the economy and the politics of the United States. We cannot make this mistake because our ideology teaches us to distinguish within a people, their constitution, or makeup, their social classes, the dominating classes and the dominated, the exploiting class and the exploited. And the lower classes in one way or another because of the system, and this is the majority of the nation, and we therefore have to see them in this light.

In other words, we have an advantage in our contact with Americans, because we do not feel hatred toward the American. Perhaps it is not the same in the United States. They may feel differently if they feel as nationalistic people only. If one thinks in terms of classes, those types of feelings can emerge, but Cubans have never felt this way and the Revolution has never encouraged chauvinistic national feelings of hatred for the American people. If we did that, we would not be true Marxists.

So that I believe we will be ready for the necessary, inevitable contact between the two social systems. I believe we will be prepared. That is our opinion.

The United States

Q. Looking at the U.S. political and economic system, what do you think is in store for the future?

A. Of course I am convinced that the last country in the world where a change toward socialism will take place is the United States, because the free enterprise institutions wield great power in the United States. It is the country where capitalism has given the maximum results, where capitalism has gone the farthest, and where the greatest economic and technological achievements have been realized. Favored by its abundant natural resources, by its political institutions, and because the parliamentary system—the republican system of government in the United States—has adapted perfectly to its economic policy, ideal conditions for the flourishing of capitalism were created. And the system enjoys prestige among the American people. If one thinks of the crises that can occur in Europe and in other capitalist countries, they will take place in those countries before they take place in the United States. The United States will be the last bastion of capitalism. Maybe you will achieve social change through parliamentary means, peaceful means. Up to now one cannot foresee a change in the United States's economic and social policy. Crises, such as the energy crisis which is now affecting the world, affect the United States less than Japan, Italy, France, England, and other countries.

Q. Why?

A. Because the United States is self-sufficient in energy sources. Eighty-five percent or more of the energy that it consumes, it produces. It produces a lot of gas, almost the entirety of its industries use gas. It has large coal reserves, it produces more than five hundred million tons of petroleum, it is the world's largest oil producer. It has developed almost all its hydraulic resources.

It is at the head of the Western world in the utilization of nuclear energy in industries, and it has a large reserve of fossil fuels. I am not saying that it is easy to manage all these resources, because the utilization of nuclear energy has its difficulties —technical problems, disposal of waste products, the resistance of the natural environment. The exploitation of coal reserves, even where those reserves are great, also has its drawbacks because it requires large investments and results in harming the environment.

In other words, the U.S. is definitely able to face an energy crisis. It is slightly dependent on the oil-producing countries because it imports one-third of the oil it consumes, and this is not the case as, for example, Japan. Japan has to import coal, gas, oil. The European countries are also forced to import their energy sources.

Energy is an important problem throughout the world, perhaps the world's number one problem today and of the future. These problems are not easily solved, neither socially nor technologically, but among the capitalist countries, the one in the most favorable position is the United States. It is in a favorably competitive position, and its technology is highly advanced. It accumulated for years, it stole brains [scientists] and developed its technology by making heavy investments in research, and this put them at an advantage over the other capitalist countries.

Q. Will the U.S. ever change its system?
A. I do believe that the system will change, and so will the society. We represent an idea of the future, and the United States represents a system of the past, which belongs to another era.
Q. Apart from those political and economic aspects,

138

what about our U.S. culture? Is there anything you like about it? (laughter).

A. To tell you the truth, I am not that familiar with American culture.

Q. Writers, novelists, painters?

A. Lately here we haven't received American books because of the blockade. Some American films come. I have seen some changes since the Revolution. Some movies which dealth strongly with civil rights issues, some critical movies. Some also that dealt with capital punishment. Very interesting movies. I can't recall the name, but there was one concerning racial problems which dealt with the problem very well.

Q. Was it called *I Want to Live*—a movie about a woman?

A. I remember some very strong movie ending in a hanging.

Q. What?

A. In the gallows—someone had committed a crime and he was hanged. I believe it was a movie condemning the death penalty. There have also been some very good movies on the issue of discrimination. *The Defiant Ones* was shown here and made a great impression. But we have had little access to American movies. We have approximately a hundred recent American movies, and we show them throughout Cuba. Of course, we are selective, and we are more critical than in the fifties. There has been a change in American films. I understand there is keen competition with television.

Q. What about American literature?

A. Well, because of political differences between Cuba and the United States a certain isolation has resulted, and we do not receive current North American literature. We are very much aware of the great technological advances made in the United States and we have bought textbooks for our universities and had them translated and printed.

We have not, however, paid author's rights. We believe that intellectual accomplishments are universal property and we therefore print these technical books because otherwise we don't have the means to bring technology here. Of course, since we have no diplomatic relations with the United States, this has not brought us any problems, and we have bought a lot of technical books but hardly any literature.

John F. Kennedy

Q. Is it true or not that relations were beginning to improve between Cuba and the U.S. back in 1963 prior to President Kennedy's assassination?

A. What happened was very interesting, and that is, a French journalist, Jean Daniel (who many years later wrote several versions, not always the truth, of course, but in general sticking pretty much to the truth), went through Washington prior to coming to Cuba and he talked with President Kennedy. When Daniel told him he was coming to Cuba, Kennedy was very interested in his trip. And he suggested several topics to Daniel, so that Daniel could bring them up in his conversations with me. Kennedy asked him to report back to him on his return to Washington. Then, Jean Daniel arrived in Cuba and we talked. I went with him to Varadero and he was explaining to me all the details of his conversations with Kennedy, the topics Kennedy had suggested, and his interest in my reply to some of these questions.

'In my opinion, this was a definite gesture on Kennedy's part to try to establish contact, an exchange with us. But as I was listening to everything Daniel was telling me about his conversation with Kennedy, the news broke over the radio that an attempt had been carried out against Kennedy's life. In reality, I tell you personally and think I speak for all my fellow revolutionaries—we all felt a reaction of pain, of great displeasure when we received the news that an attempt had been carried out on Kennedy's life. Later on we listened to the radio for hours following the developments of the state of Kennedy's health closely, until at last his death was announced and everyone was saddened. It really seemed such a shame, such a tragic ending to Kennedy's life.

Q. Did Jean Daniel carry a message from President Kennedy?

A. It could be interpreted as a message. A message, or at least . . . well, some sentiments of President Kennedy. Kennedy had expressed to Daniel his great concern about all that had occurred in the October crisis and asked a series of questions. When he knew that Jean Daniel would be going to Cuba, he told him, "Speak to Castro and come back again here, to Washington, to talk with me." When Jean Daniel was explaining all this to me in great detail, I paid close attention. I thought that Kennedy, by discussing with Daniel his trip here and his visit with me, had the objective of learning our point of view on these same problems. But it was not a formal message.

Q. But on which topics, on which subjects? What was discussed?

A. All this has been written. But I recall that one of the elements which Kennedy discussed with Daniel was the grave risk that this October crisis implied. The grave danger the entire world had faced. He also wanted to know to what extent we had also been aware of this danger. I believe it was an exploration.

Q. An exploration?

A. An exploration, really. Kennedy spoke at length about a whole series of problems. In the first place, the impression I gained was that Kennedy was questioning somewhat the policy that had been pursued towards Cuba; and in the second place, that he was exploring the positions of Cuba.

It should not be forgotten that Kennedy was in a very special situation, and that when he became

141

President, this whole plan of training troops and of invading Cuba had already been organized. And he had great doubts. In the end, still having his doubts, they convinced him to go ahead and he went ahead. Then the failure came, when all had been based on false and mistaken assumptions. It must not be forgotten, as I have mentioned, that it was Nixon who had proposed that the marines and the armed forces be used.

Unfortunately, the only indication we had of Kennedy's thoughts was the interview with Jean Daniel, and the message Kennedy sent us through him. The same day that we were receiving the message, Kennedy was assassinated.

This does not obliterate the political and ideological differences between us. We believed in two different philosophies, but above all we admit that Kennedy was a very intelligent man, who dared take certain measures. We must not forget when everyone was blaming someone else for the Bay of Pigs, he stood up and assumed the responsibility for everything. This is a gesture which must be taken into account. Kennedy had taken a courageous stand in those days, when everyone was blaming each other. He said that success had many fathers, but defeat was an orphan.

I believe that after the October crisis Kennedy started to reconsider the entire policy, to give thought to this problem. Jean Daniel spoke about this extensively, and it was the first and only time, really, that an exploratory effort of this nature was made.

Q. What do you think of Kennedy now?

A. I have an impression of Kennedy and of Kennedy's character, but I formed it over the years that he was President from different gestures, different attitudes. We mustn't forget the speech he made at American University several months prior to his death, in which he admitted certain truths and spoke in favor of peace and relaxation of tensions. It was a very courageous speech and it took note of a series of international realities. Then he talked about what had happened in the Soviet Union, of the thousands of cities that had been destroyed, of the millions of lives lost, and he compared that destruction with what could have taken place in the United States had they suffered the aggression the Soviet Union suffered. This was Kennedy after two years in the presidency, who felt sure of his reelection, a Kennedy who dared make decisions—daring decisions. I have no doubts that Kennedy would someday have reconsidered his policy towards Cuba.

Q. How would you list the main traits of John Kennedy?

A. One of the characteristics of Kennedy was courage. He was a courageous man. A man capable of taking a decision one way or another, a man capable of revising a policy, because he had the courage to do so. There are politicians who let themselves be dragged along by the current, who follow routine, without committing themselves, without changing anything.

For example, let me mention one of this kind of politician—Lyndon Johnson. That is to say, he would not question a policy—just follow the routine. But Kennedy was a bold man, a man with initiative, a man with imagination. And he was a man of courage; this is the evaluation that I have. Not because he was our friend, because we were the targets of his aggression. After all, he gave the order to go on with the expedition, he intensified the blockade of Cuba, he supported CIA activities against Cuba, the pirate attacks, the organizing of mercenary bands, he made the blockade tougher, he took many measures against us. But I speak to you in all sincerity and try to give you the opinion that I have of Kennedy. I say that truly he was one of the few men who had enough courage to question a policy and to change it. And he demonstrated this in his term as President. Moreover, the Kennedy elected President and the Kennedy of pre-presidency times was a much more conservative Kennedy. As he advanced and gained wider knowledge of the realities of the world, he went on to change his policy and his political criteria. I would say that this is a man whose political mind evolved, changing gradually and undoubtedly.

Q. And Kennedy and Latin America?

A. He drew up the Alliance for Progress. It is true that this policy was inspired by the idea of stopping the Cuban revolution, by avoiding the factors that sharpen social situations and facilitate the possibilities of Cuban-style revolutions in Latin America. But he did have an idea, he did have a strategy, and he tried to push it forward. Today, there are some North American papers which have said that Cuba is the only country in Latin America that has realized the objectives of the Alliance for Progress, because it had been intended that the Alliance for Progress would include some tax reforms, agrarian refoms, a better distribution of wealth, concern about housing, about health conditions, education, public health, and all these things —a reform program to try to stop the Revolution.

Q. And what do the Cuban people think of Kennedy? of the Kennedy name?

A. There is no such thing as a worshiping of the Kennedy name, really. Kennedy was an adversary; he is considered responsible for the measures he took against Cuba. He is not blamed absolutely for the Bay of Pigs invasion, because when he came to power it was already planned, but he was the one who decided to carry it out. Kennedy decided that the bombardments prior to the invasion should take place, and Kennedy was responsible for the subversion against Cuba. It is also true that he was responsible for the counterrevolutionary forces in the Escambray, in other provinces, for the dropping of weapons on the island, for the economic blockade, for the pirate attacks. I would not be truthful if I were to say that we have ceased to analyze critically all these factors.

144

What I am trying to do is to separate Kennedy the political man, the representative of the American empire responsible for acts of aggression against us, to separate the political leader from the brilliant man with his own ideas and initiative. He was an intelligent and able leader of American imperialism. We do not deny his many personal virtues, his qualifications. But, regrettably, we must take into consideration his responsibility for measures that were taken against us. We did not hold personal grudges against him, nor did we have reason to wish for his death, and least of all the tragic death he suffered. I say this in all honesty, in all sincerity, that we were grieved, it was very unpleasant to learn of his death, and we would have preferred that he continue in the presidency of the United States. Because if there was a President of the United States who could have had the courage to change policy, or at least to question American policy toward Cuba, that was Kennedy.

Q. Well, one rumor surrounding the Kennedy assassination was that Cuban exiles were involved in the plot, because they thought that you and President Kennedy were going to reestablish relations or were going to reach a rapprochement.

A. I don't recall very clearly, but it seems to me that I read something to the effect that this man who killed Kennedy had been in Louisiana, or somewhere around there, and had established contact with some exiles; but in reality I cannot say anything about this. I have nothing to base my judgment on. I cannot assert that counterrevolutionary elements planned the assassination. I have no proof, no basis.

Q. Another rumor concerning his death was that President Kennedy was assassinated in retaliation for an attempt against your life. Jack Anderson has written on this.

A. I have not read this in any serious American publication. You know that for a while the CIA was attempting assassination of some of our revolutionary leaders. Some say the decision was on Ken-

145

nedy's desk several times, because on all these things people have written. If the decision was to be made to assassinate the leaders of the Cuban revolution, the plans to do this existed also.

There are so many imponderables behind President Kennedy's assassination that it would be a good thing if the truth were known someday. I have heard that there are certain documents that will not be published until after a hundred years. And I ask myself why. What secrets surround the Kennedy assassination that these papers cannot be published? It is also very interesting that this man —Oswald—who was involved in the assassination, traveled to Mexico a few months prior to the assassination and applied for a permit at the Cuban embassy to travel to Cuba, and he was not given the permit. We had no idea who he was. But I ask myself why would a man who commits such an act try to come here. Sometimes we ask ourselves if someone did not wish to involve Cuba in this, because I am under the impression that Kennedy's assassination was organized by reactionaries in the United States and that it was all a result of a conspiracy.

What I can say is that he asked permission to travel to Cuba. Now, imagine that by coincidence he had been granted this permit, that he had visited Cuba for a few days, then returned to the United States and killed Kennedy. That would have been material for a provocation. Then the other mystery is that this other man—Ruby—who had no moral conditions, qualifications, no political ideals, no political passions, becomes so enraged by Kennedy's assassination that he kills the assassin right in front of the police. It was incredible, inconceivable. That does not happen even in the most mediocre of movies. Then this man is shown as a great idealist moved by this act and he comes there and . . . and kills Kennedy's assassin, who could have talked and told everything, who he was, who pushed him to do this. We have never believed in carrying out

146

this type of activity of assassination of adversaries.

Q. Even during the early stages of your own revolutionary fight?

A. Never. And our own revolutionary background proves it. We attacked the Moncada barracks, we landed on the *Granma,* we fought a war . . . against Batista for twenty-five months. We were not trying to kill Batista. It would have been easier to kill Batista than to assault the Moncada. Why? Because we do not believe that the system is abolished by liquidating the leaders, and it was the system that we opposed. We were fighting against reactionary ideas, not against men. Our Marxist policy leaves no room for liquidation of leaders of any social system through terrorist acts; this does not solve the problem of the social system. We had been attacked by Kennedy, of course, after he inherited the Bay of Pigs plans, and it is unquestionable that he carried them out and adopted measures against our country. It went against our political ideas to organize any type of personal attack against Kennedy.

This has never been the policy of the Revolution but I, of course, have never been concerned about this because I believe that the American public opinion never sought, of course, to pin the blame for the Kennedy assassination on Cubans. We understood what the implications were, and we were concerned about the possibility that an attempt would be made to blame Cuba for what had happened, but this was not what concerned us most. In reality, we were disgusted, because, although we were in conflict with Kennedy politically, we had nothing against him personally, and there was no reason to wish him personal harm. Besides, Kennedy could be followed by someone worse, and I always used to say that at least we knew Kennedy, that we had fought against him during the Bay of Pigs incidents, the missile crisis, and all that. He was a known enemy, but let me repeat that the Kennedy who was assassinated in Dallas was a much more experienced man than the one who had assumed the presidency two years before. Because he had lacked experience at the beginning of his term. He had talent, but lacked maturity and experience when he took office.

The Missile Crisis

Q. You briefly metioned the October 1962 missile crisis as one of the topics discussed between President Kennedy and Jean Daniel. In several historical works, especially in *Thirteen Days,* by Robert Kennedy, we know some of what took place during the October crisis from the American point of view. We have no data on conversations which took place among yourselves and especially between you and Khrushchev during those days.

A. To what are you referring?

Q. Well, what happened during those days, day by day, especially during the last few days?

A. I can tell you some of what happened; I am not going to tell you the entire story. What I can say is that we saw certain movements in Washington, such as the convocation, special meetings, and other certain measures, which we understood not only by instinct and smell, but by our experience with the way in which Kennedy had imposed the blockade. We declared a state of alarm and mobilized our antiaircraft weapons. When the crisis developed, therefore, we had taken all the military precautions that we could take before the two threats—aerial attack or invasion—occurred. We mobilized all our antiaircraft defenses to protect the more important, strategic spots, the missile bases included. Later we saw the alternatives open to the United States: bombardment of the bases or an invasion. We then suggested to the Soviet command that the strategic missiles be dismantled, so that they would not all be in the same position which would facilitate their destruction by an aerial attack.

There was a critical period after that. The American planes began flying very low and we understood the danger—because if we permitted these flights we were risking a surprise attack. And at a specific moment, when tensions were at a peak, our antiaircraft artillery started shooting at low-flying aircraft. That same day coincided with the shooting down of the U-2. That plane was shot down by rocket artillery.

Q. How many U.S. planes were shot down?

A. Only one plane.

Q. Only one?

A. One, not more.

Q. Who gave the order to fire on that plane? The Soviets or Cuba?

A. The order to shoot at aircraft was given by us. We had the control over the antiaircraft guns, and we had one criterion: not to permit aircraft to fly over national territory, because if the planes were allowed to fly it would mean exposing ourselves to a surprise attack.

This was possibly one of the most difficult moments of the crisis. But then at dawn, I don't recall the day exactly, the day after the order, there were planes flying at treetop level over various places of the national territory, and our batteries opened fire on the planes.

On the second day a U-2 flew over, and then was shot down by ground-to-air missiles. Of course, at that time there was no Cuban personnel that could operate these ground-to-air missiles. They were Soviet specialists. But the order to the antiaircraft to open fire was given by the Cuban side. Those were probably the most critical moments of the crisis.

Q. Who conducted the negotiations?

A. In reality, we did not handle the strategic negotiations because we lacked the means. But all our people, the entire nation, remained calm, ready for anything. I don't think any other country has seen itself in such danger, but our people were determined to stand firm without making any concessions. This was our position, everyone was ready, and then the shooting began. Everyone opened fire against the planes. Our artillery began firing against the low-flying aircraft, and in approximately twenty-four hours, twenty-four to thirty-six hours, an agreement was reached between the Soviet Union and the United States.

What I am telling you about those days and what I remember the most is the general attitude of the Cubans. We underwent an experience of great danger which tested our nation, and no one was willing to give an inch. It was truly a unique experience that we lived through during those days.

Q. Did you speak with Khrushchev during those days?

A. Yes, he kept us informed of the various steps being taken by the United States and by them. This was the truth. When the final agreement was reached, of course, we were informed by the Soviet Union with coded messages which took a long time because of the distances involved. Due to the lack of time, therefore, it was not possible to consult us with regard to the final solution. As Robert Kennedy explains, communications were quite constant between the representatives of the Soviet Union and the United States. We adopted the only position we could adopt, because we could not be hesitant or fearful, and this I can tell you has been a constant thing in the Revolution. What else could we do in the face of the antagonism and the dangers that could come from the United States?

Who is to blame for the missile crisis? If the United States had not been bent on liquidating the Cuban revolution there would not have been an October crisis. This was first demonstrated with economic aggression and then with the organization of subversive forces against Cuba, the Bay of Pigs invasion. Were we right or wrong to fear direct invasion? Didn't the United States invade the Dominican Republic? Didn't the United States bomb North Vietnam? Didn't they carry on an exhausting war for years in South Vietnam? How could we be sure that we would not be invaded? And this thought determined the setting up of strategic missiles in Cuba.

Of course, the measures we took also implied another danger, but in the final balance Cuba was not invaded and there was no world war. We did not, therefore, have to suffer a war like Vietnam —because many Americans could ask themselves, why a war in Vietnam, thousands of miles away, why millions of tons of bombs dropped on Vietnam and not in Cuba? It was much more logical for the United States to do this to Cuba than to do it ten thousand kilometers away. And this is precisely how we saw the danger, and the results of the crisis prevented this type of war against Cuba. What would have happened to us? Since the socialist countries are so far away, we had no backup defense, no direct source of ammunitions. In the end the problem of a world war was circumvented.

Q. Were you disappointed with the Soviet Union and the way the final decision was reached?

A. Well, we were not totally satisfied and we were enormously irritated. But if we are realistic, and we go back in history, we realize that ours was not the correct posture. Even though we were against making concessions, what would have happened if no concessions had been made? The Russian opinion was that two objectives would be gained from those negotiations: the promise not to invade Cuba, on the one hand, and on the other, to eliminate the danger of nuclear war.

Historically, it has been proven that Cuba was not invaded and the world did free itself from a nuclear war threat. The Revolution was consolidated and we were not attacked. The war did not take place and there was a period of relaxed international tensions. Two important political objectives were satisfied—Cuba's safety and world peace.

151

We felt very passionate and were opposed to any concessions in negotiations, but in a negotiation one has to make concessions. With all honesty I say to you now that history has proven that the Soviet position was the correct one.

We were annoyed by matters of form, by certain formalities in the conduct of the negotiations. But they are not worth arguing about, because more important than form at that time was the essence of the problems involved. What was important on the value scale was Cuba's security and the prevention of a world war. I am answering frankly and in all honesty. There is no doubt to the fact that when you analyze the results, the United States adhered to a promise not to invade Cuba—a real promise and everyone knows that. That is the truth.

Q. Who originally decided to install missiles in Cuba?

A. In reality it was decided between the two of us. We asked ourselves this question, What can we do to prevent a direct invasion? And we posed this problem to the Soviets.

Q. When was that?

A. The Bay of Pigs was in April 1961. So it was the beginning of 1962.

Q. From your point of view, was that the main reason for the missile installation—that is, to prevent what you saw as another possible future attack from the United States?

A. Yes, those were the issues, and we were willing to accept the necessary steps, of course.

Q. Did you desire the capacity for retaliation?

A. No, it was not that. We were under a protective nuclear umbrella. It was not retaliation per se, but an effective guarantee against a direct attack.

I also think that from a certain point of view the socialist camp was also strengthened, and if we expected them to take a chance for us, we had to be willing to do likewise for them. That is, we received a guarantee, and the socialist camp received an advantageous strategic position.

If these circumstances were to repeat themselves,

152

we would not do things differently. We believe
we took the right decision and it is my duty to say
so.

Today circumstances have changed. We do not
feel threatened as we did then, but one must not
forget that all those events took place during the
cold war, in the midst of the great arms race, under
very different circumstances. Those were difficult
times and I don't think anyone wishes to see them
return. They taught everyone a lesson. We came
very close to war and the world leaders were made
aware of these dangers, of those risks, and everyone became more concerned with finding a solution.

This was the turning point in the cold war and
a progressive improvement of the international
situation began to evolve. If the Soviets made concessions, then one must reach the conclusion that
we must be grateful to the Soviets for having taken
measures which prevented a war. This is a historical reality.

The CIA

Q. After the missile crisis, were there other examples
of direct U.S.–Cuban tensions?
A. Later on the pirate attacks began: the CIA-
organized bases in Central America. They had
mother ships circling Cuba, from which small
boats run by the CIA, directed by the CIA, carried
out attacks against Cuba, against refineries, ports,
warehouses, and against the city of Havana. They
would stop sixty miles from the coast. It was very
difficult to organize a defense against these pirate
boats, because they had very powerful motors and
operated in the dark. It was difficult to attack the
mother ships because they were in areas with
merchant ships. Sometimes we attacked the boats
at night, but on one occasion when we attacked
a mother ship, we hit a merchant ship.

They would launch small boats with radar and very modern equipment. They even had radars to detect our radars. In some cases we captured a few, some boats, but otherwise it was a pretty constant harassment from Miami and from Central American bases.

Considerable infiltration also went on. All this was after 1962, 1963, 1964, and all this was very irritating for us because there was an agreement against direct aggression, but the policy of harassment continued in effect.

Q. How long did this go on?

A. It all began to diminish as the United States became progressively involved in the Vietnam War, and therefore began to relax its activities against Cuba.

Q. Why was the Vietnam War an influence?

A. In the beginning, the United States had all these troops in the States and apparently the military leaders were restless to use them—those were very difficult times. Large squadrons were mobilized around Cuba, in different directions, utilizing air transports, everything, but as the Vietnam War grew in momentum, all these troops were sent there. But the pirate attacks, as well as the infiltration and landing of agents, were connected with the provocations coming from the Guantanamo base.

Q. What sort of provocations?

A. On more than one occasion shots were fired from the base, Some of our soldiers were shot at and some were killed. They said no one had fired and we were always to blame, but there were provocations coming from the base.

Q. Did this continue for a long time?

A. As the United States became more and more involved in Vietnam, it limited its activities with relation to Cuba, because it is obvious that as they diminished their troops here their troops in Vietnam increased. Our defensive capabilities also grew, and it would have been necessary to use the troops in Vietnam in any attack against Cuba.

Although there always were reserves in the United States, these were not enough to carry out a lightning attack against Cuba.

Q. Were the CIA activities the only such problems you faced?

A. Later, we faced other problems. The U.S. plane hijackings started, but that was another invention of the CIA against the Cuban revolution. During the beginning of the Revolution, hijackers, for instance, would take planes to the States; they even took helicopters. They were frequent, and this forced us to take security measures on the planes, but the precedent had been set, and what happened was that at a given time hijackings started taking place in the United States, but we had nothing to do with this. We did not even publicize the hijackings. But for various reasons, some political, hijackers started coming here from the United States. Again, another of the Americans' boomerangs was returning to them—a measure invented to operate against us became a very serious international problem. When the agreement against hijackings was concluded, we also agreed not to encourage illegal entries or departures from the country. Under the hijacking agreement, therefore, any infiltration of agents is forbidden as a violation.

After a few years, after the terrible mistake of the involvement in Vietnam, the international situation has changed and today, fifteen years after the Revolution, we can say that we enjoy a relatively peaceful climate in our country.

Q. Do you have proof of these CIA activities in '63, '64?

A. That was an everyday thing. Millions of proofs. It is not a false accusation.

Q. Who were the CIA agents? Cubans? exiles?

A. The CIA hired, recruited Cubans.

Q. And, today, are there any CIA activities in Cuba?

A. They don't carry on pirate attacks or infiltration of agents any more, but they do have their agents inside Cuba. For example, one time we discovered a diplomat from another country who was working for the CIA. They have sometimes done this, hiring people from other embassies, as well as Cubans with whom they had contact.

The CIA kept a file, with the help of those Cubans leaving the island. I believe the CIA must have information on millions of Cubans, because they were carrying out a very meticulous task then.

Q. How did the CIA collect such information?

A. If a man came from a certain factory, a little town, they would try to find out everything from him. If there were ten doctors, who they were, and how they thought; if there were five engineers, the same. Sometimes when they would send an infiltrator he would come with certain addresses from this gathered information. No one knows how much the CIA spent on its activities against Cuba. The American taxpayer paid for this. The very same taxpayer who is always complaining paid for all the CIA's activities against us. They must have spent fabulous sums. We fought the CIA for a long time, but they failed. This is the truth.

Watergate

Q. Do you see Watergate and what happened—the Nixon resignation—as a sign of strength or a sign of weakness in the United States?

A. It has two aspects. On the one hand, it revealed up to which point moral principles had been lost in the policy of the United States, including internal politics. Because generally, in its foreign policy, we had learned many things—such as the Tonkin incident, the Pentagon papers: all those were very scandalous, very immoral acts. But Watergate demonstrated up to which point all notions of morality had been lost with regard to methods and procedures of internal politics. From this point of view, it could only be said that it reflected a crisis of values.

Now, the fact that it has come to public light and has been debated amply and the consequences have been drawn, I cannot actually see it as a proof of weakness. I believe it showed a capacity to react in the face of certain problems. In short, I must tell you in all fairness that this was not a proof of weakness; I believe it was a positive act for the history of the United States. I believe furthermore that the American people and the American politicians can learn very useful lessons from all that surrounded Watergate; I would imagine that the politicians will be a bit more careful when they speak to the people to tell the truth, to tell the truth when making statements under oath. That is my evaluation.

Q. From an historical point of view, how do you view the Watergate episode?

A. Actually, Watergate is the lesser crime committed by the government of the United States because the attacks, the bombardments against Vietnam were much more criminal acts than the Watergate. This is a matter of conscience; a government with greater sense of justice would not have allowed these crimes to take place. One must admit that there are a lot of acts which weigh heavily on the conscience of the men who governed the United States —millions of Vietnamese lives lost; millions who died during the war; infinite miseries, human tragedies, blood and suffering and mourning imposed upon the Vietnamese people; millions of tons of explosives; thousands of Americans who died in an unjust war. And I ask myself which crime was of greater magnitude—the aggression against Vietnam or the Watergate affair? Of course, the Watergate affair must have shaken the moral conscience of the North American people.

Then there was the Pentagon papers affair. In the Pentagon papers, all the lies of the government of the United States were listed, and all the false

157

reasons given as justification for attacking Vietnam. The people of the United States were made fools of. American leaders told enormous lies to the people of the United States, from my vantage point. I believe this is morally worse than Watergate, all the lies the people were told. Watergate is, I believe, a logical outcome of the deterioration of moral values in American politics, and if people can be bombarded, killed, and sacrificed uselessly . . . . what else can you expect?

Q. Vietnam?

A. Vietnam, among others. If lying to the people becomes a habit, every other lie can be justified as something logical. . . .

Q. Are you referring to all of politics . . . or just Vietnam?

A. I refer to the general policy of the United States in the cold war. There is not doubt that the American people are idealistic, that they are very attached to certain principles. But the government has never questioned the morality of an act concerning foreign policy, whether it was defending peace, or humanity, or freedom, or justice. The worst crimes have been committed by the North American politicians while invoking some noble, just cause. What is happening is that the American people are becoming more aware of these problems and to what degree they can control public policy. My opinion is very personal, and I believe the American people will profit from the experience.

Q. How?

A. Perhaps from now on politicians will be more scrupulous in their behavior. This is my conclusion. I cannot be glad for all that has happened to you Americans. What one can be glad about is the fact that the public opinion of the American people exerts influence and pressure in the United States and will demand that these great mistakes not be repeated. And again, I repeat, this has not been the worst crime committed. I would like to see the American people reacting in the same fashion when they are lied to in order to carry on a war; that they would react in the same manner when in their name, in the name of the American people, crimes are committed such as those in Vietnam, where millions of people are killed.

Q. But the American people did carry on activities against the war. . . .

A. Yes, that is true, I don't deny it. I must state that the American people have had something to do with the end of the war in Vietnam. The American people, though, reacted more strongly to Watergate—even though there was no spilling of blood —than they did when Vietnam was bombarded daily. Watergate hit closer to home and the people felt their own rights were affected more directly. What I hope is that the next time such acts as in Vietnam are committed, even though they do not hit close to home, that the American people react with the same energy that they have shown in the Watergate affair. And I admit, and say with all sincerity, that the American people finally became aware of the injustice of the Vietnam War, and the participation of the American people in opposing that war was a decisive factor in bringing the war to an end. Not only us in Cuba, but the Vietnamese people, are very aware of the American people because they know the American people fought against the war.

Q. Do you think that this weakens the United States foreign policy, particularly in Latin America?

A. The Watergate scandal and the facts which brought about the scandal? Yes. The outcome, no. I believe that it would have been harmful, it would have caused you much greater harm, had all these deeds remained absolutely unpunished. The fact that they were punished and that the President of the United States was changed because of that, I sincerely do not believe that this has made you weaker.

Q. What was your impression of our government in the United States during the days of transition?

A. I believe that these days were important not only

159

to the United States but to the whole world, as there was a good deal of international expectation, observing how the events were unfolding. Of course, Nixon had been rather hostile toward us, but at present he no longer plays any part in the United States policies, and it also seems that his health is not very good. I am therefore not going to make any particular criticism of him. I had read Frank's book, *Perfectly Clear,* and I say that to me it really looks like a very illustrative work on the whole Watergate problem. To me it was very useful. Although we had reports from the press, I had not had an opportunity to read a complete study of the problem, with all the background and all of the data. Afterwards, I also received the transcripts of the tapes, which the White House had published. I was curious to see how the leaders of the United States would express themselves. Actually, my impression is that it was very serious from a legal point of view and from the moral point of view. It seems to me that, after all, you found a correct formula to liquidate the matter. It seems to me that the spectacle of a trial would have been something rather hard for the United States, and I think that in spite of Nixon's resistance, the pressures exerted on him to resign brought about results.

Q. But the resignation was a surprise. . . .

A. Well, yes, it was a bit unexpected . . . the events were rushing along headlong, with the new tapes and the new conversations that appeared. Matters became much more serious, with all the final statements he made, admitting a series of things. And it seems to me that those statements precipitated things. But what other way out and what other option was open to him? It seems to me that the only option remaining for him really was to submit his resignation; I think he resisted a good deal, but judging from press reports and the news, it became evident that the resignation was going to take place. I believe you Americans thereby spared yourselves the trial. Your forecasts on the outcome did come true, because when I talked to you during those days—

Q. In July?

A. It was in July, precisely, when we started this interview, you indeed explained to us what the situation was, and so my conclusion was that there was no way out for Nixon in this situation. I believe the U.S. resolved this in a correct manner.

Q. Didn't you meet Richard Nixon once?

A. Yes. During 1959 in an interview in Washington when Nixon was vice-president.

Q. Do you remember anything of that meeting?

A. Yes, we met in Congress. It was a very frank meeting, on my part, because I explained to him how we saw the Cuban situation, and the measures we intended to take. He, in general, did not argue, but was friendly and listened to everything I had to say.

Q. What did you talk about?

A. Of all the measures we had to take and the reasons why we found them necessary. About the unemployment rate in Cuba, the poverty, the misery, the educational and cultural lag, and in every sense, the measures the Revolution planned to take. Our conversation was limited to that. I understand he drew his own conclusions from that conversation. Because it was after that that the invasion, the plans for the invasion against Cuba, began, because they began to be formulated during the Eisenhower era.

Q. Doesn't he deal with this conversation in his book?

A. What book?

Q. *Six Crises,* no?

A. As far as I remember, he does not. I read it, but I am not sure that he deals exactly with this. Perhaps it is merely that I can't remember, because I read the book some time ago.

Q. Because he says that he immediately reported to President Eisenhower.

A. I understand that after our interview he sent President Eisenhower a report recommending quashing the Cuban revolution.

Q. And then they organized the invasion?

A. Well, I don't know if at that time the invasion was brought up.

Q. It wasn't in the book, *Six Crises,* but in an article in the *Readers' Digest.*

A. It is possible. I didn't read that article. But I do understand that after the interview he recommended taking measures against the Cuban revolution.

Q. Do you know that former President Nixon, when he was vice-president, was responsible for that proposal?

A. Yes, this is an historic fact. Nixon proposed and defended it even to Eisenhower that this method be used against us. And when, in the middle of the Bay of Pigs crisis, Kennedy consulted Nixon, Nixon —according to his own words—proposed that the armed forces of the United States be used.

Q. What do you think of the number of Cuban exiles involved in the Watergate scandal? For example, of the "plumbers," four or five were Cuban exiles.

A. I was not surprised, because a lot of Cuban exiles have been hired by the CIA.

Q. By the CIA?

A. By the CIA. They were hired, trained in espionage, sabotage, and in breaking the law. Let's remember Bay of Pigs . . . the bombardment of our air bases by planes bearing Cuban insignias. This was organized by the CIA, and everyone was surprised. In the United Nations it was said it was a consequence of an internal uprising within Cuba. These people were hired by the CIA and they have committed so many crimes that the least one is Watergate.

I understand this is a very serious problem for Americans, but from a moral standpoint, these people have committed worse crimes—they have set bombs, carried out sabotage, have attacked Cuban ports at night, have fired against our people, have killed women, children, the crippled. Among those reactionaries who were recruited by the United States, the United States has people to carry on any type of activity.

I really have no special information about those Cubans. We have read that there is such a group of Cubans. It is logical that there would be Cubans among them, because Cubans were periodically used for this type of activity. I can't recall if a certain Martinez, I can't recall the name, but I have heard.

Q. Does Bernard Barker mean anything to you, for example?

A. I can't remember very well, but I heard that some of those involved in Watergate were ex-officers in Batista's police force, but in the counterrevolutionary forces there were all kinds of people. But this is another one of history's lessons—like violations of international laws—which boomerang, such as the hijacking of airplanes, which turned into a boomerang. The same thing happened to those who were involved in acts of espionage, pirate activities, counterrevolutionary activities, who today work against and violate the laws of the United States.

Some of the people closest to Nixon, of course, had close relations with these counterrevolutionaries and logically they were utilized to perform these dirty jobs like Watergate.

Q. Ironically, the Cuban exiles being the instrument of Nixon's downfall, the Watergate Cubans, Barker, Martinez, and the two others, that is the irony of history.

A. Well, they are in prison or indicted. I imagine that today they are without a job. And unemployment is a serious matter for them. Yet it is certain that Nixon had very good relations with all these people and it is the irony of history that these people, who were prepared to conspire against the Cuban revolution, were unable to destroy the Cuban revolution, but they were able to destroy Nixon. Besides, if you train people to become spies, for

163

dirty tricks, for clandestine things, you have to use them in something, and they don't know anything else but this.

The Third World

Q. Well, let's talk now about the Third World. Do you consider Cuba a member of the Third World?

A. In a way, because of our situation and our economic development, we share many of the problems of Third World countries. And we have close ties with the African countries, the Latin American countries, and the Asian countries. Because of our under-development we have much in common with them from the economic point of view.

From the political standpoint, we now belong to the community of socialist countries. And we belong to the group of nonaligned countries together with, for example, Yugoslavia, South Vietnam—that is, the Revolutionary Government of South Vietnam, as well as the Revolutionary Movement of Cambodia. Let us say that the nonaligned countries, independently of their social regimes, are countries with common interests which belong to that movement, which is quite strong, with growing strength, as proven by such international events as in the United Nations.

Q. It is said that some of the Third World countries fear the joint leadership, for example, of the important summit meetings of the President of the U.S. and the Premier of the Soviet Union. Do you fear that the lesser developed countries will suffer from this?

A. Within the nonaligned countries, there are different political tendencies. There are socialist countries, feudal countries. Ethiopia and Yugoslavia both belong to the nonaligned countries. But since all these countries have common interests, there is an element that unites them.

But with reference to your question, the impression I have is just the opposite, because in reality one of the basic desires of nonaligned countries is the cessation of the cold war and of international tensions, and that negotiations take place between the great powers to diminish the danger of war. Because no country in this world is interested in, or desirous of, a world war. The danger of war has been one of the major concerns of all nations.

In essence, the relaxation of tensions, international tensions, has always been favorably looked upon by Third World and nonaligned countries. Of course, there are different tendencies, and from time to time, for example, issues are raised which try to or tend to split the nonaligned and the socialist countries. We have always backed the thesis that the socialist countries are the natural allies of the nonaligned countries. We have always fought the tendencies that tend to split the nonaligned and the socialist countries. That has been our position, but these are arguments that can arise in a nonaligned country or in a European country or in any other country. They are opinions that may arise, but it is not a basic idea within the nonaligned countries.

Latin America

Q. What about the countries of Latin America? Do you support the same idea of unity?

A. Actually, we are in favor of the integration and union of the Latin American countries, because the future of our peoples, the development and the technical-scientific advance of the Latin American peoples, depends on their integration and on their unity. A small, isolated Latin American country can do absolutely nothing, and I believe that we Latin Americans must fight for a community of Latin American peoples.

The world of the future is a world of large communities. The United States is a large community, western Europe is a large community, the USSR and the socialist camp of Europe is a large community, China is a large community, and in the future only the large communities will be in a position to face the great problems humanity has before it. And we, the Latin American peoples, have a community of language, of culture, of tradition, and we are peoples who must unite in the same way as the states of North America united, and we shall form a large community. If the United States had not been a large community, it would not have been able to achieve the industrial successes, the scientific successes, the economic successes it has attained. So, we believe that we must work to create a community. Not in the spirit of fighting against the United States, not in the spirit of enmity towards the United States. In the long run, Cuba and the United States are neighbors. The Latin American people and the United States are neighbors—in one way or another they have to find a way to live amicably.

But the Latin American countries must unite and we are and will be affected by any interventionist policy of the United States in Latin America.

Q. Do you believe that the military is the only way to carry out radical change? Because you were highly successful, many governments are now more aware of the dangers of revolution.

A. It was a combination of factors. The Cuban revolution has called attention to the danger of potential revolutions in Latin America. That potential danger gave rise to the Alliance for Progress and to certain worries of the governments. At the same time, it strengthened the mechanisms for fighting the armed revolutionary movement.

All these measures that were taken, however, do not prevent changes, because changes are a product of the will of men. They are a result of historical, objective necessities. Some of those military, for example, who are presently playing a progressive role in Latin America, were trained in American military academies and were exposed to Marxism through the courses they were given against Marxism. Some of the military changed through exposure to revolutionary ideas, they questioned the social order and came to the conclusion that changes were necessary. Changes have to take place because history cannot be held back.

Of course, the military already have the arms. The civilians don't have arms. That is why the civilians have to struggle to gain weapons, be it in a revolution like the Cuban revolution, or a revolution like the Peruvian or the Panamanian; weapons are indispensable, decisive. Revolutions are carried out by those who have weapons. A society cannot be changed, a revolution cannot be carried out, without arms; and in the end it is achieved by those who have the arms.

That was our case. We were not military. We had to fight the military, defeat them, and take their weapons. In the case of Peru and Panama it was the men with arms who began the revolutionary process.

Q. Then armed struggle is necessary?

A. I would say that armed struggle is necessary. Arms are necessary to carry out revolution. Otherwise you cannot effect social change.

Q. Is that a lesson from the Chilean experience?

A. The Chilean case is more a proof than a lesson. Why couldn't the *Unidad Popular* implement its revolutionary program? The oligarchy defended itself through the parliamentary majority, and through the armed forces. It stopped the process abruptly and established a fascist dictatorship in the country, one of unbelievable cruelty.

How did the U.S. gain its independence? It did not win it in Parliament. It won it by revolutionary struggle; and in the end, how was the slave issue

167

resolved in the States? Was it not solved in a violent war?

Armed struggle is not one of my ideas. I wish all changes could be achieved peacefully, and I don't doubt that under certain circumstances in some countries peaceful change can be achieved. But, as a rule, historically, all major social changes have been produced revolutionarily.

Q. But why does force have to be necessary?

A. Because the ruling social regime stays in power through force. The new social regime also has to impose itself through force, there is no doubt about that. The ruling classes do not give up their interests, they do not give up their privileges peacefully, and they are the ones who employ violence. Historically, the oppressed did not invent violence. Violence was thought of and developed by the oppressors, the vested interests within each society, and throughout history these interests have been protected by force.

This does not arise out of a love for arms. We do not love arms.

And again I repeat, I wish change could be promoted within societies through peaceful means, but history teaches us otherwise. The French revolution, the major changes, the coming of age of liberal ideas against feudalism, did not take place peacefully. The Russian revolution, the new social order, did not come about peacefully. The Chinese revolution was not accomplished peacefully. Those are realities. The time may come when, under certain circumstances, certain countries will effect change even through parliamentary means.

Let's take the European case. There, the legal institutions, parliamentary institutions are very consolidated. Since the Paris Commune, more than one hundred years have passed. Since the Versailles troops, supported by Bismarck's troops, repressed the first European socialist revolution, which resembled the Paris Commune, there have been no social changes in western Europe. But today these are countries where parliamentary institutions are strong, and today, in today's world, with the present correlation of forces, it is possible to conceive change through electoral means, through parliamentary means. Because fifty years ago the so-called Holy Alliances existed between governments to prevent revolutions. Wherever a revolution could have started in isolation, it would have been crushed violently. It is difficult to imagine, nevertheless, that just fifty years ago Italy or France or the Europe of today faced a situation similar to Chile's. I say difficult, not impossible, but it is also difficult to imagine a greater, a more flagrant violation of popular will and a more violent suppression of the institutional rhythm in any of those countries than what has taken place in Chile.

With the circumstances under which we have had to operate, and with the difficulties we have had to face, and the enemy we have encountered it is the revolutionary form in which we have proceeded. But I am not going to say that the formula we Cubans have utilized is the only valid formula.

Q. But you have said that the Chilean experience teaches us that socialism cannot be achieved through a parliamentary system?

A. The Chilean experience has proven this. Look, the *Unidad Popular* of Chile tested the possibility of making a change by peaceful means and by parliamentary means. Actually, Allende was very respectful of Parliament, he was very respectful of the opposition parties, and was very respectful of the opposition press and of the constitution and of the laws. It is absolutely false and absolutely baseless that Allende tried to establish a single party, that Allende tried to destroy the opposition parties, that Allende tried to destroy the opposition press and that Allende tried to destroy Parliament. I knew Allende very well and I can assure you that Allende scrupulously respected the law, the con-

169

stitution, and the institutions of Chile. It is simply a lie to try and justify the intervention that took place there in Chile. Allende tried to carry out social reforms with a parliament, with the parties, and through absolutely legal and absolutely peaceful means. And what they did was to conspire, to obstruct the government, to sabotage its work, and in the end, violate the constitution, cause a coup d'etat, assassinate Allende, establish there a regime of terror—one of the most cruel known in the history of this hemisphere. And I believe that to make a revolution you need the people, and force is also needed and power is needed, the power of arms is needed.

Q. Would you care to explain the Peruvian revolution, for example, carried out by the military, traditionally the repressive forces?

A. Very well; that seems to be the Peruvian case, a new revolutionary road. Someone said that many roads lead to Rome, and it seems that many roads also lead to revolution. The Peruvian military have very special characteristics, because many of the officers and generals of the Peruvian army come from very humble backgrounds. It does not have an oligarchic origin. This factor is influential. The situation of the sixties also led many of these military men to think, to consider, to analyze deeply the causes of social discontent, and they reached the conclusion that really what was needed was deep major structural changes in the country. They took power and began to change the structure, and the first thing they did was implement agrarian reform which was much more radical than the agrarian reform we initially passed in Cuba. It put a much lower limit on the size of properties; organized cooperatives, agricultural communities; immediately adopted measures in defense of national interest and of its natural resources. They also have been pushing other fields—in the field of education, social development, industrialization, and, most importantly, on measures to recover its natural resources.

Previously, before the Peruvian revolution, the army was a guardian of the status quo.

But we must also see the example in Portugal where the military just played a decisive role in political change in that country and are on their way to finding solutions. They may not have found them yet, of course, because I don't believe there can be any other solution to the colonial war than granting independence to the colonies, for example. But you see that in Portugal the military have played a progressive role, without a doubt, and the Peruvian example is very important because one cannot say now that the military will always be the guardians of established order.

We have another experience, that of Panama, where the military are playing an important role —politically progressive—and have raised issues relative to national rights. They are claiming the reinforcement of their legitimate rights over the Canal Zone and are also carrying out social reforms. So that we have two concrete examples— Peru and Panama—where the military are acting as catalysts in favor of change and in favor of the revolution. The armed forces have been playing a revolutionary role for a number of years, and they can carry on with it, because they can count on the support of arms. If a revolutionary process is to be carried through without the support of arms, then it does not march forward, and what happens to it is what has happened to Chile. This is the lesson we can draw from the Chilean experience.

Q. And what about other Latin American countries?

A. If the arms are in the hands of the civilian or military revolutionaries, then a revolution is possible; otherwise, the revolutionary process is overthrown, as happened in Chile. But there are many possibilities. Perhaps the Italians will do it differently from us—their traditions, their points of view. The

171

French may do it differently, the English, the Americans. We had our own very particular conditions and we had to follow this road. I am not saying it is the only way.

Q. Is there any possibility at all of a government which would meet your definition of a social reform government now being elected anywhere in the hemisphere?

A. Well . . . there might be an exceptional case if, for example, the government received broad popular support, can count on a parliamentary majority, and can count on the support of the armed forces, that is, firm, unconditional support of the armed forces. It would then be possible to carry through some social changes, some revolutionary changes. Theoretically, these conditions could exist.

Q. Then you don't see that developing anywhere now at the moment, in a particular country. But could you name two or three countries where you think that that might happen, conceivably? Venezuela?

A. Well, to make such a profound change as the revolutionary changes in Cuba—no.

Q. No?

A. No. But look, in Venezuela certain circumstances prevail. We would speak of an elected government with a parliamentary majority that proposes to carry out some measures of nationalization, such as the nationalization of iron and the nationalization of oil. I believe that these measures enjoy great national support, enjoy a sense of great national sympathy. And I include among those having this national feeling, the armed forces of Venezuela. I am sure that these changes, at least the measures of nationalization of iron and of oil, can perfectly well be implemented by the present government of Venezuela. These are important measures. But a profound social revolution such as the one that took place in Cuba, it creates more complex and more difficult problems, because then a struggle of interests begins. . . .

172

Q. And of classes?

A. And a very fierce struggle between classes. I believe that inasmuch as the measures proposed to be carried through include the defense of natural resources, the defense of national interest, then they are measures that can count on the support of all the people and they can be put into practice. But as soon as certain internal interests that have great influence and have much power are affected, then these interests decide to resist the revolutionary changes. As long as they are not touched, things can go on one way or another. When these interests are powerful politically, are powerful in all the areas affecting them, that is when conspiracy and counterrevolution starts to be organized.

Q. Is the capitalist system doomed in Latin America?

A. There is no future for Latin American countries along the capitalist route.

Q. Why?

A. Capitalism helped develop certain nations—England, the United States, Germany, France, Japan, they were the initiators of industrial development. In those days, to start an industry you needed only five thousand dollars. Technology was fairly simple so that hardly even engineers were required. This is not the case today, where industry requires high efficiency, enormous investments, complicated technological research, so that small underdeveloped countries cannot compete successfully with the industrialized nations, commercially, financially, technologically. We have to take an historical jump, and it cannot be done unless resources are utilized in a very rational, organized manner.

There is no room for waste, for free competition, to reach a level of economic development. There is no alternative but to plan the economy, centralize and pool raw materials, and gain in a few years what would take another system one hundred, two hundred years. I believe that the underdeveloped countries, in order to overcome the enormous technological gap from the developed world, must plan their economics along socialistic principles. How can they succeed against illiteracy, ignorance, disease, under the capitalist way? Brazil today is a haven for multi-national companies which receive all the facilities and favorable investment conditions. Its production increases while its education suffers, decreases, its public health is impaired, poverty grows as wealth increases. What is the purpose of augmenting wealth if this wealth will not bring justice among men? If it will not even provide the minimal needs of a human being? If some other political system is not adopted, these problems will not be solved. What does this mean? It means that historical realities prove to the peoples south of the United States that they need a system other than the capitalist system, and it will have to be the socialist system.

The Alliance for Progress

Q. Some scholars have dubbed you the Father of the Alliance for Progress.

A. Scholars? Where? Who do you call scholars?

Q. Well, professors, students of Latin American history . . .

A. In reality, one can say there is a direct connection between the Cuban revolution and the idea of the Alliance for Progress. Many of the measures brought forth as necessities by the revolutionary program in Cuba were later seen as necessities under the Alliance for Progress, because the goal of the Alliance was to effect social reform which would improve the condition of the masses in Latin America. That was the spirit of the Alliance for Progress, which included the agrarian reform concept, fiscal reforms, better distribution of national wealth, all those palliatives which might slow

174

down the revolutionary processes in Latin America. Our program under the first phase of the Revolution sought these very same goals: to establish a better distribution of wealth and a regime of social justice, to eliminate the injustices and the exploitation which had existed in our country. But time has passed and the Alliance solved nothing. History has demonstrated that it was a useless hope because the oligarchies in Latin America are not willing to allow reforms. I won't deny that the idea of the Alliance for Progress was an intelligent strategy. But it had a very weak point, because those in charge of seeing that the agrarian reform was implemented in Latin America were the very owners of the lands, and they were unwilling to carry out an agrarian reform or a fiscal reform, or to enforce more equitable distribution of wealth. Also the Alliance for Progress concept was closely tied to development through foreign investments. Foreign investment is interested in gaining greater wealth and not in solving social problems within a country. Basically one has to admit that the idea of the Alliance for Progress was an intelligent one; however, an utopian one.

Q. How do you mean?

A. I am talking theoretically . . . from a theoretical point of view. It is true that if social reforms which diminish the exploitation of the agricultural worker are carried out, agricultural development encouraged, if the rich are adequately taxed, and national wealth better distributed, the reasons for popular discontent diminish. Looking at it from this angle, I think it was a very intelligent strategy, much more intelligent than repression. There were basically two criteria: one, a policy of repression, the other, of social reforms. The Alliance for Progress presented some social reforms. It is in that sense that I believe it was a politically wise concept put forth to hold back the time of revolution.

But it was utopian in the sense that revolution-

175

ary changes in Latin America are inevitable. Resources were mobilized through the Alliance for Progress, road-building plans were drawn up, some dams, housing, schools were built, but the Latin American problem is not solved by that type of reform. That is unquestionable. It can change, it can be a palliative for a social situation, but it is not a deep solution of the problems. I am not saying that, from the revolutionary point of view, the strategy of the Alliance for Progress was a good one. From the United States's point of view, it was an intelligent policy.

I do not agree with this type of reform. I am not sympathetic with that reform. I support more radical measures. The idea of the Alliance for Progress had the objective of preventing the Revolution. Historically, that was the goal of the Alliance; but it was an intelligent formula—that is what I said, that it was politically intelligent.

Cuba and the Soviet Union

Q. But how are relations between Cuba and the USSR defined?

A. We have political, friendly relations; we have common political philosophies and an important economic exchange.

Undoubtedly, our commerce with them is less important to them than it is to us, but that happens to many countries. The day our economy and our people are integrated with the rest of Latin America, we will constitute a self-sufficient community, much more so than today.

I can assure you that in very few instances has a small country received as much aid from a country that is so distant as we have received from the Soviet Union—aid which has not been based exclusively on economic interests, for we also have commercial exchange.

These past few years have been so difficult, so hard for us, that we could not have survived without this aid. Who can say this aid has hurt us? What would we have had to do without this aid? Could the Latin American countries have helped us? Unfortunately, no, they could not have helped us, because the Latin American countries bowed to the American dictates. Could the African countries help us? They did not have the resources. The members of the Common Market? They had no reason to do so. And if we have been able to carry through our economic development program, our public health program, our education and anti-poverty programs, we cannot forget that it was precisely thanks to the aid we received from the Soviet Union.

We cannot look upon that as a tragedy for Cuba, but rather as a favorable factor. Our country was fortunate to have received this aid, as equals, with mutual respect, with absolute consideration for our country, without exploitation and without having acquired a single property here. We have received, continue to receive, and in the future will receive additional aid from Russia. And this is in agreement with our political philosophy and that of the Soviet Union. We appreciate that aid very much. You in the U.S. are still grateful for the aid you received from the French during your War of Independence, and you feel a great deal of admiration for Lafayette because he helped you during those difficult years. Even after two hundred years, you still remember this experience with gratitude.

Q. Some critics allege that you have traded one dependency for another, from the United States to Russia.

A. We are all dependent, in one form or another, upon

others. The U.S., for example, depends on the oil-producing countries for oil supply; it depends on the raw material supplies for your iron ore, copper, nickel, and other products.

Q. Bauxite?

A. Bauxite, for example. You Americans depend on the foreign market to sell your excess production. The Soviet Union constitutes our major market. How can one compare the relations we have with the Soviet Union and those that existed with the United States? The Soviet Union has given us easy payment terms, has helped us obtain credit elsewhere, and has had the greatest consideration for us in financial matters. With reference to the United States—the United States owned our mines; the United States owned our electrical plants, our telephone company, our major means of transportation, our major industries, our best lands, our bigger sugar mills. They owned our banks and controlled our foreign trade. In other words, they owned the Cuban economy. The Soviets don't own a single mine in Cuba, a single factory, a single sugar mill, or an hectare of land, a bank, a business, or any public utility enterprise. So that all the natural resources, all the industries, and all the means of production are in our hands. Our relations with them are totally different. We depend on the Soviet Union, depend on the other socialist countries, just like other countries have relations of interdependence, and I don't think there is a country in the world that escapes this. Even the United States is now debating whether they should become self-sufficient in oil and are considering the cost this would involve, human and environmental. This was proven by events when the blockade came into effect and this is very interesting, because the United States invented the blockade. And now with the energy crisis, other countries learned the lesson which the United States gave them, and applied the oil embargo. The United States learned

178

what it means to be blockaded, and the Americans in general did not agree with this.

We have no energy sources, no oil, coal, or hydroelectric power. We will always have to be dependent upon others for the supply of energy, of many raw materials and of some foodstuffs, just as other countries depend on us for their supply of sugar, nickel, and other products. The entire world is interdependent. That argument, therefore, that Cuba traded one dependency for another is nothing but an empty phrase.

Q. When you see the United States and the Soviet Union's leaders meet warmly in Moscow and talk over world problems, how do you see it—just as an expression of a desire to relax tensions and nothing else?

A. We realize that it is necessary for world leaders to meet. Logically. We are not surprised that they greet each other amiably, because that is part of elementary courtesies in relations between statesmen.

Q. Symbolically speaking?

A. We are not concerned because these meetings take place. We have very well-defined policies on the subject. We do not want war, of course.

Q. When the U.S. President and the Russian Premier meet, for example, don't you think they may discuss Cuba?

A. I do not know if they discuss Cuba or not.

Q. Don't you wonder if they do?

A. It is not the Soviets who have a cold war policy toward us. It is the government of the United States that applies a cold war policy toward Cuba. I suppose they agree on the topics that they will discuss and it is always necessary to come to an agreement on those topics. But I know that Soviet statesmen are reasonable on the need for easing of tensions and peaceful coexistence and we, on the other hand, have unlimited trust in them. We trust them completely, the loyalty of the Soviet leadership toward the Cuban revolution, and we have no concerns, worries, on this subject. We trust them—that is the truth. We can state that during this period when tensions between the United States and the Soviet Union have relaxed, our relations with the Soviet Union have improved. They are better than ever at this time. Our relations, therefore, with the Soviets have not been affected by the policy of peaceful coexistence and easing of tensions.

Q. But to quote Metternich, "A nation has neither permanent allies nor permanent enemies, only permanent interest."

A. We do not agree, because we believe there are basic principles which unite peoples.

Q. Which principles?

A. The relations, for example, we have with socialist countries, and basically with the Soviet Union, are based on international principles and revolutionary principles, and I believe those are long-lasting. Metternich's quote is a strictly chauvinist policy, and we Marxists are not strict nationalists. We see patriotism as an integral part of internationalism. That is, there are national interests and there are international interests and the ties we have with the socialist countries are based on those principles. We therefore believe in the permanence, durability, of these ties.

Don't forget that Metternich lived with nineteenth-century principles, and that during the period of the Holy Alliance there was no Marxist conception of the world and policy.

Q. Do you accept the current move toward detente?

A. I think there has been a general acceptance of the policy of relaxation of tensions. We have lived in the past few years in a period of more peace and everyone has welcomed the end of the cold war. However, the cold war is still imposed partially on some countries. With Cuba a cold war policy is applied. Up to now, there has been no relaxation.

Q. It has not changed?

180

A. It has not changed for us in that sense, but we nonetheless see with satisfaction the cessation of the cold war, thinking not only in our interests, but in universal, worldwide interests. Some people are in favor of relaxation of tensions, others of cold war.

Q. Who, for example, is in favor of cold war?

A. Well, everywhere. In the United States, for instance, there are some who oppose the policy of relaxation. The cold war had its supporters—the reactionaries everywhere—who were not realistic, because the world's present-day problems cannot be solved through war. We are not in 1914 or 1939 —we are living in an era when technology in the area of armaments makes world war impossible. And this has been an influential factor—and people have taken the problems of peace much more seriously. Never has peace concerned people as much as now, because a war today would mean the annihilation of mankind and suicide for the human race.

The cold war was a stage after World War Two I think it was a stupid policy, a reactionary policy, a repressive policy, a gendarme's policy, in which the United States arrogantly assumed the role of keepers of world order and tried to prevent changes in the world. In essence, that has been the basic reason for the cold war.

World Economy

Q. Do you blame the United States for the current state of world economy?

A. Well, I do not think that only the United States is to be blamed.

Q. Not it alone.

A. I believe that in general the entire industrialized world is responsible for this. But, in our opinion, there is no doubt that the United States has a responsibility, because actually, the United States directed the world economy after the last war. The International Monetary Fund was organized by the United States; all the financial organizations were organized by the United States. That gave the United States a very privileged position, because it turned its paper currency into the currency of the whole world. It was able to effect a vast expansion of its economy; it was able to invest fabulous amounts of money abroad, and to buy numerous industrial companies in England, in Europe, all over the world.

But it also seems that not only has the U.S. influenced the world economic situation, but the problems of the cold war have influenced this, too. Nobody can believe that after the Second World War the Soviets would not be interested in reconstructing their economy. The basic interest of the Soviet Union, which had been totally destroyed by the war, was to rebuild its economy and repair the damage done by the war. That was an excellent moment for devising a policy of peace in the world. Yet, in spite of this, the Soviet Union was surrounded by military bases, nuclear bases, a whole series of military pacts were organized, the arms race was started, and for this fabulously enormous amounts of money have been spent. In addition to all this, there was the Vietnam War, for which the United States is responsible, too, and which cost more than a hundred billion dollars. On what was this money spent? On causing destruction and death in a small country. The military budgets, which in the United States now run at more than eighty billion dollars, are generating inflation. The world became filled with U.S. dollars and the inflation resulted as a consequence of their being in existence more money than production goods.

Q. Has this inflation affected Cuba also?

A. We have also had inflation, and the inflation has forced us to take certain measures. We established rationing when faced with this inflation, and

182

achieved a more equal distribution. For a capitalist country, it is much more difficult to put into place a measure of this type. Next to this, the capitalist industrialized societies have developed an economy that can be called a waste economy, which calls for ever more, more raw materials, more energy resources. Now then, no country in the world had the raw material and the energy resources that the United States had, thanks to which the United States attained its enormous economic and industrial prosperity. But the oil it produces is not enough for the United States; the energy it produces, the hydroelectric energy, the coal, all that is not sufficient, and therefore it has fallen into a situation of dependency on other countries.

Q. What about the rest of the world?

A. Now then, the situation became worse in the countries of Europe and Japan when they started to increase the consumption of oil to huge quantities. They abandoned coal, because oil is much cheaper than coal, oil can be handled easier than coal, it is a cleaner fuel than coal.

When World War Two ended, the world was consuming about five hundred million tons of oil. In 1950, it already consumed a billion tons; in 1960 two billion. It seemed as if oil resources were unlimited, that they would never become exhausted. The large petroleum companies made enormous profits, obtaining very cheap oil in the Middle East, in Venezuela, and other countries, and selling it in the United States at prices at which the oil of the Gulf Coast was sold. So that the raw material was cheaper than coal, but it was still sold above the production costs. That is why we say that the habit of establishing monopolistic prices for oil is not an idea devised by the oil-producing countries, but rather by the oil companies.

Q. Is this situation the same with other basic materials?

A. The same thing as with oil happened with the rest of the raw materials: iron, copper, aluminum, tin.

183

What was the trend during the past thirty years? The products of the industrialized countries increased in price every year. The products of the underdeveloped countries fell in price every year, all those years. So, at any given moment, you needed twenty-five tons of sugar to buy a truck; than later you would need thirty tons, forty tons, fifty tons, a hundred tons of sugar to buy a truck. This phenomenon, therefore, has impoverished all the underdeveloped countries.

Q. What effect has all of this had on the underdeveloped world?

A. As a result of this, there is enormous resentment in all the underdeveloped world because of the conditions of exchange between the developed and the underdeveloped world. The developed world became ever richer and the underdeveloped world ever poorer. This situation could not continue. We have now reached a point where the countries producing these raw materials which the industrialized countries need have become conscious of their strength and really demand and require a more just treatment in the exchange between the developed countries and the underdeveloped countries. This is the question which is at the heart of the oil problem. The energy problem is, of course, a very complex problem, undoubtedly, which concerns the whole world. It has been calculated that within fifty or fifty-five years, the world might have fifteen billion inhabitants, and calculating the consumption of oil at a rate similar to the one the United States has today, all of the oil and all of the coal of the world would be exhausted in less than one year.

Q. What about other sources of energy?

A. There are no alternate sources of energy that could immediately replace oil. Coal can replace it only in part. There remain no other sources except nuclear energy and solar energy Nuclear energy has not had a very extensive technical development and it raises certain problems with its residues, certain very serious environmental problems. It is calculated that within sixty years, twenty-four thousand nuclear power stations would be needed to satisfy the energy requirements of the world, for a population of fifteen billion inhabitants. On this we can agree with President Ford, namely that the energy problem is one of the most serious and most fundamental ones.

Q. How can this problem be solved?

A. It cannot be solved by force. I believe that the problem of raw materials and of oil can be solved through negotiations, where the poorer countries will unquestionably demand something that is just, a just price for their raw materials; because what is happening with oil will also happen with copper, with aluminum, with almost all the raw materials produced in the underdeveloped world. Now, the present policy of the United States is to unite the industrialized countries and to divide the underdeveloped world. Why? Because among the underdeveloped countries there are countries that have oil and countries that do not have oil.

Q. Does not that situation create new problems?

A. The oil-producing countries will acquire great financial resources. Either they use it in the developed capitalist world, as some of them do, or they use it in the underdeveloped world. Our thesis is that these financial resources should be invested in aid to the underveloped world.

Q. But thus far the oil-producing countries—above all, the Arab countries—have not extended aid to the poor countries.

A. Up until this moment, the oil-producing countries do not have a clear and decided policy of aid to the underdeveloped world. That is true. But I believe that the only intelligent path that they can follow is to seek the support of the underdeveloped world in this struggle.

Q. But what must come first, the support of the underdeveloped countries, or the aid from the oil-producing countries?

A. Well, actually, as a matter of principle, we must

185

support the oil-producing countries. Because to support oil means to support the other raw materials. Because if at first we leave them to themselves, then most probably they can be divided and can be defeated. And the underdeveloped world does not agree with the defeat of the oil-producing countries. This is our point of view. Now, I believe that the oil-producing countries understand that they need the support of the underdeveloped world; that if they don't have or seek support of the underdeveloped world, the capitalist countries can isolate the oil-producing countries.

It is, of course, they who must take a decision one way or another. Whether they allow themselves to be isolated, if they yield to the demands of the capitalist countries, or seek the support of the rest of the underdeveloped countries. The strategy we outlined in the speech of September twenty-eighth[1] is that of the unity of the underdeveloped world. There is no doubt that it is the oil-producing countries that today have a stronger position. This is our thesis: that the resources derived from oil, the surplus, which they don't need for their development, that instead of investing that in the industrialized capitalist countries, they invest it in the underdeveloped world.

Now, to return to the first question. I believe that the United States has a great responsibility in all this worldwide economic crisis. Not it alone, because the rest of the capitalist world followed the American model. It abandoned coal, abandoned other energy resources, and flung itself into the consumption of a very cheap energy source, a very short-sighted policy.

Q. Do not the Arab countries also share responsibility for this crisis?

A. No doubt about it. Undoubtedly, from my point of view yes, because lately in the last decade, Europe has greatly increased the consumption of oil. And

---

[1] See Appendix 1.

it developed its entire economy on the American model. Japan did exactly the same. And suddenly they find that they depend on the oil-producing countries. For many years, the oil-producing countries let themselves be exploited by the oil companies, but at a given moment they became aware of their power to defend their interets. Up until that moment, the only powerful ones in the world were the captalist industrialized countries. They determined the prices they would pay for raw materials and the prices to be paid for the finished products. This situation has changed in the world, because the world is undergoing a revolutionary process. Today, the countries unite, they group, they become aware of their strengths and are taking measures to defend their interests. I believe that this conflict cannot be resolved by force. I believe that this conflict can be solved only through cooperation and negotiation, and I believe that it should embrace not only the interests of the industrialized countries and the interests of the oil-producing countries, but all the interests of the underdeveloped world. On this basis alone a solution could be found for this problem. Now, I have no doubt that the capitalist industrialized countries will—of necessity—have to make sacrifices.

The exchange relations which have existed during all these years cannot be maintained further. And we know that. We, the underdeveloped countries, know this. Because we have seen the prices increase for trucks, tractors, industrial equipment, technology, all this extraordinary increase in prices, and during many years we have been seeing the prices for our products go down.

Cuba:
The Revolution
in Place

Some chiefs of state—even some dictators—are rarely
seen in public, and are rarely seen to take an active
part in the day-to-day decision making that is involved
in the art of government. A problem in Cuba is that
Fidel Castro may be seen too often, and that he not
only knows about the daily decisions of government,
but that he seems to make almost all of them.

But before we get into a discussion of the command-
ing role played by this one man in Cuba, perhaps it
might be best to give some background on what you
are going to read in this chapter. For a total of almost
six weeks on three separate trips—which would not be
enough time to learn everything, but which can be
enough time to learn a lot—we traveled through Cuba
and visited every major city. We saw whatever we
wanted to see and talked with whomever we wanted to
talk, and formed a number of impressions. They are
not presented from the vantage point of economists or
sociologists, nor do they pretend to be an expert summary of all that is happening in a very complex country
which combines modern revolutionary development
with an ancient colonial heritage. What follows is
simply what we saw and the conclusions we drew.

Neither of us had been to Cuba before—not even
before the Revolution—but we had both read a great

deal of pro-Castro and anti-Castro literature, we had both traveled extensively in other countries in Latin America—and not as tourists but with the Peace Corps. We felt and still feel competent to make judgments and comparisons—not as competent, perhaps, as some who have acquired more expertise in technical areas, or as those who have been in Cuba more often and longer, but competent nonetheless.

To return to the question of Castro's command of the scene: as our interview indicates, he almost seems to know everything that is happening on the island and to have a suggested plan of action for it.

He does know, for example, and is prepared to discuss with a casual foreign visitor or a project engineer the annual construction rate of schools, housing, factories, and hospitals. He knows the number built and being built, their scheduled dates for conclusion, and the building plans projected for the next five to ten years. He knows the number of students at each level of the educational process, is familiar with the curriculum, knowns how many graduated from one class to the next last year, how many will graduate this year and in 1980, and 1985. He knows the standards for promotion from one school to the next and what they will be in the future.

He knows the monthly water temperatures at the fishing ports and when they are most favorable for catching various fish. He knows how many feet can be spanned by concrete—and at what stress. And he knows sugar—probably better than anyone in the world. He knows the harvest of every year—although lately the size of each harvest is kept secret, perhaps for reasons of worldwide economic competition, and perhaps (as some others suggest) because of a desire to avoid comparison with the size of prerevolutionary harvests. He knows, almost hourly, sugar's price on the world market and is familiar with its fluctuations. He knows the agricultural cycle for sugar, and in what year and in what months of its growth it can be maximized.

He also is intimately familiar with the governing

structures in towns, cities, and provinces, as well as the more recent decisions—and the method of reaching those decisions—in the state-owned factories, businesses, and services.

Castro's encyclopedic knowledge does not extend only to things Cuban. He is obviously an enormously quick study, and on our visit in 1975 he outlined—over an hour or so—his understanding of the combined program President Ford offered in his State of the Union message in January to combat both the growing economic recession and the energy crisis.

It was clear from the conversation that Castro understood the program and all of its interrelated parts better than Ford's experts—at least those who had commented on it publicly—and probably better than the President did. Not only that, he defended it vigorously and eloquently. According to Castro, Ford made the transition from fighting inflation to fighting recession and unemployment—and made it in fine style.

What's more, he thinks the Ford program for fighting the energy crisis—increasing the tariff on imported petroleum—is probably also the best that can be done. It will increase prices, he agrees, but he thinks Americans will not tolerate rationing. And, finally, he agrees with Ford that if the President's policy is enacted—and stuck to—the U.S. *will* be self-sufficient in petroleum within a decade. If the White House advisers were really courageous, they'd bring Fidel Castro up to cut some TV spots; in our opinion the Ford program will never be more eloquently defended.

Castro's knowledge of Cuba gives him tremendous advantages. It enables him to cut short extended discussions and reach quick decisions. It also has an incalculable advantage in terms of his relationship with the Cuban people. In conversation with a school teacher or with the head of a construction brigade, he appears to know—and indeed *does* know—as much or more about the matter at hand than the person to whom he is talking. And if he does not know something, he learns it very quickly.

But there are dangers inherent in the situation. For

190

example, there is a widespread belief that Fidel is "numero uno" in everything. More than one Cuban told us that Fidel is as popular as he is—and neither of us ever encountered a Latin American leader more popular with his people—because they believe him to be the best at everything. "He can tell us about cutting sugar cane," said one young man in a responsible government position, "because he is the best sugar cane-cutter in the country. He can talk about sports, because he was the best baseball player, and he can talk about other things because he is the best at those, as well."

In the early interview, Mankiewicz asked Castro if he thought that his presence in Cuba was so dominant that there might be a problem of succession. Castro—as we have seen—turned the question into one about the Revolution, and proceeded with an eloquent answer about the things that had grown "in the shade of the Revolution," but the impression remained that he sensed the dangers in his dominant position.

One danger is the "cult of personality." Our guess is that Castro works diligently against the expression of such a cult, because in a country as thoroughly dominated by the personality of one man as any in the world, there is little public evidence of that dominance.

The large photos on billboards and signs—particularly in the weeks prior to July 26th—are seldom of Fidel, but usually of Che Guevara, and sometimes Camilo Cienfuegos, both dead revolutionary heroes. The portrait of honor in middle- and working-class homes, a picture of Christ in much of the rest of Latin America, in Cuban homes is of Che, never Fidel. In our travels we saw only a few pictures of Castro, mostly on the office walls of government officials, and in each case a picture of Castro and the official himself.

In Santiago, for example, preparations for July 26th included twenty-five-foot-high plywood representations of Che and Camilo. Considering that Castro is a son of Santiago, it would have seemed a reasonable place for at least a temporary statue of the Prime Minister, but there was none. Those few times that Castro is depicted publicly, it is in an historical setting, such as the landing of the *Granma*. There is no Fidel Castro Boulevard in Havana, although there used to be main streets named not only for his predecessor, Fulgencio Batista, but also for Batista's wife.

This is a problem of which other Cubans are aware as well. As one government official told us, "We have to take care and deal with this problem. Fidel will not be with us forever and there are some who think he is a god and that Cuba cannot and will not be able to function without him. We are trying to cope with this situation and this attitude."

But Fidel Castro is forty-seven, and he must think very little about the question of succession. Perhaps he believes that by the time he *must* think of it, the Revolution will have created situations and personalities of strength and knowledge sufficient to assume a leadership role.

One thing that appears very clearly from at least the view we have of Cuba is that *everybody* takes part in the affairs of the country—in the economy, in the government, and in social programs. Nearly everyone who is able-bodied has a job. Women work, thanks largely to an extended and apparently excellent program of day-care centers, all of which appear to be far more ambitious than the "storage centers" one so often finds in urban America. Now more than four hundred centers exist in Cuba and day-care is available for children aged forty-five days and older. Even in the smaller and more remote towns in Camaguey and Cienfuegos provinces, the day-care centers are complete with modern playground equipment, toys, and what certainly appeared to be expert and trained supervision.

In addition to his job, every worker has a part in the proliferation of committees, councils, and other group activities that contribute to decision making at the industrial level. Thus, at a machine shop we visited in the interior, runoff elections were being held for membership on the production committee, and the genaral plant committee was conducting worker education courses in a part of the factory building set aside for that purpose. Castro himself commented on all this activity at one point during our discussion, when he remarked, only half jokingly, that he thought perhaps the workers—women especially—had too many organizational duties connected with their jobs and their communities.

A teacher, for example, would not only carry a full work load, but also serve on a faculty committee, be expected to take an active part in the teachers' organization (not only at the level of the school but of the school system), and perhaps serve on a committee or two of the teachers' union.

In addition, he or she will be expected to take part in community activity, perhaps as a member of a Committee for the Defense of the Revolution, or a community or block organization responsible for polio shots, traffic control, or perhaps preparing a float for a civic parade or carnival.

Every young man must serve three years in the armed forces, and every able-bodied person is armed and takes occasional training as a part of the militia— to be mobilized on such occasions as the invasion at the Bay of Pigs or the missile crisis of 1962.

Women and young people seemed to form a larger portion of the work force than one expects to see, perhaps because older people formed a disproportionate share of the self-exiles who left Cuba in the sixties.

One device by which there will—according to plan— be far more direct participation at the community, regional, and provincial levels is the proposed expansion of what is called *Poder Popular*—literally, "People Power."

In 1974, for the first time since the Revolution, Cuba held an election. For that matter, it may well have been the first unrigged, unbought election ever, whether before or after the Revolution. It was only a pilot operation, confined to the province of Matanzas, neighboring Havana, a small province with low population and problems more easily managed than the others, but the results have persuaded Castro and his colleagues to propose expanding the experience to the whole country in 1976.

In Matanzas, elections were held in each of the country's smallest districts, the *circonscripción*. From each of these 1,050 units, one delegate to a municipal assembly was elected. The rules required that there be at least two candidates in each race, nominated by neighborhood meetings which anyone could attend, and at which anyone's name—sixteen years and older —could be proposed. Significantly, only half the candidates were members of the Communist Party, and many of them were defeated. But all the candidates elected were strong supporters of the Revolution. Less than five percent of those elected were women.

This municipal assembly proceeded to elect from its membership a regional assembly and a provincial assembly. The provincial assembly, with a paid staff of professional planners, runs much of the local government. Thus, it sets local production quotas—even to the extent of deciding whether, within the national planning parameters, Matanzas will build, let us say, another bakery or another movie theater. It can also assign quotas among the various production units, but it may not make decisions in areas which have been determined to be "national" in scope. Thus, health standards, school curricula, or anything to do with sugar production are off limits to *Poder Popular*.

But that still leaves a wide area of authority that finds its roots in local, precinct-level elections. They are not ideal elections, from a classic political science viewpoint. A designation by the Party is undoubtedly crucial. A Communist candidate is stronger than one who is not. Support from the local officials of the Party and the government probably counts about as much as designation by the local power structure in a midwestern town in the United States, and probably counts less than an endorsement by Reform clubs on the Upper West Side of New York.

It is a good start toward decentralization, if not toward democracy. And the aim of the Cuban government is toward decentralization. For that reason, the success of *Poder Popular* in Matanzas means that it will be on the agenda of the First Communist Party Congress when it convenes late in 1975. And that means that elections on this model will be decreed for every province in 1976. The provincial assemblies thus elected will then create a national assembly, and from that meeting will undoubtedly emerge the first post-revolutionary constitution.

Several things remain to be seen about *Poder Popular*. It is not clear, for example, whether a decentralized system which can work in a small province without a really large metropolitan area, can work in, let us say, Oriente or Havana—where urban problems are substantial, and where the national/local differences are not nearly as apparent.

Poder Popular is the latest in a series of what would be called "experiments" in a non-Communist society. It is one of the refreshing things about viewing Cuban history in the past fifteen years that there has been no consistent Communist line, no ideological "turns" to fit sudden and unexpected developments in the Soviet Union. It must also be refreshing to Castro to look back on the period and discover that somehow each of the "failures" was followed by enough good fortune and flexibility of the government and its willingness to change in order to keep the Revolution on the path.

The first phase, immediately after the triumph of the Revolution, was a heavy emphasis on cooperatives, especially in the agricultural sector. Coming out of the Sierra Maestra, Castro and Che were convinced that the support and *élan* of the campesino could be transferred easily to support of and participation in cooperatives.

The expectation was wrong. Cooperating enthusiastically in the Revolution did not prove at all to be an automatic harbinger of cooperation in whatever economic system the new leaders prescribed. Cooperatives were utterly foreign to the Cuban experience, where even under Batista the government had set fairly rigid production quotas for sugar.

With the failure of the cooperative experiment came

195

a period in 1962–63, under the administration of Che Guevara at the National Bank, in which the apparently correct decision to industralize was taken, and there followed an attempt at a "Great Leap Forward" in which Cuba tried to break the shackles of a one-crop economy and an underdeveloped industrial plant. But not only was the industrial capacity down, but many of the ablest technicians had fled in the first wave of refugees. The result was that poor industrial capacity was further depressed by a lack of industrially skilled workers, and in the process good sugar land was destroyed as well.

Through those first four or five years, a sort of hit-or-miss political development was taking place as well. One month after the Bay of Pigs invasion by the United States, Castro first announced his allegiance to the principles of Marxism-Leninism, and simultaneously turned to the Soviet Union as the source—for a while, the only source—of economic and military aid.

The Communist Party of Cuba had been anointed early in the days after the Revolution as the party through which Castro would express the government's political policy. There seems little reason to believe that Castro sought this affiliation, and practically none to suggest a link prior to the Revolution, but the dynamics of the Cuban situation were similar to those found elsewhere—most recently in Portugal. After years of repressive dictatorship, only the Communist Party emerges relatively intact, and with the discipline and—above all—the international connections necessary to play a governing role.

By 1960, the other Cuban parties, particularly those of the left, were shattered and quarrelsome, and the Communists moved with Fidel's blessing into the vacuum. But over the next three or four years, a serious split was to develop between Castro and the Communist leaders. The old-line secretary-general of the Party was Anibal Escalante, and Escalante was not only an old-fashioned Communist, he was an old-fashioned Cuban as well. He eschewed much of the moral fervor that animated those early *Fidelista* years, and stuck to the idea that material incentives were the best spur to production.

Worse, from Castro's point of view, Escalante and his old Bolsheviks stayed firmly entrenched in their positions in the party, and very few of them had left to go and fight with Fidel in the mountains. (One significant exception was Carlos Rafael Rodriguez; alone among the old Batista-era Communists, he remains an important figure in the government, probably ranking just after Castro and his brother Raul.)

This situation resulted in a "purge" of Escalante and his followers, most of whom were simply retired or "promoted" to nonpolicy jobs in 1962 and 1963. Escalante himself was first appointed ambassador to an eastern European country and only later officially disgraced.

The years of the mid-sixties were transitional years, in which the material incentives of Escalante were replaced by a moral striving and an operational code which relied heavily on the creation of the "new socialist man." This man, according to the then-prevailing belief, would do extra work without extra pay, and could do the work of ten because his heart was pure. This was also the time of support and solidarity for revolutions around Latin America—the basis for the charge that Castro was "exporting revolution." He wasn't really; but he did not ignore a chance to further it whenever a likely proposition appeared in Latin America.

By 1965, Castro had reorganized the Communist Party. He had moved out the old-line leadership and most of their followers, and replaced them with his own people. That done, he changed the name from the PSP to the *Partido Comunista Cubano,* its present name. What Fidel had done was to take the shell and the apparatus of the old party—which he had used to carry out his original program but which he had not armed—and to create a new one, retaining the trappings and little else except a sense of historical continuity.

After Che Guevara's death in 1967, the change was

virtually complete. By January 1968, Castro could tell an International Cultural Congress that "the old Marxist-Leninists have become ecclesiatical, and the old ecclesiatics have become revolutionary." He was referring to the increasing radicalization of the younger priests, particularly in Colombia, and the increasing stodginess of Communist parties, particularly throughout Latin America. It was the closest he came to an independent (of the USSR) Marxist line, and the closest identification he was to make with radical neo-Maoists in the international cultural community.

By August, however, Castro defended the Soviet invasion of Czechoslovakia and moved back to a more orthodox line. His position was a curious one; there was no *legal* justification for the invasion, he said, but it was necessary because the Communist bureaucracy in Czechoslovakia, as elsewhere, had become remote from the people, and, in any event, to do otherwise would have invited an imperialist takeover. The European intellectuals abandoned him almost to a man (and woman), and have not significantly supported the Cuban revolution since.

By 1969, Cuba had turned back toward incentives. Now the "volunteer" workers in the construction projects would be compensated for their extra work, and the economy developed a blend of moral and material compensation equated by a blend of sugar and other agriculture, and by a reasonable mix of industrialization.

This time, with five more years of education for the Cuban technician (often in eastern Europe), and massive assistance and technical help from the Russians, it began to work. Only one more turn back toward the "pure" model was attempted, and as Castro admitted later himself it turned out to be a failure. In 1970, Castro announced that Cuba would produce a sugar harvest of ten million tons, an amount almost forty percent above the average and thirty percent above the previous all-time record.

Almost every resource, mechanical and personal, in

the country was mobilized, largely with moral incentives as a spur, and in the end it failed. The harvest reached eight and a half million tons, an astonishing figure for any year, but in the course of the mobilization almost everything else in the country suffered. (In an interesting irony, Castro now points out, publicly, that at today's prices, 1970 would have represented a twenty-million-ton year. The capitalist lesson of enforced scarcity as a road to higher profit, however, has not been adopted—the figure remains an irony and nothing more. This year, as before, a considerable effort has been systematically organized to *optimizar* the harvest, even in the face of a serious drought.)

The moral component is still present in the Cuban economy, but now work is paid for, and extra work receives extra money. As a matter of fact, the billboards around Havana in 1975 read like the posters at an IBM company party. "More Goods of Better Quality in Less Time," and "To Reward Those Who Fulfill Their Tasks Is to Stimulate Others to Fulfill Theirs," are only two fair samples. Production, efficiency, and quality are the watchwords now, the always-high absentee rate is significantly down, unemployment has been replaced by labor shortages, and the impression is everywhere that things are working.

There is no one in Cuba today who will say that Cuba has not made mistakes in the last fifteen years. In fact, Fidel Castro is the first to criticize. History clearly shows that the hardest task of a revolution and its makers is the governing of the country that follows.

Fidel Castro was thirty-two years old when he assumed power. The country's treasury contained only seventy-five million dollars; much of the professional class had left or was about to leave; the most powerful country in the world was embarking on an invasion, to be followed by a strict economic and political blockade. These problems were added to the normal ones of solidifying and uniting an underdeveloped country after a revolution. There is little question that Castro and the Cubans have made mistakes and that the first year of their power were ones filled with experiments that did not all work. But after fifteen years, one inescapable impression is that Castro has learned and indeed has landed on some formulas that up to now are working.

Castro commented that he thought great progress has been made in the battle against racial discrimination. This appears to be true, if the presence of black Cubans in management and supervisory positions is a reliable index. Certainly social discrimination against blacks— once widespread—seems to be almost totally eliminated, and there are no longer racial barriers at any of the "luxury" hotels, beaches, restaurants and clubs.

Cubans are active. Six days a week, it often appears that everybody is working or at least engaged in some kind of activity. Indeed, Cubans are active elsewhere than in Cuba. In a situation somewhat reminiscent of the early days of the Peace Corps, more than two hundred Cuban doctors are in North Vietnam, a team of engineers is building schools on the Cuban model in Tanzania, and other technicians are elsewhere in Africa and Asia.

Castro cites this activity as an answer to what would happen to the revolutionary *élan* of Cuba once the necessities had been provided. Would not Cubans then begin to adopt some consumerist values? Would not people begin to think about a *color* television set, a private automobile, foreign travel? Castro thinks that foreign service would take up some of the slack.

"We produce," he said, "one thousand doctors a year, and even though we have not yet met our own needs we send two hundred to other countries. When we begin to produce two thousand, then more than two hundred—perhaps five hundred—will be working to help other countries."

However optimistic that might seem, the reality so far is on track. The chief engineer of the giant new city Alamar, for example, had spent two years in Chile working with his Chilean counterparts in developing ideas for similar projects there, and he seemed to regard it as a very natural part of his career.

The Cuban people—and this seems to have been true before the Revolution as well—are extremely neat and clean, and the Revolution has encouraged these traits. There is almost no debris on the streets. One evening we spotted some ice cream wrappers in the gutter on a side street in Camaguey. The next morning they were gone, and the street was immaculate.

The leveling effect of the Revolution is apparent almost everywhere. In no casual meeting is it possible to tell what level job or position a Cuban occupies. The upper class and the upper middle class no longer exist, nor is there apparent urban poverty. In some rural areas, where families still live on—and off—their own small plot of land, and where the housing is barely adequate, there still appears to be a subsistence level existence. But it is rapidly disappearing, and in the cities there is little of the grinding poverty one finds elsewhere in the western hemisphere.

The new housing that has been built since Castro took power is dramatic. Either of the two major housing projects—Alamar, outside of Havana, and José Martí, outside Santiago—would make almost any large U.S. project look small. To call Alamar or José Martí just a housing project might even be unfair; they really are the equivalent of new cities. Alamar, with 30,000 residents now, will eventually house 125,000. All the housing structures are identical, but we did not get any sense of congestion or sameness. They are adequately landscaped and colorfully painted. They are equipped with an olympic-size swimming pool, day-care centers, stores, restaurants, schools, playgrounds, and small factories. Public transportation is plentiful. Most of the people in Alamar work in Havana and once occupied substandard housing. They carefully tend to their new apartments and grounds, and these massive complexes are as clean as the rest of the country.

In fact, Castro's Cuba has acted on a theory often advanced but never acted upon elsewhere in Latin

America, where each capital city is ringed by a belt of misery—hundreds of thousands of people who have moved from the countryside to live in packing boxes, straw huts with dirt floors, or improvised shacks made of boxes and flattened cans. The theory has been that if life could only be made more attractive in the countryside, it would slow or stop the migration to the capital. People come to the city, knowing the desperation of life in the slums there, only because life is even more desperate in the rural areas they leave. But revolutionary Cuba *acted* upon the theory, and for at least the first ten years virtually starved Havana of development funds and spent almost everything that was available in the countryside.

It is out in the country that roads are newly paved, the medical posts exist in every small town, hospitals in every city, and new schools and small factories are everywhere. The result is that migration to Havana is minimal, and it stands today as the only Latin capital not surrounded by the ring of misery that threatens to strangle every capital in the developing world.

Outside Santiago, we drove by what most resembled the shantytowns that always surround Latin cities. Our foreign ministry guide explained that "we have so much to do, and there are big problems remaining. We have a lot of work to do still."

As for housing in the rural areas, the strategy has been to encourage people to leave their wooden, dirt-floor *bohios* and move to newly created towns and housing projects. The new housing in such places as Mayari Arriba and the *Plan Genetico* outside Matanzas provides furnished apartments complete with television sets and refrigerators—rent-free.

In those mountain areas where the terrain makes it most difficult to operate, the government is providing now upgraded *bohios* more strongly built as an intermediate step toward the day when those people too will be integrated into more convenient communities. Roads are being extended to the deepest and highest parts of the Sierra Maestra in order to bring bus transportation to the remotest villages.

In addition, Castro's government made an important decision with respect to luxury. The large tourist hotels, particularly in Havana and at the beaches, as well as the restaurants once attended only by the rich and the Americans, might have seemed a tempting target for typical Communist bureaucrats. One imagines, for example, that in the Soviet Union or in East Germany the great hotels would have been converted into dormitories or barracks, and the style of living and the food reduced to some common level and made available to all.

But in Cuba, the "luxury" is maintained. One dines at the great hotels off the same thick tablecloths and with the same gleaming silver and stemware as must have once delighted Meyer Lansky and his friends. The same superb Daiquiris are still available as one takes one's ease beside the swimming pool; the only difference is that all of this is now available to—and used regularly by—the ordinary working people of Cuba. The hotels and restaurants—with very few exceptions—are subsidized, so that our suites at the Hotel Riviera, which went in 1958 for twenty-eight dollars per night, are now available at five dollars. The price of meals is similarly scaled, and the famous Daiquiris can be had for twenty-five cents. The result is that at the next table in the fine restaurants, one is likely to see a black dock worker on vacation with his wife, or a group from a provincial sugar mill in for a holiday they have earned.

This is one of the "consumption" items which tend to spur production; the factories, for example, reserve a number of tables at the famous Tropicana nightclub each weekend, and they are used by workers who have been nominated for the honor by their comrades on the various committees.

One comment heard often from Americans who have visited Havana is the "rundown" condition of these hotels. It is true that the carpets are a bit threadbare, the sofas a bit worn, and maybe the silver-plated serving dishes are often dented. But those same people who miss "the good old days" also fail to mention that the Cubans make no pretension that the condition of the hotels is a major concern of theirs and certainly not a top priority. Cuba has simply taken the money once used to maintain this luxury for a few and spent it on services for the poor. Now they just do the best they can with what has existed in the hotels since 1959. And in reality, the air conditioning, the dining rooms, and the swimming pools function well with one difference—the Cubans think it is great even if foreigners think it is just not the same.

Everyone in the country, according to Castro, earns between 100 and 700 American dollars per month, and he says the government is anxious to narrow even that gap. The result is that no one can be found who seems to be living very well, but more important to Cubans, at least for now, hardly anyone can be found who is living badly.

Rationing is considered the great leveler by many. It is another factor about Cuban life that receives a lot of attention from visitors—"long lines, small quantities, and little variety." All of that is basically true, but Cubans will sometimes remark that the United States has had its own long lines and rationing problems with gasoline. And in fact we never did see long lines outside of stores. The Cubans now assign specific days to specific people.

When most Americans think of rationing, the image that first comes to mind is "not enough." In Cuba this can be an inaccurate definition. In the rural areas, for example, we visited produce markets that were piled high with several varieties of vegetables. Rural residents are allowed 180 pounds of produce per month for a family of four. Their ration is never used up. And even in the urban areas where the shortages are most likely to occur, a family of four with two children receives the ration allotment for the entire family even though the children are at school and receive all their meals away from home. In fact, the allowable ration for four

204

is rarely used up by the family of two. The ration book, therefore, in practice is not necessarily a firm limit.

Most things are within the means of even the lowest-paid workers. Rent, for example, ranges from free to ten percent of income. Medical care and hospitalization are free. Education is free, and public transportation is either free or only five cents.

As Dan Rather pointed out, if there is a favored class in Cuba, it is the children. One of the highest priorities of Castro and the Cuban government is education and the construction of schools. We visited several types—primary, elementary, secondary, and technical. The new primary and secondary schools are as well equipped as any in the United States. Brightly painted classroms, well-stocked libraries, new desks and chairs. In some of the classrooms, there are tables of different shapes and design as experiments in learning techniques.

The secondary and technical schools are located mostly outside the city and none will be built in urban settings in the future. The work/study program that Fidel outlined in detail in the interview is indeed the future for education as Cuba sees it today. All the schools will be identical in size, shape, and style. Fidel feels that he has found a system that is right for Cuba and sees no reason to vary the physical characteristics of the schools. He says that this approach will save money and time.

The students at these schools do not seem to mind working in addition to studying. In fact, many told us that they were grateful for the opportunity to study and feel that they should contribute to the country with their work.

If the results of the first generation of the new Cuban citizen are any indication, this effort has been well worthwhile. The young professionals we met all seemed to have the kind of spirit, patriotism, and dedication to their job and their society which should be the envy of every capitalist country.

In addition to the young, the mentally ill have received a great deal of attention. One of the first acts of

205

the Castro government in 1959 was the construction of a new mental hospital. It was, perhaps, the most impressive single project we visited. We both have visited mental hospitals throughout Latin America. They all were human garbage bins. Old and young were thrown together. If there were beds, there were enough for only a few—most slept or huddled on the floor surrounded by their own feces. If a doctor ever visited, it was to give shock treatment to patients considered little more than cattle to be prodded. We were told that such was the case in Cuba until 1959.

Today, in a large, spacious facility outside Havana, there are clean beds for all, private shower and toilet facilities, a swimming pool, a fully-equipped track—there is a special olympics every year—a beauty parlor, a barbershop, and a pedicurist. There are shops and handicraft facilities for artwork, weaving, and sculpture. Great emphasis is placed on work therapy—all voluntary. There is a chicken farm, carpentry, and construction. Almost all of Lenin Park was built by voluntary labor from the mental hospital. The doctors feel that patients should be and need to be considered individuals with a contribution to make to their country.

Inevitably, in considering a Communist dictatorship such as Cuba (Castro is the first to admit that Cuba is presently in the stage of Communist development known as "the dictatorship of the proletariat"), the Westerner's mind turns to the question of political freedom. When we asked Castro about freedom of speech, he seemed surprised and said, "Of course, there is criticism of the government. Go out in the street or go into the factories, and you will hear it everywhere."

It is true there are complaints about one's job, some problem in rationing, or the distribution of things, but this was hardly the freedom of speech we were talking about.

When it came to freedom of the press—part of this exchange appears in the transcript—Castro was very firm. It is a revolutionary society, he pointed out, and "all the people support the Revolution." It would therefore be absurd, he said, to permit counterrevolutionary groups to publish material whose aim was the destruction of the Revolution. "But," asked Mankiewicz, "if all the people support the Revolution, then what is the risk of permitting an opposition press?" Castro smiled. "It is not a question of risk," he said, "it is a matter of principle. We will not permit it."

These are facts of Communist life which might make it extremely difficult for Americans, even those whose material life might be improved by the change, to want to live in Cuba. The custom of saying "no," even if sharply limited for many in the United States and of doubtful value for some, is still a strong one. And there is no room for those who say "no" and want to change the fundamental political structure of post-revolutionary Cuba.

But if one compares Cuba's lack of political freedom and social mobility to any other Latin American country, then to all but a handful of landed aristocrats it must seem a very desirable place indeed. To those parts of the world where for centuries the poor have supported a small rich class with their labor and the lives of their children, the Cuban revolution holds out great promise. In fact, the distinct impression one gets— even after short visits such as ours—is that this is what a Latin American country was meant to look like after ten years of the Alliance for Progress. If one is looking for ironies, there is the greatest one.

There *is* some opposition remaining in the country, but it appears to be minimal and confined largely to the grumbling of older Cubans who elected to stay, live off their property, and take no other part in society. This decision of Castro's to permit *rentiers* to remain and to keep their property until their death—private property can be retained, but it cannot be sold—seems to have been a wise one. The result is a small number of people who actively oppose the Revolution (they are called *gusanos* or, literally, "worms"), and spend most of their time selecting a restaurant in which to eat the next day. They are public, they speak of their preference for the old days, but no one seems to feel

207

they have either the desire or the power to change anything.

There seems little doubt that the few remaining pockets of private property will be turned over to the state within a generation. While some prerevolutionary farmers refuse to turn their small plots of land over to the various agricultural plans, their children seem far more disposed to join the Revolution.

The pressure to capitulate comes in the form of material benefits. A farmer who gives up his land moves from his dirt-floored, straw-roofed shack to a furnished apartment with electricity, running water, and good schools nearby. We met no official who worried that private property would catch on in popularity—at least not in the foreseeable future.

We visited farmers who retained their land and decided not to participate in the group activities of their peers. Their families still receive free education and medical services. They are just left outside the mainstream. But it is one thing for an old peasant to reject the Revolution; it is quite another to expect his children to follow.

Another factor in the creation of a population almost entirely in favor of the Revolution was Castro's decision that anyone who wished to could leave. Between six and seven hundred thousand Cubans—they would make up nearly ten percent of the population—left, mostly for Miami and the United States.

If Cuba had followed the policy of other Communist countries and forbade emigration, then you might see some of the trappings of a typical Communist state in Cuba. But there are no labor camps, no ever-present secret police, no brooding presence of the State which one senses in a Communist country, let us say, in eastern Europe. It could be said that next to sugar Cuba's most successful export has been dissent and opposition.

In fact, even Castro's Marxism seemed faintly suspect to us. He spoke all the requisite words and was highly skilled in arguing the Marxist position, but he did so only when pressed and it seemed to us that his

208

ever-present sense of humor made it difficult for him to speak seriously and at any length about—for example—the "withering away of the state."

By contrast, the "new" Cuban generation is much more dogmatic and didactic in its Communist commitment, and the young men and women of the foreign ministry who were our guides were ready at a moment's notice to argue the advantages of Marxism-Leninism and the fatal flaws of capitalism, and to do so with all the enthusiasm of an American college student of the thirties who had just read his first Marxist tract.

There is a remarkable absence of any Russian presence in Cuba. We had expected to see more than we did, and the only visible signs are in the Havana port. Our hotel window looked out on the pathway into the Havana harbor. There was hardly a time when we could not see a ship entering or leaving—and most of those ships bore the hammer and sickle. Many Cuban professionals freely admitted with a sense of pride that they had been trained by the Soviet Union. Maybe it is as Castro says—Russians do not flaunt their presence as do Americans.

Another significant difference between Cuba and other Communist countries—at least to our eyes—is that while it is clearly and admittedly a *dictatorship,* it is not *totalitarian.* Totalitarian societies, by definition, are *total* and the governments lay their hands upon every aspect of human life. In the Soviet Union, there are Communist art, Communist music, Communist films, Communist dance, and one departs from this "socialist realism" at great peril. Recently in Moscow, Soviet bulldozers destroyed an open-air exhibition of modern art because the paintings were nonobjective and did not meet the present standards the government had imposed for what is "proper." Such an event would be unthinkable in Cuba. We visited a number of workers' art schools, and the students were encouraged to paint as they pleased. Some chose representational art, others chose Cubism as a model, and it was apparent that no orthodoxy was being enforced. The music one hears in Cuba is either traditional, when it is played

209

by the amateur groups that exist in every village and neighborhood, or "decadent" when played on the radio in Havana and by the Muzak in the hotels, where the favorites still seem to be Viennese waltzes and 1950s American-style swing and early rock. Cuban movies often have a revolutionary theme but sometimes do not, and American "escapist" films are much in demand. The local television resembles American television in the pre-cable days, complete with live soap opera and variety shows.

Castro expressed his disappointment that practically no women were elected in the *Poder Popular* elections in Matanzas. He thought this represented a traditional Latin feeling about the role of women, which he said he was anxious to change. That led him into a discussion of a peculiarly Cuban Communist experiment—the promulgation of a new family code. This is an extremely -advanced document, even by American liberationist standards, and proclaims the equality of the sexes, not only on the job and in society, but at home as well. It requires men and women to share equally in domestic responsibilities, including all the traditionally female tasks of child rearing, home maintenance, cooking, and laundry. Castro expects a fairly long period of discussion of this code before it is put into effect, and he anticipates considerable opposition from Cuban males. But he is determined to carry it through, and the force of his personality and leadership is such that even (as one suspects) if he meets opposition within the Cuban Politburo, he will have his way.

The discussion of the family code and Castro's personal convictions on the matter recall Castro's answer when Mankiewicz asked him, seeking an admission that Cuba was really run by Castro himself, "Has any proposal of yours ever been rejected by the political committee of the party, which makes the decisions?"

"It could happen," Castro replied, with a generous smile which seemed to indicate that it had not happened yet.

On balance, then, Castro's Cuba is prosperous and its people are enthusiastic, reasonably content, and optimistic about the future. Perhaps the overriding impression of three trips to Cuba is the enthusiasm and unity of the Cuban people. They are proud of their accomplishments and sing songs about themselves and their country that reflect this self-pride. The feeling of inferiority so prevalent in other Latin countries where centuries of domination and repression have stifled individual self-esteem is apparently gone from Cuba. The people work together and work hard—for what they believe to be the good of their neighbors and therefore their country. This feeling was best summed up by an army sergeant who explained, "I have a ninth-grade education, all of which I acquired after the Revolution when I was fifteen and illiterate. I would feel that it would be my responsibility to help educate my neighbor who might only have a fourth-grade education, even though," he added, "if by doing so I ran the risk that he could one day take my job or my place." As long as there is a labor shortage, he may not yet face that dilemma, but it is significant that he believes he would do so.

Cuba is by no means a model Western democracy, but neither is it a stereotyped model Communist dictatorship.

As to relations with the United States, Castro seems eager that we end our economic blockade, but he is not prepared to make any sacrifices to achieve it. He has patience, he says, and he observes correctly that history seems to be on his side. He seems anxious to assume a position of leadership in a new organization of Latin American countries, one which would exclude but not necessarily be hostile to the United States, and he is careful to draw a distinction between American leadership and the American people. He and all the Cubans we met seemed genuinely friendly to Americans, and anxious to learn more about their neighbor.

We came away convinced that it would be in the interest of the United States, as well as that of Cuba and the rest of Latin America, if we were to bring our Cuban policy in line with the rest of our foreign policy, drop the blockade and resume economic and diplomatic

211

relations with Cuba. In the first place, it would end a period of our history which has brought us censure and hostility from increasing majorities in Latin America and the rest of the world, and it would promote a closer relationship between the two countries and eliminate what appears to be a hostility stimulated largely by the United States. Time will tell, of course, but time seems to be on the side of Cuba and Fidel Castro.

Appendix 1

Speech by Commander-in-Chief Fidel Castro at the meeting commemorating the XIVth Anniversary of the Committees for the Defense of the Revolution, Havana, September 28, 1974

Invited guests;

Comrades of the leadership of the Party and the Government;

Comrades of the Committees for the Defense of the Revolution:

Exactly a year ago in this same square, on another anniversary of the founding of the Committees for the Defense of the Revolution, the gigantic solidarity meeting with the Chilean people and in homage to heroic President Salvador Allende took place *(Applause)*.

Since then, the Chilean people have lived under one of the bloodiest and most horrible tyrannies known to modern times. Since September 11, 1973, tens of thousands of Chileans have been tortured, assassinated, imprisoned or exiled by the vicious and blood-thirsty government that came out of the fascist military *golpe*. Hundreds of thousands of workers have lost their jobs. The nationalized industries, for the most part, have been returned to their former owners, and Chile's doors again opened to penetration and domination by the foreign monopolies. Finally, as an additional service to imperialism, in recent days the fascist junta has shamefully violated the Cartagena Agreements by granting special privileges for foreign investment and threatening the very survival of the Andean Pact in which many South American countries have placed their hopes for development and economic integration. The fascist junta has given all that its imperialist bosses could have expected from it, and the bitter fruit that the outraged opinion of the whole world foresaw from the terrible events.

Editorial de Ciencias Sociales, Instituto Cubano del Libro Calle G N Q 505, Vedado, Habana 4—CUBA

The enormous wave of solidarity in all countries of the world as a result of the Chilean tragedy has not weakened over the course of time. On the first anniversary of the heroic death of President Allende, his stature in the eyes of world opinion has grown enormously and the people are redoubling their condemnation and disparagement of the fascist junta.

There is really no event in recent times that has so injured world sensibility and produced such unanimous revulsion in all corners of the world. No government is as unpopular and morally isolated as the fascist government of Chile.

And what is it that has capped the indignation of world public opinion at this particular time? What is it that makes the role played by the fascist clique of Chile even more grotesque and repugnant? The full confirmation and confession of the participation of the United States government in the process that culminated in the otherthrow and death of President Allende. *(Exclamations: "Fidel, seguro, a los yanquis dales duro!"* ["*Right, Fidel, hit the Yankees hard*"])

At that time the United States authorities hastened to deny what all the world suspected: the responsibility of the government of that country for the events in Chile. At the end of a year, a wealth of details has come to light, proving that the CIA interfered shamelessly in Chilean affairs on orders of top US authorities over a period of ten consecutive years, first in order to prevent the triumph of Popular Unity; to obstruct handing over the government after the triumph; and, finally, to work actively in the overthrow of President Allende.

Today it is known, through the release of the testimony of CIA Director William Colby before the Intelligence Subcommittee of the Armed Services Committee of the House of Representatives on April 22, 1974, and through other revelations by CIA agents published by the North American press itself, that in the 1964 elections, the CIA gave Christian Democracy $3 million to support its candidate Eduardo Frei against Salvador Allende; that in the 1970 elections, the CIA invested large sums of money in order to again prevent the triumph of the popular candidate; that after the victorious elections of the popular forces that same year, it invested $350,000 to bribe the

Chilean Congress not to ratify Allende's election; that immediately after the constitution of the Popular Unity government, the CIA spent $5 million between 1971 and 1973 in order to disturb and sabotage the Popular Unity government; that in the 1973 parliamentary elections, the CIA spent a million and a half dollars in support of the opposition candidates and to influence the mass media; and, finally, that in the summer of 1973, the CIA financed the counterrevolutionary demonstrations, the truck owners' and businessmen's strikes in which tens of thousands of fascists participated, and other actions that led directly to the criminal and traitorous *golpe* of September 11th of that year. These large sums of money were manipulated on the black market, above the official exchange rate, contributing to speculation and aggravating monetary difficulties.

Without beginning to consider the close relations the Pentagon had with the Chilean Armed Forces, which it continued to supply with arms while the popular government was denied all credits in the United States and the international financial organizations it controlled, the CIA clearly played a decisive role in creating the conditions and preparing the ground for the fascist *golpe* which has cost the Chilean people such grief, blood and tragedy. The responsibility for the thousands of Chileans tortured, assassinated, imprisoned and exiled, and for the dreadful conditions of repression, unemployment and misery that millions of people in that fraternal country are suffering today, falls directly on the Central Intelligence Agency and the top authorities of the United States who propitiated and fanned the flames of this policy. The pure, revolutionary and heroic blood of Salvador Allende *(Applause)*, assassinated on September 11th, forever stains the United States' rulers in the pages of history!

In the long list of that country's aggressions against the peoples of Latin America, dating from the invasion and occupation of half of Mexican territory in the last century, up to the present, including the pillage of the Panama Canal Zone, the interventions in Cuba, Nicaragua, Mexico. Haiti, Santo Domingo, Guatemala, etcetera—some past, some present; open or undercover—in order to first seize and then plunder the natural resources of our countries and subject them to their dictates and interests, few have been so repugnant, sordid and perfidious as this impudent interference in the internal affairs of Chile.

Although it is true that the responsibility for these deeds falls on previous administrations of the United States, the new President, to the surprise and astonishment of Latin-American public opinion, has declared that such deeds were carried out in the best interests of the United States. That is, the government of the United States, at this level, openly proclaims the right to intervene by any means—however illicit, dirty or criminal—in the internal affairs of the peoples of this hemisphere, as long as the reactionary and mean interests of that country deem it advisable.

Isn't this in flagrant contradiction to all the norms of international law and the fundamental principles that rule the United Nations Organization? Isn't it contrary to the agreements and international treaties imposed by the United States on the peoples of this hemisphere?

What does the shameful OAS, the discredited OAS, the prostituted OAS say of this? (Boos) Can anyone imagine that there remains even an atom of decency or moral authority or reason for this ridiculous and wretched institution to exist?

Let us say it with complete frankness: those who were accomplices of the United States in its aggression against other peoples of Latin America are to a great extent guilty of these deeds: those who tolerated, covered and even supported events such as the overthrow of Arbenz in Guatemala, the massacres against the students and people of Panama in the Canal Zone and the invasion of Santo Domingo by the Yankee Marines in 1965.

What is to be said of the very history of United States and OAS aggressions against the Cuban Revolution? What is to be said of the economic blockade, the invasion of Playa Girón, the pirate attacks from Central-American countries and from Miami; the subversion, terrorism and sabotage that the CIA has promoted against our people over many years?

It cannot be forgotten that, in its policy of aggression against Cuba, the United States bought the humiliating complicity of numbers of governments, and divided the sugar quota and the plunder of the Cuban economy among them. What then is so strange, that with this elemental lack of respect and consideration it feels toward our peoples, the United States today confesses and justifies the intervention in Chile, at the same time that it threatens Venezuela and Ecuador—among other oil-producing countries

—with reprisals of hunger and even worse, if they do not give in to its demands to reduce the price of oil? Will the OAS, instrument of the worst form of neocolonialism, defend the peoples of Latin America, integrate them and unite them politically in the face of the prepotency and the domination of the United States? *(Exclamations of "No!")*

The countries of Africa have their organization of African States in which South Africa, Rhodesia and Europe are not included. And those African peoples, recent arrivals to the world of independence and incomparably poorer than those of Latin America, nevertheless have a much higher and more worthy concept of the sense, functions and role of a truly regional organization *(Applause)*.

The United States on the one hand, and the Latin-American and Caribbean peoples on the other hand, form two worlds as different as Europe and Africa. They do not fit into the same community. Over there, they are separated by Gibraltar, which is a minuscule stretch of sea; here the Río Bravo and the Florida Straits separate us; in both cases a technological abyss, and absolutely different cultures.

The United States is already a large community; the peoples of Latin American and the Caribbean have before them the historic task of forming theirs, as an unavoidable condition for liberty, development and survival. And that can never be achieved in unworthy promiscuity and by mixing with the United States *(Applause)*. Together, our peoples will have the force sufficient to provide us with the security and guarantee that no Inter-American Treaty of Mutual Assistance and no OAS have ever offered us in the face of the domination, the aggressions and the interferences of the United States.

A moment ago I mentioned the threats the United States has made to the oil-exporting countries—two of them Latin-American: Venezuela and Ecuador—demanding the reduction of prices. As the question has been stated, in unusually harsh terms, by the President of the United States and other leaders of that country, in the United Nations and in the IXth World Energy Conference in Detroit—where, by the way, the Yankee authorities, by denying visas, prevented Cuba's participation—the question of oil assumes dramatic proportions.

In a concerted and perfectly executed action, the leaders of that nation have demanded that the oil-producing countries reduce the prices, blaming them for the imminence of a world economic crisis, and threatening them with various possible reprisals. The North American news agencies themselves have taken on the task of especially emphasizing the dramatic nature of these statements, and they have not lacked the basis for doing so.

In Detroit, the President of the United States said that, and I quote, "throughout history nations have gone to war over natural advantages such as water or food, or convenient passages on land or sea. But in the nuclear age, when any local conflict may escalate to global catastrophe, war brings unacceptable risks for all mankind." Then he added: "In the nuclear age there is no rational alternative to international cooperation." Further on he said:

Sovereign nations try to avoid dependence on other nations that exploit their own resources to the detriment of others. Sovereign nations cannot allow their policies to be dictated, or their fate decided, by artificial rigging and distortion of world commodity markets. No one can foresee the extent of the damage nor the disastrous consequences if nations refuse to share nature's gifts for the benefit of all mankind. I told the United Nations General Assembly last week that "the attempt by any country to use one commodity for political purposes will inevitably tempt other countries to use their commodities for their own purposes."

At the end of the speech, he concluded that "it is difficult to discuss the energy problem without lapsing into doomsday language."

The statements by the President of the United States were complemented by similar declarations on the part of the Secretary of State and the Secretary of the Treasury of the United States.

United States strategy is very clear: to group the developed capitalist countries tightly under its control, to divide the nations of the Third World and isolate the oil-producing nations with the objective of imposing its conditions on them. To this end, it threatens not only with reprisals of food supplies, but also with war.

In the first place, it is unjust to blame the oil-producing countries for world inflation and the international monetary crisis. The responsibility for such problems falls basically on the United States itself. They imposed on the community of nations the monetary system that gives the dollar a privileged position over all other monies; they have inundated the world and the central banking reserves of almost all countries with North American bills that greatly exceed their gold backing; they blockaded and isolated the socialist community from international commerce; they began the Cold War; they unleashed the arms race; they and their allies in military pacts invested billions each year in armaments over a quarter of a century; they promoted the Viet Nam war, that cost more than $150 billion. The war budget of the United States surpasses the figure of $80 billion a year, and the CIA alone spends billions a year. In this dismal imperialist policy lie the roots of inflation and the monetary crisis that arose considerably before the increase in oil prices. Finally, they imposed the consumer society and the unlimited waste of the peoples' natural resources. The increase in oil prices, at most, sharpened a situation of crisis already unleashed by the imperialist society itself.

In the second place, the Organization of Petroleum-Exporting Countries arises as a just reaction on the part of the producer countries which belong to the underdeveloped world, in order to defend themselves from unjust prices, unequal exchange, and the exorbitant profits of the big multinational companies which are essentially North American. The big oil companies and not the producer countries were the ones that set the monopolistic prices of oil way above the costs of production and thus obtained fabulous profits for the benefit of the imperialist metropolis.

Over many years, oil suffered the same fate as all the raw materials the underdeveloped world produces. But oil is a special raw material, because iron, aluminum, tin, copper, nickel, uranium, chrome, manganese and many other products are consumed almost uniquely by the developed countries; on the contrary, oil is a product that all the peoples of the world need to consume to a greater or lesser degree. Among the raw materials, it is the most essential and the most indispensable. In this lies the force, and also the weakness, of the countries that produce it, in this confrontation with imperialism.

As soon as oil prices rose after the last crisis in the Middle East, the developed capitalist countries sharply increased the prices of equipment, technology and industrial products way above what the cost of energy added to production costs. They immediately responded to the increases in oil by raising the prices of their exports. They resort to this in order to meet their problems; but there are many countries in the world that are not industrialized and do not have oil, and whose agricultural products or raw materials do not compensate in price for the tremendous increase in industrial products and energy.

That is why the imperialist strategy takes into account that the demand to reduce oil prices may find acceptance in many poor countries. This could result in tremendous division among the countries of the Third World and, therefore, a defeat for the oil exporters; a defeat which, in the long run, would be that of all producers of raw materials and would signify a worsening in the unequal exchange that imperialism has imposed on our peoples.

Oil enjoys a privileged position among all raw materials; that is why it plays a vanguard role in this struggle. But it imposes an immense responsibility on the countries of the OPEC. If all the underdeveloped countries are to make the battle of petroleum theirs, it is imperative that the oil-producing countries make the battle of the underdeveloped world theirs (Applause). It is not by investing the income from oil in the industrialized capitalist countries or in the international financial organizations controlled by imperialism that the support of the underdeveloped world can be won. These resources must be invested essentially in the Third World, in the struggle against underdevelopment, so that the petroleum battle really becomes a banner and a hope for all the peoples of the world that have been marginalized. Otherwise, a large part of the underdeveloped world would have nothing to gain in this battle but instead would have to pay more dearly for manufactured products and energy and be resigned to greater impoverishment in an already critical situation.

Neither the oil producers nor the other underdeveloped peoples can permit themselves the luxury of losing this historic opportunity. This is the hour in which all the countries of the Third World must unite their forces and confront the imperialist challenge. If the oil-producing countries remain united and firm (Applause), if they do not allow themselves to be intimidated by the threats of the United States, if they seek the alliance of the rest of the underdeveloped world, the industrialized capitalist countries will have to accept as inevitable the disappearance of the humiliating and unjust exchange conditions they have imposed on our peoples.

The non-aligned countries could meet and give a firm, united and categoric reply to the threats and pressures of the United States *(Applause)*. Against the imperialist strategy of division, the most resolute union is necessary *(Applause)*. In that way, international cooperation, which is imperative, would not be imposed in the terms the imperialists demand, but rather on the basis of the most legitimate aspirations and interests of all the peoples of the world.

The government of Venezuela has replied with energy and dignity to the speech by the President of the United States *(Applause)*. Nevertheless, only a few Latin-American countries, several of them oil producers or potential future exporters, have given Venezuela their backing. Many governments have remained silent. When Venezuela nationalizes its iron and oil in the near future—as its government has proclaimed—imperialist policy toward Venezuela will probably harden. This is the historic hour in which Venezuela needs the support of the peoples of Latin America, and Latin America needs Venezuela! *(Applause)* We must see in her battle a battle of all our peoples!

At the same time, Venezuela, with the extraordinary financial resources it can mobilize as the fruit of a firm and victorious oil policy, could act for the union, integration, development and independence of the peoples of Latin America, just as the soldiers of Simón Bolívar did in the last century *(Applause)*.

Cuba, which with the generous aid of the Soviet Union *(Applause)* has not felt the energy crisis, and whose development marches ahead in spite of the imperialist blockade and the cowardly action of many governments of this continent, does not hesitate to proclaim its support for the fraternal people of Venezuela *(Applause)* and the government of that country, in its just position with respect to the intentions of the United States!

May the Venezuelans profit from the example of the Cuban Revolution which, under the most incredible conditions of blockade, hemispheric solitude and isolation, firmly and unhesitatingly resisted all the assaults of imperialism *(Applause and exclamations of: "Fidel!" and*

"Fidel, seguro, a los yanquis dales duro!"), emerging after fifteen years, victorious and invincible, as an irreversible factor on this continent. Venezuela will not be alone in this hemisphere as Cuba was *(Exclamations of "No!")*. And perhaps destiny again reserves for the people of the illustrious Liberator an outstanding and decisive role in the definitive independence of the nations of Latin America!

Patria o muerte! Venceremos! *(Ovation)*

Appendix 2

Speech by Commander-in-Chief Fidel Castro at the closing session of the Second Congress of the Federation of Cuban Women, Havana, November 29, 1974, "Year of the XVth Anniversary."

Dear guests;

Dear comrades of the Party and the Government;

Dear comrades of the Federation of Cuban Women:

We have reached the end of this beautiful Congress. And it is not easy to evaluate an event so filled with accomplishments and hope.

In the first place it has not been entirely our Congress; we have shared it amply with a worthy and representative delegation of the revolutionary women of the entire world.

The presence at this Congress of such prestigious comrades as Fanny Edelman, Valentina Tereshkova, Angela Davis, Hortensia Bussi; the presence of numerous women from the fraternal countries of Latin America; the presence of the Arab women, and especially the delegation of the heroic Palestinian people; the presence of the women of Indochina and among them, of the thousand times heroic Vietnamese people *(Applause);* of the Korean women, of the women of the revolutionary and progressive people of Africa, of the women from our sister socialist countries, and the representation of the working women of Western Europe, doesn't this tell us that the representatives of the noblest and most just causes in the whole world have gathered here?

Across oceans, boundaries, languages, the representatives of the progressive women of the entire world have joined hands in this Congress. And there is no need to use the term "foreigner" to characterize these delegations, because at all times we have experienced the feeling that

Editorial de Ciencias Sociales, Instituto Cubano del Libro Calle G N Q 505. Vedado, Habana 4—CUBA we are part of the same homeland, of the same people: th universal homeland, the human population. This proves that nothing except exploitation and injustice separates people, and nothing unites people more than the community of ideals and the aspiration to justice.

The topics that we have been discussing in this Congress have a truly universal interest. They are not just the problems of Cuban women but the problems of the vast majority of women in the world.

It is clear that women need to participate in the struggle against exploitation, against imperialism, colonialism, neocolonialism, racism; in a word: in the struggle for national liberation. But when the objective of national liberation is finally achieved, women must continue struggling for their own liberation within human society *(Applause)*.

We have brought along some data from a report made by the United Nations Department of Statistics which reveals women's situation in most of the world.

Women represent 34% of the work force; that is, 515 million workers. By the end of the present decade, it is estimated that this figure will rise to 600 million, and in the year 2000, to 842 million.

In Western Europe and North America, women constitute between 30% and 40% of the work force.

In spite of the increasing number of women in the ranks of the employed, particularly in professional and technical posts, the United Nations report points out that they are underpaid in comparison to men. "Although it is true," says the report, "that the legal barriers against equal job opportunities for women are few and the principle of equal pay for equal work is now universally accepted, in practice the situation demands the urgent application of measures to eliminate such discrimination."

In many industrialized countries, women's wages are approximately 50% to 80% of men's for the same hours of work. In the developing nations, the low salaries for women indicate that women are engaged in the lowest levels of work and jobs in terms of skill and pay.

In general, this report refers to the question of wages. Of course, it does not analyze the infinite number of problems that affect women in the class society of the capitalist world.

Naturally, in the socialist countries woman has advanced a long distance along the road of her liberation. But if we ask ourselves about our own situation: we who are a socialist country with almost 16 years of revolution, can we really say that the Cuban woman has acquired full equality of rights in practice, and that she is absolutely integrated into Cuban society?

We can analyze certain data, for example. Before the Revolution, there were 194,000 working women. Of them, according to a report I have here, 70% were in domestic work. Today we have three times more women working. The figure for women in civilian state jobs, which as you know include the majority of productive activities, services and administration, is 590,000 women out of a total of 2,331,000 persons working. That is, 25.3% of the workers are women. Nevertheless, the number of women holding leadership posts in all this apparatus of production, services and administration, is only 15%. Feminine membership in our Party is only 12.79%. A notably low figure. And the number of women who work as Party cadres and officials is only 6%.

But we have an example that is still more illustrative and is related to the elections held for People's Power in the province of Matanzas. The number of women selected as candidates was 7.6% and the number of women elected was 3%, to which the comrade from Matanzas referred.

The figures are really something to be concerned about, to make us do something about this problem. Because in those elections the candidates were proposed by the masses, and the masses only proposed 7.6% women candidates, when women make up approximately 50% of the population. And the masses elected only 3% women.

Who here at this Congress, what invited delegate who has been here with you for a week can understand, imagine or conceive how, with such a strong and such a politically advanced feminine movement, only 3% women were chosen in elections?

And these figures reflect nothing more than the reality that after more then 15 years of revolution, we are still politically and culturally behind in this area.

The reality is that there are still objective and subjective factors that discriminate against women.

Naturally if we compare our present situation with what existed before the Revolution, the advances are enormous. It isn't even possible to make any kind of comparison between women's situation before the Revolution and their

225

present situation. And that situation which the Revolution encountered, fully justified the creation of the Federation of Cuban Women. Because our experience teaches us that when an underdeveloped country such as ours liberates itself and begins to construct socialism, a mass organization like this one is necessary, since women have innumerable tasks to face up to within the revolutionary process. And for this reason we believe that the decision to develop this feminine movement, to create this organization that was born on August 23, 1960, was really a wise decision because the work this organization has done could not have been carried forward by any other means.

What would the Party have done without this organization of women? What would the Revolution have done?

It is true that we have other magnificent mass organizations, such as the trade unions, the CDRs, the peasant organizations, the youth and student organizations, the Pioneers and even the organization of the nursery schools. But what organization could have fulfilled the tasks that the Federation of Cuban Women has accomplished?

Comrade Vilma gave a significant historical account of those innumerable tasks, but it is sufficient to recall, first of all, the struggle to develop culture and political understanding in Cuban women, because in capitalist society women really remain culturally and politically downtrodden, they have even fewer educational opportunities than men, and many women in class society are deceived precisely because of that low political level and are frequently used against revolutionary processes.

It is enough to recall that among those tasks were some of great importance. In the first place, the tasks related to the defense of the Revolution and the homeland, the struggle against illiteracy, the struggle for the education of peasant girls, the struggle in preparing domestic workers for productive jobs, the struggle against prostitution, the struggle to incorporate women into work, the struggle to create nursery schools, the tasks of support for education, the public health campaigns, the social work, the deepening of political and ideological consciousness among women and the struggle for the development of an internationalist spirit in the Cuban woman.

The Federation has worked in all those fields and has successfully completed all its tasks. And only the women

226

themselves could have carried out those activities with such efficiency.

But now, in this present stage of the Revolution, the woman has a basic task, a historical battle to wage.

And what is that task? What is that battle? Could you give the answer?

What was the crux, the center of the analysis and the efforts of this Congress? The struggle for women's equality (*Applause*). The struggle for the full integration of Cuban women into society!

And that is really a historical battle. And we believe that this objective is precisely the focal point of this Congress, because in practice, woman's full equality still does not exist (*Applause*).

And we revolutionaries must understand this, and women themselves must understand it. It is not, of course, only a task for women. It is a task for the whole society! (*Applause.*)

But no one need be frightened because women's equality in society is being discussed, although some were frightened when the discussion of the Family Code draft was launched (*Laughs and applause*).

And Blas explained to us here the many conversations he has had with certain male comrades who didn't understand, and he summed up his ideas with a beautiful argument that man's happiness was not possible without women's happiness (*Applause*).

And we don't see why anyone should be frightened, because what should really frighten us as revolutionaries is that we have to admit the reality that women still do not have absolute equality in Cuban society (*Applause*).

What must concern us as revolutionaries is that the work of the Revolution is not yet complete.

Of course in this lack of equality, in this lack of full integration, as I said, there are objective factors and there are subjective factors. Naturally everything that prevents the incorporation of women into work makes this process of integration difficult, makes this process of achieving full equality difficult. And you have seen that precisely when the woman is incorporated into work, when the woman stops performing the traditional and historical activities, is when these problems begin to show up.

In conversation with some of the delegates to this Congress, they expressed their great satisfaction and joy that, during these days of the Congress, many of their husbands had remained at home taking care of the children so they could come to the Congress *(Applause)*. It is unquestionable that if those women had not been integrated into the Federation and had not carried out this work, if they had not been revolutionary militants and had not been participating in this Congress, such a problem never would have arisen in their homes, and the opportunity for those husbands to become aware of such a necessity and of such duties would never even have existed.

Among the objective factors that still hinder women's incorporation into education and work, some were pointed out here, such as the lack of sufficient nursery schools, of sufficient day boarding schools, of sufficient boarding schools, problems concerning the hours in which the schools function, to which we can add such factors as the lack of sufficient jobs for women throughout the country and, of course, the fact that many women do not have the level of qualification for that productive work.

In this area, as far as the nursery schools and education are concerned, over and beyond the great efforts that the Revolution has already made, during the next few years—and particularly in the next five years from '76 to '80—a still greater effort will be made, in the first place, to satisfy the growing educational needs of our people and at the same time to facilitate the incorporation of women into work.

The present capacity of nursery schools is approximately 50,000 children. In the first version of the next five-year plan, the idea of constructing 400 nursery schools with state brigades has been considered, apart from those the micro-brigades construct *(Applause)*, in order to increase the capacity to 150,000 children. That is, three times the capacity we now have.

We are also proposing to construct 400 day boarding schools for 300 pupils each, or the equivalent, in order to increase the capacity by 120,000 children; to construct no less than a thousand high schools with a capactiy of more than a half million additional boarding school students.

Special attention will also be given to a type of school that you know is very important, the special schools for pupils with certain problems. The proposal is to build capacity for 40,000 more pupils in this type of special education.

228

At the same time, the Revolution will continue developing the public health sector in the next few years: 49 new hospitals, 110 polyclinics, 19 dental clinics, 51 homes for the aged, and 16 homes for the disabled will be built throughout the country.

The total investment in education and public health in the next five years will be approximately 1,650 million pesos *(Applause)*. We believe this is good news for the members of the Federation *(Applause)*. And it does not mean starting something new, but rather increasing the rhythm of what is now being built, because more than 180 high schools accommodating 500 students each are now being built per year *(Applause)*.

The hospital construction program is moving ahead; the first brigades for the construction of nursery schools have also been organized. And the brigades necessary to contruct the 400 nursery schools programmed and to construct the special schools, the polyclinics, the homes for the aged, homes for the disabled and the day boarding schools at the primary level, those brigades that are still lacking, will be organized beginning in 1975.

This program is in progress and we are perfectly sure that it will be carried forward.

During the discussion we could appreciate the enormous importance that you attach to these problems and especially to the problems of education. It can be said that a large part of the discussion in the Congress revolved around these questions. Yet in the fields of education and public health our country already occupies first place among all the countries of Latin America *(Applause)*.

And we are really just beginning. It is precisely in the last years that it has been possible to provide a great impulse to school construction. And there were not enough installations nor enough cadres, nor enough teachers. How many difficulties the Revolution has had to confront in order to carry forward these educational programs and to carry forward the public health program, when out of the 6,000 doctors we had, almost all of them concentrated in the city of Havana, they took 3,000 from us. One of the many forms the imperialists use to carry out their crimes; because if in other places—as in Viet Nam—they shell and bomb in order to kill people, here they tried to take away all the doctors so the people would die, just as they blockaded us and still blockade us to try to kill the people by hunger.

Of course today we already have 9,000 doctors, and they are magnificent doctors *(Applause)*, and more than 6,000 youths studying in the Schools of Medicine *(Applause)*. So that not only are we able to satisfy our medical necessities, and do so with increasing quality, but we have also even been able to organize medical brigades to help other fraternal people *(Applause)*. And in the years to come we will graduate some 1,000 doctors each year *(Applause)*, and some of those doctors will be able to offer their internationalist services *(Applause)*. And our medical services will go on improving in quality and will go on conquering disease and will continue eradicating some of those diseases.

The Minister of Public Health explained what the infant mortality rate is now: 27.4 per thousand live births. In Brazil—where there aren't even mortality statistics—it is estimated that it may be between 150 and 200. And unfortunately this is what takes place in many other Latin-American countries. This means that, for every infant that dies in Cuba, four, five, six and seven infants die in other countries of Latin America. The same is true of many other problems: mortality at other ages—because we are talking about mortality in the first year of birth—medical care in general, education.

The Minister of Education explained the figures that reflect the progress of education in Cuba: all children enrolled in schools, the growing number of those graduating from the sixth grade and the explosion we are already having at the high school level, with the result that all the constructions we're building aren't enough.

But now in the years to come the problem will be not only the number of children studying, but also the quality of our education. And our education will improve in quality year by year, with the new system that is being projected and with the growing number of young people studying to be teachers and joining the Pedagogical Detachment.

So that if we now already occupy the very first place among Latin-American countries in education and public health, what will it be in five or six more years? What will it be in future years, given this rhythm of construction, this rhythm of advancement we now have?

And this is the blockaded country, the country against which the imperialists have committed their crime of blockade. And we might ask ourselves: why the blockade? And what has happened in the countries they didn't blockade? What has happened in education? What has happened in public health? How many illiterates are there? How many children without schools? And how many children die each day for lack of food, medicine, medical treatment and everything?

Then, what did imperialism want for the peoples of Latin America? To maintain that situation! And what did they want for Cuba? To prevent us from doing what we are doing! And, it is true, they have achieved one objective, yes: keeping Latin America in that humiliating present situation. But on the other hand, with all their crimes and their blockades, they haven't been able to prevent the social successes of the Cuban Revolution (*Prolonged applause*).

And these truths, these realities, can no longer be hidden, no matter what desperate measures imperialism and its lackeys resort to. And these truths are beginning to become known throughout the world.

And on the other hand, what is left of the Alliance for Progress, if anyone remembers it? Nothing! Frustration after frustration. And nevertheless, the imperialists and their lackeys are determined to maintain the blockade of Cuba, even against a broad majority of Latin-American countries.

This presents no problem for Cuba. But for the Yankee imperialists it does present a problem, because the Revolution is advancing and imperialism is moving backwards. And the longer they maintain the blockade the greater will be the infamy of the imperialists and the greater will be the merit of our people and of our Revolution! (*Applause.*) The OAS isn't even worth mentioning. It met a few days ago. Nobody paid any attention! (*Laughs.*) A group of Latin-American countries that don't even have relations with Cuba, put up a battle against the blockade: Venezuela, Colombia and Costa Rica. It is true that the Costa Rican government publicly stated that it wasn't as concerned about the blockade of Cuba as it was about the OAS sinking, and that if the blockade continued, it was completely sunk. Let the OAS, the Inter-American Treaty of Mutual Assistance and all those things disappear!

But it is true that they put up a battle, especially Venezuela and Colombia, with the support, of course, of the growing number of friendly governments we already have in Latin America. Twelve governments voted against the blockade, three voted in favor. And what models of government: *(Laughs)* Chile, Paraguay and Uruguay. The three typically fascist governments of the continent, and also the most super-discredited in the whole world. And the Yankees? They abstained. Just in order not to stop being pharisees and hypocrites *(Applause)*. And Brazil abstained.

But what they say about the OAS and about certain governments in this hemisphere is interesting:

They say that the sponsors of the initiative to lift the blockade had 15 votes. The Yankees have invented a mechanism by which a two-thirds vote is required. And the sponsors of this initiative had 15 votes: the 12 that voted against the blockade and, in addition, Haiti, Guatemala and Bolivia. And according to all the news, these governments shamelessly sold out to the United States government. Not to vote against, but rather to follow the new formula: to "abstain" *(Laughs)*. And the result: three for, six "abstentions"—which is the new form—and 12 against the blockade. So, in accordance with the laws of imperialism, the blockade persists.

Now we don't know what some of the governments that don't have relations and yet voted against the blockade are going to do in the face of this shameful maneuver, this humiliation, in the face of this effrontery by the imperialists.

One can't even count how many times certain Latin-American countries have already been bought. The case of Haiti is historical. The situation in Haiti couldn't be more horrible, with hunger, illiteracy, poverty; the Haitian people are suffering the most terrible calamities a people can suffer. They are our neighbors. And the other time, in order to take measures against Cuba, they bought them; and now they've bought them again! And each time they hold a meeting, the Haitian government starts thinking how many votes they lack and how many votes they have, and how much they're going to pay for the vote. They bought them the other time and now they've bought them again.

And they call this an international organization, a regional organization.

But those who think that, in effect, the OAS and the ITMA are going down the drain have all the reason in the world on their side. And we can't help but feel satisfied and happy that the OAS is finally going under! (*Applause*). And you can all rest assured that we will never lift a finger to save it—if it is possible for a corpse to be saved. And we will wait with patience and perseverance until it finally sinks, now or whenever that happens once and for all. And we will maintain our position and our principle that this imperialist instrument has to disappear. And we know that if the governments of today don't make it disappear, the peoples will make it disappear one day! (*Prolonged applause.*) And I do not believe that all the governments of Latin America at this moment are very enthusiastic about the OAS. The more independent and more progressive their position, the greater their scorn for that institution.

However, the Cuban Revolution must take into consideration the governments that voted aginst the blockade, although they do not have relations with Cuba. And we take this occasion to express our acknowledgment and our respect (*Applause*). And if any of those governments should make the decision to reestablish relations with Cuba, we would have nothing against reestablishing relations with them (*Applause*).

Faced with the crime and the imperialist humiliation, they can only reply with a courageous position. And that is what history will write in the future: that governments had enough determination to take a courageous position at this moment! (*Applause.*)

For the rest, what's our hurry? Why should we be impatient if we are winning, if we are triumphing, if now more than ever the country is advancing in spite of the blockade, if all our projects are carried out in the face of the blockade? And all those hospitals and polyclinics and dental clinics and schools and nursery schools and universities, we have planned to build all those in the face of the blockade (*Applause*).

So our country can continue its march forward serenely and confidently. These 15 years have not passed in vain. And the Revolution is more secure today than it has ever been before, the Revolution is more solid today than it has ever been before, and the Revolution is advancing today at a rhythm it has never had before.

I have said all this, speaking of the objective factors that hinder the integration of women, referring to schools, hospitals, etc. And I really simply wanted to express to you the ideas and the projects related to the solution of these problems.

You come from all over the country. There are comrades here from Guane, from the Isle of Pines, from the province of Havana, from Matanzas, Jagüey, the Escambray, Santi Spíritus, Sola, Veguitas, Guantánamo (Applause); and you know how the Revolution's schools are springing up all over, transforming the landscape and the life of our countryside (Applause). And we will march forward at this rhythm.

The question has been raised here as to whether the same measures were being applied to the junior high schools in the countryside as to the day boarding schools with respect to the children of working mothers, and actually there are some regions where all the pupils, all of them, are now in the junior highs in the countryside, all the pupils of that level. There are various regions in the country where of course this problem no longer exists because all the youth are taken care of.

The Minister of Education explained the factors that hinder this, taking into consideration the objective of having not a single youth without a corresponding high school, not one sixth-grade graduate who does not go on to a higher level; the same principle for the difficulties involved can be applied to these schools as well. But we believe that, even so, something can still be done to favor the children of working mothers, high school students, in certain regions, in certain provinces; because many times they take out a complete school in order to put a primary school there, for example, and they have to find locations for those pupils in any case.

But this proposal was a just proposal; that is, the aspiration expressed here by some comrade delegates, and at the same time it is also very just that the Ministry's difficulties be taken into account, since its problem number one is to make all the changes and combinations possible in order to achieve the objective of having no sixth-grade graduate left without a school.

We also believe that, in the long run, the question of auxiliary teachers will have to be solved. We believe that the country will have to face up to the necessity of employing a specific number of comrades in this task, and that it will be necessary to analyze the economic considerations, and also the facilities that those auxiliary teachers must be given.

If there are presently close to 600,000 working women, and 250,000 more are to be incorporated in the next five years, there will be no other solution than to attack those problems related to the hour that the primary schools and the day boarding schools begin to function, and the problems of Saturdays.

The question of vacations was also raised. And we believe that the country has the resources to deal with this problem of summer vacations, since we are building hundreds of junior high schools in the countryside, and those installations could also be used for vacation plans. They are magnificent installations, and we are analyzing the possibilities of using them during the summer for vacation plans.

Many of these problems that you have raised here can be resolved with what we already have today. And in the long run, all these questions that hinder the incorporation of women into work, as the most certain way for the advancement of Cuban women along the road of their own liberation, we will overcome all these objective difficulties sooner or later.

There are others that weren't mentioned, at least in the discussions of the Congress, such as questions relating to the laundries, etc., etc. But we will go on solving these material difficulties.

And now there remain other difficulties, which we would consider to be of a subjective character. And what are those subjective difficulties? The problem of an old culture, of old habits, of old mentalities, of old prejudices.

There are administrators, for example, who whenever they can, give the job to a man and do not give the job to a woman, for a number of reasons; because they begin to think of the problems of job slotting, the problems of maternity, the difficulties of absenteeism a woman may have. The reasons, the factors, are many; but the fact is that the woman is discriminated against in terms of job opportunities.

At one time Resolution 47 was decreed, which froze a number of positions, certain positions, to be filled only by women. Later, that question was analyzed in the Workers' Congress and it was proposed that Resolution 47 be abolished, and at the same time, that Resolution 48, which prohibited women from taking certain jobs, be studied more deeply.

In any case, this problem must be attacked, if not in the form of freezing these jobs—which has raised certain difficulties, because many times the qualified feminine personnel for the job didn't turn up—at least in job slotting in work centers, the positions in which women will be given preference must be noted; and in every new industry, every new work center, these job slots must be noted. And the Party, the workers' organizations, the mass organizations and public administration, in judging the efficiency of those work centers, must take into account whether the job slottings that give preference to women are really, in effect, occupied by women.

And in every new factory built in any Cuban town, it must now be indicated what work is to be given to women *(Applause)* so there will be time enough to proceed with the selection and training of those women.

The rules and policy of the Party and of the mass organizations must be careful to maintain and insure the conditions for women to be incorporated into work. First, it is a question of elemental justice; and second, it is an imperative necessity of the Revoution, it is a demand of our economic development, because at some point, the masculine work force will not be enough, it will not be enough!

And for that reason it is necessary to wage a consistent battle against that mentality of discrimination against women in their job opportunities.

Here in the Congress, you pointed out other types of difficulties women have, related to the home, related to child care and related to old habits. And you have suggested ways to overcome those difficulties.

In the investigation that was made, it was shown that there are attitudes held by men, negative attitudes, and that there are also negative attitudes held by some women, and that this requires a special educational effort.

We believe that this struggle against discrimination of women, this struggle for women's equality and for women's integration, must be carried out by the whole society. And it is the task of our Party, in the first place; it is the task of our educational institutions and it is the task of all our mass organizations.

We were very pleased by the statements made here in the name of our youth, and how they committed themselves to wage the battle to overcome prejudices, and the mentality that persists. Perhaps these subjective factors imply an even greater struggle than the objective elements. Because with the development of our economy, we will overcome the material difficulties and one day we will have all the nursery schools we need, and we will have all the day boarding schools we need, and all the boarding schools we need, and all the services we need *(Applause)*.

But we still have to ask ourselves when we will eradicate the age-old ways of thinking, when we will defeat all those prejudices. Of course, we have no doubt that those prejudices will be defeated. It also seemed very difficult to overcome the concepts of private property that existed in our society before the Revolution. It was impossible to conceive of life without private property. And today it really isn't possible to conceive of life without socialist ownership of the means of production *(Applause)*.

But many habits remain from the times when women were also property within society. And these ways of thinking have to be eradicated. And we understand that the Family Code itself, which has produced so much discussion, is an important legal and educational tool in helping to overcome those habits and those prejudices.

But in order to achieve those objectives, women and men must struggle together, women and men have to become seriously and profoundly aware of the problem. They have to wage that battle together. And we are certain that it will be waged and that it will be won! And we believe that you are also certain of that! *(Applause.)* And the argreements of this Congress will be magnificent tools in that struggle.

I believe that all the resolutions are very worthy and very important. The resolution on the working women, on the young woman, the peasant woman, housewives, and the role of the FMC, the role of the family in socialism; the special resolution on the participation of women in physical education, recreation and sports; the resolution on International Women's Year, on solidarity, and the inspired appeal to Cuban, Latin-American and all women of the world, in solidarity with Chile. All those resolutions are resolutions worthy of this Congress.

And we believe that all those documents must be taken

237

up and studied. And studied not only in Federation circles, but also by the other mass organizations and by the Party (*Applause*).

Because those resolutions represent a real program of work for this historical struggle, for this historical battle you have before you in order to fulfill this revolutionary duty.

One of the things that our Revolution will be judged by in future years is how we have resolved women's problems in our society and in our homeland (*Applause*), even though that is one of the Revolution's problems that demands more tenacity, more firmness, more constancy and more effort.

On the question of prejudice, we told you once what happened in the Sierra Maestra when we went to organize the "Mariana Grajales" platoon, and the real resistance we encountered to the idea of arming that women's unit, which reminds us how much more backward we were a few years ago. Some men believed that women weren't capable of fighting.

But the unit was organized, and the women fought excellently, with all the bravery that the most valiant of our soldiers could have shown.

Nor was that the first time in history that this occurred. In the underground struggle women carried out an infinite number of tasks that, on occasion, placed them in greater danger than the dangers on the front line of fire. And during World War II, during the fascist aggresion against the Soviet Union, thousands of women fought in antiaircraft units, in fighter and bomber planes and even with the guerrillas and at the front. But still the old prejudices seek to impose themselves.

And nature made woman weaker physically than man, but it did not make her morally and intellectually inferior to man (*Applause*). And human society has the duty to prevent this difference in physical strength from becoming a cause for discrimination against women. This is precisely the duty of human society: to establish the norms of coexistence and justice for all.

Of course the exploiting societies, the class societies, exploit women, discriminate against them and make them victims of the system. Socialist society must eradicate every form of discrimination against women and every form of injustice, discrimination of any kind (*Applause*).

238

But woman also has other functions in society. Woman is nature's workshop where life is formed. She is the creator par excellence of the human being. And I say this because, instead of being the object of discrimination and inequality, woman merits special consideration from society.

I mention this point because there is something that we must bear very much in mind: that the struggle for women's equality and full integration into society must never be converted into lack of consideration for women; it never means the loss of habits of respect that every woman deserves (*Applause*). Because there are some who confuse equality with rudeness (*Applause*).

And if women are physically weaker, if women must be mothers; if on top of their social obligations, if on top of their work, they carry the weight of reproduction and child-bearing, of giving birth to every human being who enters the world (*Applause*), and if they bear the physical and biological sacrifices that those functions bring with them, it is just that women should be given all the respect and all the consideration they deserve in society (*Applause*).

If there is to be any privilege in human society, if there is to be any inequality in human society, there must be certain small privileges and certain small inequalities in favor of women (*Applause*).

And I say this clearly and frankly, because there are some men who believe they have no obligation to give their seat on the bus to a pregnant woman (*Applause*), or to an old woman, or to a little girl, or to a woman of any age who gets on the bus (*Applause*). Just as I also understand it to be the obligation of any youth to give his seat on the bus to an old man (*Applause*).

It is this sense of the basic obligation we have toward others: on a bus, in productive work, in the truck, others always have to be given special consideration, for one reason or another.

It is true with women and must be so with women because they are physically weaker and because they have tasks and functions and human responsibilities that the man does not have (*Applause*).

For this reason we appeal to our teachers, we appeal to parents, we appeal to our youth organizations and our Pioneers, to give special attention to this type of behavior in children, to this type of behavior in our youth.

239

Because it would be very sad if, with the Revolution, there wasn't even the recollection of what certain men in bourgeois society did out of bourgeois or feudal chivalry. And instead of bourgeois and feudal chivalry, there must exist proletarian chivalry, proletarian courtesy, proletarian manners and proletarian consideration of women *(Applause)*.

And I say this with the certainty that the people understand it and share it, with the certainty that every mother and every father would like their son to be a chivalrous proletarian *(Applause)*, that type of man who is respectful of women and considerate of women, capable of making a small sacrifice that dishonors no man but on the contrary exalts and elevates him *(Applause)*.

And here, at the closing of this Congress in which the question of the struggle for women's equality and integration has become the center of Cuban women's political and revolutionary activity for future years *(Applause)*, I say this so that one thing isn't confused with the other. I am saying what I really feel.

And we constantly run up against even verbal, linguistic forms of discrimination against women; the comrade who spoke here in the name of the workers, Agapito Figueroa, spoke of the discriminatory terminology used. And we must be careful even about this. Because sometimes we use a slogan that seems very pretty, that says: "Woman must be man's comrade"; but one might also say: "Man must be woman's comrade" *(Applause)*.

There is the linguistic habit of always making the man the center and this is inequality, or it reflects inequality, it reflects habits of thinking, although language is the least important in the final analysis, words are the least important. There are times when words remind us of something in the past although they no longer have that meaning. Deeds are what are really important!

Many things about this Congres have impressed us. As always, first of all, the enthusiasm, the joy, the interest you have shown; but very especially the political level this Congress reflected, because this Congress expressed the political development of the Cuban woman. The cadres that are rising in the Cuban feminine movement impressed us; the mental sharpness, the depth, the security and the conviction that the delegates to this Congress reflected.

I know our invited guests were impressed because they

saw the Minister in discussion with you here and you in discussion with the Minister; they were impressed by the great frankness, the great naturalness, the great spontaneity with which the debates evolved. And all this, of course, in a very disciplined atmosphere.

We weren't really so impressed by those things, because we are all accustomed to this, and there's nothing extraordinary in the fact that the Minister and anyone else discusses matters with you, or discusses them in a student assembly or a workers' assembly or anywhere else; he discusses with the masses and, if necessary, gives the masses a thousand and one explanations (*Applause*).

The Revolution's force lies in this proximity, in this identification between the masses and the Government, between the masses and the State, between the masses and authority. This is what gives the Revolution an invincible force, because the masses see in everything—in the State, in the Government—something that is theirs; not someone else's, not a foreign thing nor a strange thing. And no leader can view positions, functions, authority as his own (*Applause*). But in any case it has been highly flattering for us to see how our invited guests have commented about the form and character of the Congress.

For me, the advances Cuban women have made are what impressed me especially, their present political culture and the values that are developing among the masses. It pleased me—and I am sure other comrades too—to see the magnificent leadership that has developed, the magnificent cadres directing this movement headed by Comrade Vilma Espín (*Applause*), the very worthy leaders the organization has: their experience, their seriousness, their depth, along with their human qualities. And to see that in the provinces, in the regions and in the municipalities, that type of cadre is arising, that type of leader is arising. And to see that the working masses sent such magnificent and brilliant delegates to this Congress (*Applause*).

We are gratified to see the force the Revolution has in women (*Applause*); we are gratified to confirm the revolutionary quality of Cuban women (*Applause*), the self-sacrifice, the discipline, the enthusiasm, the passion for the Revolution, for just ideas, for the just cause of Cuban women, demonstrating their virtues which—as we have said on other occasions—are virtues demanded of the revolutionary militant and that women have to a very

241

high degree *(Applause).* And so we believe that our Party must rely more on that force *(Applause),* that our State must rely more on that force *(Applause),* that our productive apparatus must rely more on that force *(Applause).*

The Revolution has in Cuban women today a true army *(Applause),* an impressive political force *(Applause).* And that is why we say that the Revolution is simply invincible *(Applause).* Because when women acquire that level of political culture and revolutionary militance it means that the country has made a very great political leap, that our people have grown extraordinarily, that our country's march toward the future can't be stopped by anyone. That things will only be better all the time, that things will only be superior all the time. And that is why the Revolution is so strong; because of its mass organizations, because of the people's political consciousness, and because of its vanguard Party *(Applause).*

There is something worth emphasizing in one of the agreements you made, and that was the agreement about the pound of sugar each month for one year *(Prolonged applause).* Because this move came from the masses in an absolutely spontaneous way *(Applause).* No one in the government hinted or suggested or proposed that this request be made to the people.

It was done once before in regard to the problem of Chile. The Party and the government proposed to the people that there should be an effort to aid Chile when its economic difficulties became known.

This time, as soon as the fact that there had been a very severe drought was mentioned, that it was necessary to make the most of the sugar harvest and that sugar prices were very high, many citizens began to talk in many places, simultaneously and spontaneously, about how desirable it would be to reduce our sugar consumption a little.

Evidently, many calculated that internal sugar consumption at present prices is worth more than 500 million dollars. And spontaneously, this initiative arose from the masses. And we propose: if it comes from the masses, if it is coming from the base, it should be discussed and analyzed; if all the organizations, if all the people agree to it, then we accept it because we believe it is good, it is positive, it is correct.

But much more important than the sugar that can be collected and the value of this sugar, is the gesture of our people, the concern the people have for the affairs of the Revolution. Go to a capitalist country and see if you find anything like that!

And now they have problems of inflation, problems of depression, problems of all kinds, problems of the cost of living and strikes of every type. Compare this situation to ours in which such an initiative comes from the masses in a really spontaneous way.

We believed that initiative should be discussed with the other mass organizations, in all assemblies, so that it will really be a unanimous feeling of all the people (*Applause*). That would mean—at the present prices and even at slightly lower prices—between 40 and 50 million dollars. Many things can be done with 50 million dollars.

We spoke here of 100 junior high schools in the country-side. Now each school of this type costs about a million pesos, but in terms of direct import components it costs some 80,000 dollars So in direct import components, with 50 million dollars, 300 or 400 schools could be built.

With 50,000 tons of sugar at these prices, a textile factory can be bought, for example, which could produce 60 million square meters a year, six additional square meters of cloth per capita (*Applause*).

In any case, in the first version of the five-year plan, construction of three more textile factories is under consideration in addition to increasing present textile capacity, that of the present factories, by some 100 million square meters. Because it is evident that one of the problems we must try to resolve in the more or less near future, is the question of cloth and the per capita amount of cloth for the population. We are not thinking as they do in consumer societies, but there is no argument about the fact that we need a few more clothes. This is unquestionable. And we have many needs, in pillow cases, in sheets, in towels and all these things. We know that perfectly well (*Applause*). Not only cloth to dress ourselves, but also to make the bed and all that (*Applause*). We know the amount per capita that now exists and which, unfortunately, we have not been able to increase. But now in the next five-year plan, we are contracting for some of those factories. Unfortunately the process, from contract to construction and full production, takes years. Unfortunately.

In other areas we are going ahead much more rapidly; but we are relatively far behind in this aspect of a textile

243

industry. And one of those three factories—or any other industrial installation—that is in the original version of the plan, could be acquired with that sugar. Many things can be acquired that are very useful for the people. And those 50,000 tons over a year will help finance the 1976–1980 plan. Some comrades suggested a longer period of time. It seems to us that it needn't be any longer. What you have proposed is correct, the proposal of a year, because it coincides with two years of severe drought we have had, which of course has affected production. We would have a much higher production if we hadn't had two years of drought. And especially the last drought. And the proof of that is that the reservoirs throughout the country were empty at the end of spring. That had never happened before. Had it not been for the effort made in agriculture, there is no telling what the effect would have been. And if the effect is not greater, it is because of the magnificent work that has been done in the sugar cane fields. In a normal year, under other conditions, that wouldn't even have been necessary; but what is extraordinary is the people's sharpness in understanding the connection between a year of drought and prices. Why? Because sugar commands a respectable price now. And naturally that helps us and makes us happy.

In 1970 we tried to harvest 10 million tons and couldn't; but the sugar harvest of 1975, at today's prices compared to those of 1970, is the sugar harvest of 20 million tons (*Applause*). Of course, this doesn't mean that we're suddenly going to become millionaires (*Laughs*). Many of the products we import are also very costly. If there is more income, it has to be used well. Because we have to take into account the fact that sugar prices sometimes dropped to three cents, to two-and-a-half cents and yet we had to bear that without affecting consumption, without affecting anything. If we now have higher prices, this helps stabilize our finances, consolidate our economy. It doesn't mean that we consume it all now, no! To work for development. I believe we are all clear about that, right? (*Exclamations of "yes!"*) It isn't a question of living like rich people one year (*Exclamations of "no!"*), but rather of building the future.

So you see: those who blockaded us are now going without sugar (*Applause*). How much will sugar cost the imperialists in the year 1975? Billions of dollars! So they are not only going to have to pay a high price for oil, they are also going to have to pay a high price for sugar. It is costing the Yankee imperialists billions of dollars. That's their problem! (*Laughs.*) As long as sugar stays at that price, we are delighted (*Laughs*). They're now going around putting up signs over there: "Don't consume sugar." They're going to use artificial sweeteners again. But the sweeteners produce cancer, so they don't know what to do. And for sugar they have to pay high, high, high! (*Applause.*)

Of course it isn't Cuban sugar. Cuban sugar has markets and very good markets. We aren't in a hurry to sell the Yankees sugar. If one day they want to buy it . . . we won't blockade them (*Laughs*). We will sell them the sugar. It's closer, there's less transportation . . . well, part of the sugar, right? Because we have our sugar commitments which must be met first of all. But the blockade is theirs. Now they are self-blockaded in sugar.

And our country is doing well. Going ahead, going well, and work on all fronts is improving.

But this contribution you have made is a help, it is aid that has an important material significance. But it has a still greater importance from the moral point of view. This is what is called political consciousness, this is what is called revolutionary consciousness, this is what is called ideological depth! And after this, who is going to deceive us? (*Exclamations of "no one!"*) Who is going to tell us stories? (*Exclamations of "no one!"*) Who is going to detour us? (*Exclamations of "no one!"*) No one! And every year that passes will be better. Every year that passes we will have a more educated, more aware, more revolutionary and more internationalist people (*Applause*).

So these are the impressions we take from this historical Congress. We think that you are also content (*Exclamations of "yes!"*), that you are also satisfied (*Exclamations of "yes!"*), that you are proud of the Congress (*Exclamations of "yes!"*). I can tell you that our Party is also proud of the Congress, is satisfied with the Congress (*Applause and songs*).

Sometimes you say that you have learned from us, but the reality is that we have learned much more from you (*Applause*), we have learned much more from the people, from the masses. Because they always renew and fortify our confidence, our faith, our revolutionary enthusiasm.

245

You help to educate us and when I say, us, I speak not only as leader of the Party, I also speak as a man (*Applause and slogans*). You help us all, all men, all revolutionaries, to have a clearer awareness of these problems. And you help the Party and you help the leaders of the Revolution; a Party in which there is a very high percentage of men in the leadership (*Laughs*), a Government in which there is a very high percentage of men, so that it might seem to be a Party of men and a State of men and a Government of men (*Laughs*). The day has to come when we have a Party of men and women (*Applause*), and a leadership of men and women, and a State of men and women, and a government of men and women (*Applause*).

And I believe that all the comrades are aware that this is a necessity of the Revolution, of society and of history.

The great contemporary revolutionaries always understood the role of women: Marx, Engels, Lenin.

Lenin said what has been repeated here several times, that the full victory of the people could not be achieved without the complete liberation of women.

And Martí, the Apostle of our Independence, had very high ideals and said very beautiful things about women; and not only beautiful but profound and revolutionary. As when he said that the campaigns of the people are only weak when they do not enlist the heart of women, but when women move and help, when women stimulate and applaud, when educated and virtuous women anoint the work with the sweetness of their love, the work is invincible (*Applause*). Or when he said that women's natural nourishment is the extraordinary. Or when he said that women, by instinct, divine the truth and precede it. Or when he stated that women will live as an equal of men, as a comrade, and not at their feet as a pretty toy (*Applause*).

May we be worthy followers of the idea of Marx, Engels, Lenin and Martí (*Applause*).

And I know that your just aspirations and ideals, those of Cuban women, will penetrate deeply into the heart of revolutionaries and the heart of the entire people.

Patria o muerte! Venceremos! (*Ovation.*)